More Praise for *The Embodiment of Leadership*

"This path-breaking book extends our view of leadership theory and practice by seeing leadership as 'performance' and 'physicality' and by doing so provides a new and robust leadership framework for practitioners and scholars alike."

—Georgia Sorenson, visiting professor
of leadership studies, Carey School of Law,
University of Maryland

"This book presents unconventional ideas, creatively explored with great sympathy for the subjects of enquiry: quite a unique tone for a book on leadership; something new is happening. Leaders who are fed up with idealised images of what they *ought* to feel and do will recognise their actual experience here and find words given to what has hitherto been almost improper. It will do more for leadership development than could ever be imagined in any number of competency models."

—Jonathan Gosling, professor
of leadership studies, University of Exeter
Business School, United Kingdom

"This timely collection 'embodies' the important research and development work that is required to create a more human understanding of leaders and a more humane practice of leadership."

—Brad Jackson, Fletcher Building Education
Trust Chair in Leadership, The University
of Auckland Business School

"Between the covers of *The Embodiment of Leadership* readers will find contributors from around the world who provide an extraordinary synthesis of interdisciplinary concepts to craft a new lens of the body's place in leadership. With it scholars and practitioners will discover hidden dimensions of the processes, development, and relations of leadership and see anew their familiar dimensions."

—Richard A. Couto, distinguished senior
scholar, Union Institute & University

"From examining the way in which Michelle Obama takes up her role as first lady to what we can learn about leading through attending to dance, this volume offers a much-needed and exciting perspective on leadership as an embodied practice. Its challenge to traditional ideas about what it takes to be a leader literally made my spine tingle!

—Donna Ladkin, professor of leadership
and ethics, Cranfield School of Management,
Cranfield University, United Kingdom

The Embodiment of Leadership

Edited by
Lois Ruskai Melina

and

Gloria J. Burgess, Lena Lid Falkman, and
Antonio Marturano

A Volume in the International Leadership Association Series
Building Leadership Bridges

International Leadership Association

JB JOSSEY-BASS™
A Wiley Brand

Published by Jossey-Bass

A Wiley Imprint

One Montgomery Street, Suite 1200, San Francisco, CA 94104-4594—www.josseybass.com

Jossey-Bass books and products are available through most bookstores. To contact Jossey-Bass directly call our Customer Care Department within the U.S. at 800-956-7739, outside the U.S. at 317-572-3986, or fax 317-572-4002.

Wiley publishes in a variety of print and electronic formats and by print-on-demand. Some material included with standard print versions of this book may not be included in e-books or in print-on-demand. If this book refers to media such as a CD or DVD that is not included in the version you purchased, you may download this material at http://booksupport.wiley.com. For more information about Wiley products, visit www.wiley.com.

Library of Congress Cataloging-in-Publication Data

The embodiment of leadership / edited by Lois Ruskai Melina and Gloria Burgess, Lena Lid Falkman, and Antonio Marturano.
  pages cm. — (Building leadership bridges)
  Includes index.
  ISBN 978-1-118-55161-5 (pbk.); ISBN 978-1-118-61575-1 (pdf);
  ISBN 978-1-118-61566-9 (epub); ISBN 978-1-118-61565-2 (mobipocket)
    1. Leadership.   I. Melina, Lois Ruskai.
HM1261.E44   2013
303.3'4—dc23

2013002878

Printed in the United States of America

FIRST EDITION

PB Printing   10 9 8 7 6 5 4 3 2 1

Contents

Contributors

Ray Batchelor, PhD, MA (RCA), FRSA, is lead coordinator for teaching and learning at Buckinghamshire New University, High Wycombe, Buckinghamshire, England. A passion for the Argentinean tango has led him to dance it, then teach it, and subsequently explore its wider social and political dimensions. He also teaches the history and theory of design to designers and has written about design and mass production. He has a particular interest in design and human evolution. He promotes effective learning and teaching.

Julie Burge, MPH, MCMI, is senior lecturer and course leader for the academic programs leadership and management in multiagency settings at Buckinghamshire New University, High Wycombe, Buckinghamshire, England. She has twenty years of experience in leading academic programs in the United Kingdom, the United Arab Emirates, and Australia. She is interested in the role of social, organisational, and professional culture on the understanding and embodiment of leadership, and her current role is to design and deliver programmes of learning in leadership development for public sector organisations and enabling skills in evidence-informed practice. She has a particular interest in dialogic approaches to learning engagement.

Gloria J. Burgess is professor of leadership at Seattle University and the University of Washington. Her research arenas include arts and leadership, spirituality and leadership, and intercultural praxis and leadership. Her scholarship includes numerous invited keynotes, journal articles, commissioned poems, and three volumes of poetry. Books include *Dare to Wear Your Soul on the Outside*, which focuses on legacy-centered leadership (2008). This is Burgess's second collaboration for the Building Leadership Bridges series.

Skye Burn is director of the Flow Project, which applies principles and practices of art making in resolving social and cultural challenges. An award-winning poet, Skye has also worked professionally as an illustrator and fine woodworker. Her research interests include the relevance of art making to leadership and governance. She is an associate member of the UNESCO Chair in Comparative Studies of Spiritual Traditions, Their Specific Cultures and Interreligious Dialogue; associate member and community board member for the Center for Intercultural Dialogue; and contributes to In Claritas, bringing creativity to governance.

Lionel Cox, MA, BSc (Hons), PGDip Ed, is senior lecturer and course leader for criminology programs at Buckinghamshire New University, High Wycombe, Buckinghamshire, England. He has twenty-five years of experience in operational and project management in dealing room environments and financial institutions. This management background in cutting-edge environments prompted research interests that revolve around the methodological lens and social application of chaos, tipping points, fuzzy logic, and fuzzy sets. This exploration of nonlinear dynamics has led to in-depth study of the leadership and followership dialectic in "occasions of power."

Kathryn Goldman Schuyler has more than twenty-five years of practice in leadership development, organizational consulting, and somatic learning. Author of *Inner Peace—Global Impact: Tibetan Buddhism, Leadership, and Work* (2012), she earned a PhD in sociology from Columbia University after a Fulbright

Fellowship in Paris. Dr. Goldman Schuyler is a professor at Alliant International University, San Francisco, California, and has years of personal experience with both Buddhist practice and the Feldenkrais Method. She has published widely on leadership and change.

Maylon Hanold teaches in the sport administration and leadership master's program at Seattle University within the Center for the Study of Sport and Exercise. Her courses include sport sociology, leadership, human resources, and organizational behavior. She holds an EdD from Seattle University and has published in the *Sociology of Sport Journal* and *Advancing Women in Leadership Journal*. She is the author of *World Sports: A Reference Handbook* (2012). She competed for the United States in the 1992 Olympics in Whitewater Slalom.

David Holzmer is a doctoral student at Union Institute & University, Cincinnati, Ohio, where he is pursuing a PhD in interdisciplinary studies with a concentration in leadership. His research examines leadership as a social construct that integrates complexity, relationality, and human development to address challenges in organizations and the world. David lives with his wife in southern New Jersey and works in a position of leadership with a midsized nonprofit organization. He can be reached at DavidHolzmer@gmail.com.

Kate Katafiasz is senior lecturer in drama at Newman University in Birmingham, UK. She holds a PhD in drama from the University of Reading and publishes internationally on Lacanian approaches to embodiment, aesthetics, and intermediality in applied drama and theater. She has a particular interest in the collaboration between Big Brum Theatre in Education Company and dramatist Edward Bond, and Dorothy Heathcote's Mantle of the Expert inquiry-based learning system.

Lena Lid Falkman is a scholar at Stockholm School of Economics, Sweden. She has a Marie Curie Fellowship from the European Commission and will spend 2013 at ESADE, Barcelona, Spain. Lid Falkman's interests are value-based leadership, global leadership, rhetoric, and communication. Her PhD thesis has received awards in both the United States and Europe. Lid Falkman has fifteen years of experience teaching master and executive education, and she is often an invited lecturer to companies, departments, and NGOs. She can be reached at Lena .Lid.Falkman@hhs.se.

Stephanie Guastella Lindsay is an educator, performance artist, and choreographer. Her passion, research, and work in the world focus on using personal mythology to help leaders explore the ongoing themes and patterns of their lives. A graduate of Gonzaga University's doctoral program in leadership studies, she teaches and performs nationally and abroad. She currently teaches in Gonzaga's Theatre Arts Program.

Antonio Marturano (PhD) is adjunct professor of business ethics at the Sacred Heart Catholic University of Rome, Italy. He researches and teaches on applied ethics and philosophical foundations of leadership. Antonio has published in several international journals (such as *Leadership, Philosophy of Management,* and others) and in edited collections. He has coedited with Jonathan Gosling the book *Leadership: The Key Themes* (2008). Antonio is the editor in chief of the journal *Leadership and the Humanities.*

Lois Ruskai Melina is full-time faculty and chair of the Ethical and Creative Leadership concentration in the PhD program in Interdisciplinary Studies at Union Institute & University, Cincinnati, Ohio. Her research uses performance theory and narrative inquiry to explore both leadership and social movements. As an educator and a leadership consultant, she uses both movement and the arts to explore and understand ideas and ourselves in unique ways. She holds a PhD in leadership studies from Gonzaga University.

Nora Méndez holds a master's degree in women's studies from the Universidad Central de Venezuela and currently is pursuing an advanced degree in feminist theology from Escuela Feminista de Teologia de Andalucia in Spain. She worked for many years in community development in impoverished metropolitan areas and was also a pastor in Caracas, Venezuela, in the Vineyard denomination. Her current research interests are in women's leadership and feminist theology. She can be reached at currucita@gmail.com.

Fernando Mora has been professor of management at the MBA in International Business and Health Management of St. George's University, Grenada, since the inception of these programs in 2009. He served on several research commissions for the Venezuelan Ministry of Science and Technology. At St. George's University he coordinated the creation of the PhD in management. His research interests are in the field of leadership, organizations, and social participation systems. He can be reached at fmora@sgu.edu.

Arja Ropo is professor of management and organization at the School of Management, University of Tampere, Finland. Her research interests include aesthetic approaches to leadership, embodiment in leadership, and leadership in creative organizations. She has widely published in European, North American, and Australasian journals and books. She is an editorial board member of *The Leadership Quarterly*, *Scandinavian Journal of Management*, and *Organizational Aesthetics*.

Perttu Salovaara, PhD, is a researcher at the School of Management, University of Tampere, Finland. With a background in philosophy, his research interests focus on leadership's epistemological and ontological questions. His recent publications include a documentary film, *Leadership in Spaces and Places*; a coauthored book on arts and leadership (in Finnish 2010); a dissertation on leadership; and articles on embodiment in leadership research. Prior to his academic pursuits he worked as a management consultant and leadership trainer for fifteen years.

Elizabeth D. Wilhoit is a doctoral student in organizational communication in the Brian Lamb School of Communication at Purdue University. Her research uses a phenomenological approach to understanding the role of the body, material, and space in organizational settings and organizing processes.

Helle Winther, PhD, is a body and dance psychotherapist in the dance therapy form Dansergia and associate professor in the Department of Exercise and Sport Sciences at the University of Copenhagen, where she was Teacher of the Year in 2010. Her research and teaching interests include embodied leadership, the language of the body in professional communication, movement psychology, dance, and dance therapy. She has coauthored and edited six books and anthologies and authored many articles in journals and books.

Kimberly Yost holds a PhD in leadership and change from Antioch University. Her interests include looking at popular culture, particularly film and television, for the ways in which leaders are depicted and how those depictions influence the understanding of leadership.

Introduction

Lois Ruskai Melina

Throughout much of the world, leaders are memorialized as bodies, carved in marble, cast in metal. Some are readily recognizable, a few known only to locals. Words spoken by the leader may be etched at the base of a statue, but the leader's weight is conveyed primarily through the depiction of the body.

In life, leaders have bodies that think, move, act, have emotions and desires, age, hurt, and sense. This corporality is raced, gendered, cultured, sexual, instinctual, and emotional. Too often, however, in both academic literature and mainstream media, leaders are treated as disembodied, their leadership qualities referred to in ways that not only suggest leadership involves only cerebral functions but fail to recognize that cerebral functions originate and are actualized in the body. Monuments to leaders and their leadership, as well as our desire to pilgrimage to them, remind us that leadership is in the body and known through the body—the bodies of leaders as well as our own.

Ropo and Parviainen (2001) pointed out that leadership practice originates in and is informed by bodily experiences—experiences situated in social, cultural, historical, and deeply personal contexts. This practice is conveyed through the leader's body and experienced through our own, in a profound exchange of knowledge mediated and informed by, among others, identity, beliefs, fears, race, age, gender, psychology, family dynamics, birth order, language, illness, and appearance. Jemsek (2008), for example, suggested that the experience of disability can contribute to a healthy and much needed awareness of vulnerability in leaders. With this kind of understanding of the role of the body, for example, pregnancy and motherhood are not simply human resource issues that require policies; they contribute to the way some women constitute their leadership. With this acknowledgment, rather than hiding the fatigue felt working sixty-hour weeks and the fear of losing their edge, aging leaders can examine how the existential questions that one of my students has called the "midlife crisis of leaders" (R. Sarver, personal communication) can show up in shadow form or as a new set of life and organizational priorities.

Approaching embodiment as an artist would, through the senses, Springborg (2010) described another important contribution that the body makes to leadership. Springborg challenged the notion of "sense-making" by leaders as something *produced* through an intellectual analysis of observed and experienced data, arguing instead that meaning is *received* through the senses, creating what we know as our experience. He suggested that the leadership function that we call sense-*making* is more accurately depicted as *describing* the meaning.

The importance of embodiment to leadership is not new. Nearly one hundred years ago, Mary Parker Follett (1924/1930) wrote that reason, wisdom, sense-making, and other essentials of leadership originate in the body and emerge through the activities of our daily lives. Further, she said, the integration of new ideas, particularly those arising from differences, must take place at a bodily level: "The question all leaders, all organizers, should ask is not, how can we bring about the acceptance of this idea, but how can we get that into the experience of the people which will mean the construction of new habits" (p. 200).

This notion of embodiment is not something that can be reduced to a language of gesture, posture, and facial expression, easily learned in a weekend workshop. Nor does the awareness that leadership is embodied knowledge mean that knowledge is readily converted into usable form (Ropo & Parviainen, 2001). This volume presents not only some of the ways to conceptualize the relationship between leadership and the body, but some of the ways to take on the challenge of articulating and translating the embodied knowledge of leadership.

Although the field of leadership may have suffered, as other disciplines have, from a privileging of the realm of the intellect, it would be a mistake to overcorrect and place too much emphasis on the physical aspects of leadership. Indeed, many of the submissions we received for this volume articulated the importance of an integrated mind–body approach to the theory, practice, and development of leadership.

Paradoxically, perhaps, the notion of embodied leadership offers the potential to contribute to an important and overdue direction in leadership studies, that is, the idea that leadership is not something "housed" in an individual (a person with a body) but is a discourse that is performed by a person with a body, in relationship with others who are also performing an embodied discourse that both reveals and constitutes identity. These discourses are informed not only by experiences (Ropo & Parviainen, 2001) but by social, cultural, and personal narratives (see, for example, Shamir, Dayan-Horesh, & Adler, 2005; Shamir & Eilam, 2005; Shaw, 2010; Sparrow, 2005).

The performance of these discourses both reveals and constructs what we know as leadership and followership. In this way, leadership as well as followership are embodied texts that can be "read" (through the senses) for their personal and cultural meanings. Indeed, anthropologist Victor Turner (1986) suggested that it is through performance situated in the body that we not only reveal meaning but reveal ourselves to ourselves and others and acquire wisdom.

We received seventy submissions for this volume, with interpretations of and approaches to the notion of embodiment that ranged from discussions of archetypes and metaphor to leadership lessons learned through physical activity; from broad, theoretical, and abstract conceptualizations to specific activities for leadership development. With the collaboration of the associate editors, these were winnowed to twenty-eight. We then reviewed those before selecting the twelve essays in this book. The range of treatments is broadly captured in the three part headings, introduced by the associate editor for that part: the theory and interdisciplinary studies of "Leadership Thresholds," Gloria J. Burgess, editor; the relationship of leaders to their bodies in "Leaders Are Their Bodies," Lena Lid Falkman, editor; and the experiential dimensions of leadership development, "Leadership By and Through the Body," Antonio Marturano, editor.

I thank the International Leadership Association (ILA), its board of directors, President Cynthia Cherrey, and Director Shelly Wilsey for their commitment to exploring contemporary issues in leadership research and practice through the Building Leadership Bridges series. Debra DeRuyver, ILA's director of publications and special initiatives, provided gentle guidance and strong support of the process. I am particularly grateful to JoAnn Danelo Barbour, who edited the previous two volumes and generously shared notes and experiences that allowed for a transition that I hope was as smooth for others as it was for me.

I am indebted to Gloria J. Burgess, Lena Lid Falkman, and Antonio Marturano, associate editors, for their collaborative work across the full range of time zones. I also want to thank Jeffrey Zacko-Smith for his contributions early in the selection process.

My thanks also go to the many leadership scholars and practitioners who participated in conference calls outlining the scope of the project—your questions and ideas helped me broaden my thinking. I particularly thank those authors who submitted work for their insightful and often beautiful explorations of the multiple facets of this topic.

References

Follett, M. P. (1924/1930). *Creative experience.* New York, NY: Longmans, Green, & Co.

Jemsek, G. (2008). Vulnerability and shifting leadership values. *Reflections, 8*(4), 20–29.

Ropo, A., & Parviainen, J. (2001). Leadership and bodily knowledge in expert organizations: Epistemological rethinking. *Scandinavian Journal of Management, 17*(1), 1–18. doi:10.1016/S0956-5221(00)00030-0

Shamir, B., Dayan-Horesh, H., & Adler, D. (2005). Leading by biography: Towards a life-story approach to the study of leadership. *Leadership, 1*(1), 13–29. doi:10.117/1742715005049348

Shamir, B., & Eilam, G. (2005). "What's your story?" A life-stories approach to authentic leadership development. *The Leadership Quarterly, 16*(3), 395–417. doi:10.1016/j.leaqua.2005.03.005

Shaw, J. (2010). Papering the cracks with discourse: The narrative identity of the authentic leader. *Leadership, 6*(1), 89–108. doi:10.1177/1742715009359237

Sparrow, R. T. (2005). Authentic leadership and the narrative self. *The Leadership Quarterly, 16*(3), 419–439. doi:10.1016/j.leaqua.2005.03.004

Springborg, C. (2010). Leadership as art–leaders coming to their senses. *Leadership, 6*(3), 243–258. doi:10.1177/1742715010368766

Turner, V. W. (1986). *The anthropology of performance* (1st ed.). New York, NY: PAJ Publications.

Part One

Leadership Thresholds

Gloria J. Burgess

Now more than ever, leaders stand at the threshold of myriad unknown and unknowable frontiers that can be daunting if not downright terrifying. But when we welcome them, thresholds can be places of allure, hospitality, and companionship. As pioneering scholar and soul curator Thomas Moore (2000) reminded us, there, "in these liminal narrows, a kind of life takes place that is out of the ordinary, creative, and once in a while, genuinely magical" (p. 34).

Part One presents innovative practices, ideas, and insights on embodied leadership from several interdisciplinary thresholds or perspectives. The authors explore ways that leaders might befriend and traverse these thresholds, beginning with reflections on the singularity of the leader's journey as embodied story and concluding with a summons to leaders everywhere to embrace the world body as a singular collective because our very survival depends on it. In between, the authors invite us to sojourn, offering a way station for beleaguered travelers—leaders in the throes of ever-accelerating change, leaders in search of new maps, new coordinates to navigate pervasive ambiguity, disorientation, and dislocation.

We begin with a chapter by Stephanie Guastella Lindsay, who investigates the interconnections of metaphor, embodiment, and personal mythology. Delving into the heart of these intersectionalities, she invites leaders to embark upon a heroic journey, a voyage inward so that they might discover and reflect on their personal metaphors and how they are expressed through the language and behavior of their personal and professional narratives.

Continuing with a chapter by Kate Katafiasz, we are ushered into the domain of dramatic discourse as she examines the work of actor, educator, and transformational leader Dorothy Heathcote, whose legacy to leadership theorists and practitioners is a vast body of work that suggests how drama can assist leaders in generating the creative flow that is necessary to challenge the status quo and become transformational leaders, equipping teachers and others to become transformational leaders themselves.

In his contribution on the nexus of leadership and performative discourse, David Holzmer reminds us that in a radically destabilized world, leaders must shift their mind-sets and habits to continuously adapt and flourish. To equip them in making and mediating these shifts, Holzmer offers fresh perspectives for leaders on navigating the interlocking thresholds of pervasive uncertainty and disruptive upheaval.

This part concludes with Skye Burn's chapter, which moves beyond leading in the contexts of corporation, organization, institution, system, and community. With the conjoined sensibility and perspective of creative artist *and* social artist, Burn's context, canvas, and corpus is the world. She calls for nothing less than our conscious awareness and aligned stewardship of our precious planet as singular body.

As leaders cultivate the capacity to embrace thresholds not as threat but as opportunity, they prepare themselves for their most significant and enduring act of leadership, that is, being conscious stewards of our organizations, institutions, and communities, for the sake of our children, our children's children, and the many generations to come.

Reference

Moore, T. (2000). Neither here nor there. *Parabola*, 25(1), 34–37.

Chapter One

The Anatomy of Leadership

Stephanie Guastella Lindsay

Therefore, if one administers the empire as he cares
for his body, he can be entrusted with the empire.

Lao Tzu

Metaphor, Embodiment, and Personal Mythology

Metaphors are deeply entrenched in our everyday language. We explore untested waters by getting only our feet wet rather than diving right in, enjoy the fruits of our labors, and get all nerved up when things are up in the air. When metaphors ring true, they help us make sense of our lives. Because metaphors are plentiful, a fallacy exists that they are just words, that they are not important. Although they typically operate below conscious awareness (Johnson, 2007, p. 139), the nearly six metaphors per minute (Geary, 2011, para. 3) we use in our everyday language dictate to a large degree how we live our lives.

The words we use to describe our experiences reflect the physical structures and functioning of our bodies. We say *we grasp an idea* or *love slips through our fingers* because our hands and fingers are anatomically made to hold and let go. Two metaphors of embodiment that have been used to describe leaders, for example, are *having one's feet on the ground* and *holding one's ground*. The ability to solidly hold up well on two feet has to do with the "great significance" we give to "standing up, rising, and falling down" (Johnson, 2007, p. 137), which, of course, have to do with the body's basic ability to maintain verticality and balance. The ability to stand upright and maintain balance, actually and metaphorically, can ensure a leader's survival. We trust leaders who are upstanding or who take a stand.

Cool-headed, hands-on, tight-fisted, and *cutthroat* are a few more examples of the nearly infinite number of metaphors of embodiment that can be used to describe a leader's performance. Self-referential metaphors of embodiment like *I'm just a pretty face* or *I've got a good head for numbers* hint at and reveal essential aspects of our autobiographical selves, our personal mythologies. Personal mythologies evolve from memory and imagination. Acting as narrative blueprints, personal mythologies are the "vibrant infrastructure[s] that inform" one's life (Feinstein & Krippner, 1988, p. xi). They are brought about by significant pleasurable and painful events we are certain did happen, events that we may be uncertain about having happened, things that we had hoped would happen but did not, and events that did happen but that we wish had not.

Rather than an accurate historical record, our personal mythologies are experienced as a Gestalt from which not only the meaning of our lives can be made, but upon which we base our actions. Sometimes our personal mythologies are inaccessible to us—our psyche holds them at arm's length; at other times, they are in our face. Stephen Wolinsky (1991) proposed that people create self-image identities that reflect "core beliefs about [their] performance and worth" (p. 220). Self-image identities manifest as specific behaviors (p. 221) that can be either life affirming or life negating. By early adulthood, we become so identified with these "patterns of behavior" (p. 8) that we actually become them. We perform our lives according to these identities that we ourselves have written and embody. Our "attention becomes reduced to those few inner realities that define the identity" so that we "experience all the thoughts, feelings, emotions, and sensations of that limited state/identity" (p. 221).

As a physical, literal, and concrete living structure that takes up space and moves through time, the entire body takes in and chronicles data from the outside world, then interprets and stores them. Our bodies contain our entire life stories just as surely as "they contain bones, muscles, organs, nerves, and blood" (Halprin, 2003, p. 17). If we purposely attend to and examine our own metaphors of embodiment, we can apprehend them as linguistic indicators, vignettes, of the internally held stories of our lives. The person who reports many experiences of love slipping through his or her fingers may develop a personal mythology based on the core belief that he or she is, indeed, unlovable. The person might then intentionally or unconsciously embody the personal mythology of unlovability in ways that will ensure that romantic love will be elusive. Metaphors of embodiment, then, are simple linguistic indicators of deeper, complex personal mythologies.

A convincing argument has been made that metaphors have real-life consequences like "war and peace, healthcare, environmental issues, and other political and social issues" (Lakoff & Johnson, 1980, p. 246). It makes sense, then, for people in positions of leadership to attend to the self-referential metaphors of embodiment that spill from their lips. When leaders disregard these metaphors as just words, they are likely to disregard the personal mythologies that accompany them, and the roles both play in their performance of leadership. When we listen closely to the metaphors of embodiment we use and then consciously seek out the stories behind them, we open the way to self-understanding and apprehending our deepest reasons for doing what we do.

The leader who declares that he or she stands firm on his or her decisions, or who is known for holding his or her ground, for example, may have a personal mythology more tied to an aversion to appearing weak in public than to any inborn quality of stubbornness. Standing one's ground only becomes a negative quality for a leader when it results in an inauthentic performance of self.

Self-referential metaphors, then, can manifest in life-affirming or life-negating personal mythologies.

Dualism and Embodied Metaphor

Rational philosophic thought has conceptualized thinking as coming from a disembodied intellect that we call the mind (Johnson, 2007; Lakoff & Johnson, 1980, 1999). Dualism traditionally divided human experience into mind and body. On the one hand, the mind became the seat of logical thinking—the place where Absolute Truth could be sorted out. The body, on the other hand, was linked to the "imaginary, unreal, [and] unscientific" (Pert, 1997, p. 18), the "devil's handiwork, animal instincts, and lower forms of life" (Hanna, 1987, p. 9). Hunger, thirst, exhaustion, elimination, reproduction, and illness are some of the body's never-ending list of baser functions in which the loftier mind seemingly has no interest or involvement. The mind has been conceived of as rising above the messiness of the body. Emotions—also messy—arise from the physical body, get us all stirred up, and cloud our judgment. Finally, the body ages, dies, and decays.

When we say that someone needs to *use his or her head*, has *lost his or her head*, or is *out of his or her head*, we are really referring to the person's mind. The notion that the mind is located in the head, where the brain is, and where thinking is thought to occur, is conventional wisdom (although Empedocles once taught that the heart was the seat of intellect and Aristotle thought the brain was the body's cooling system) (Gross, 1995). According to dualism, abstract concepts like consciousness, morality, and time, and more concrete concepts like language and leadership, arise from a purely reasoning human mind, and are "in no way dependent upon our embodied, phenomenal selves" (Johnson, 2007, p. 7). If we believe that language springs spontaneously from a pure and disembodied mind, it becomes easier to believe that the self-referential metaphors leaders use are merely linguistic symbols—extensions of disembodied thinking—and that the body plays no role in a leader's deeply personal ways of being, decision making, and acting. The idea that thinking takes place somewhere in a mysterious inner space of the body called the mind is so ingrained in Western thinking that it is almost impossible to "think about mind in any other way" (Lakoff & Johnson, 1999, p. 266). It makes the notion that the body thinks and has a logic all its own seem absurd.

Embodied Minds, Enminded Bodies, and Many Minds

While dualism has contributed significantly to our understanding of the world, we seem to be embracing more holistic attitudes toward and accounts of mind and body. Contemporary science is engaged in "refuting traditional" ideas of dualism by "validating accounts of consciousness that relate body, self, mind, and emotion" (Fraleigh, 2000, p. 55). Language is now thought to depend on a "core consciousness" that is envisaged as a spiraling "bodymind axis" (p. 61). Psychoneuroimmunology has furthered the nondualistic basis of phenomenological inquiry, which has traditionally rested upon the concept of "the lived body" and the sentiment that dualism has been an error, that the "traditional division of body/mind [is] false" (p. 55). Cogent arguments for the embodiedness of mind (or enmindedness of body) have been provided: "What we call 'mind' is really embodied. There is no true separation of mind and body. These are not two independent entities that somehow come together and couple. The word *mental* picks out those bodily capacities and performances that constitute our awareness and determine our creative and constructive responses to the situations we encounter. . . . Mind is part of the very structure and fabric of our interactions with our world" (Lakoff & Johnson, 1999, p. 266, italics in original). "There is no disembodied logic at all" (Johnson, 2007, p. 181).

Perhaps we do not have one mind but many. Research suggests that the mind "travels the whole body on caravans of hormone and enzyme, busily making sense of the compound wonders we catalogue as touch, taste, smell, hearing, vision" (Ackerman, 1991, p. xix), and kinesthesia. Mind, then, might be conceptualized as numerous embodied biological systems that extend into and derive information from the world. Data are stored in the filing drawers of organ, bone, muscle, and nerve. Our organs and musculoskeletal, nervous, cardiovascular, respiratory, and endocrine systems, then, can each be conceptualized as having minds, and stories, of their own.

Metaphors of embodiment are evidence of the enmindedness of the human body. Our hair stands on end, chills run up and down our spines, and our skin crawls when we are fearful. We love people from the bottom of our hearts, we get choked up, and no one makes it through life without feeling as though his or her heart was breaking at least once. Our blood runs cold, we waste our breath, we get cold feet, and we feel things in our bones. We become flushed with love and feel the heat of anger. We change our minds.

That self-referential metaphors of embodiment provide "true statements about our inner lives" suggests that these metaphors "conform in significant ways to the structure of our inner lives as we experience them" (Lakoff & Johnson, 1999, p. 288). Leaders perform real actions in the world, with good or bad results, and the metaphors they use contextualize and explicate to themselves and others why they do the things they do. It makes sense, then, to pay close attention to the metaphors of embodiment that come from and circulate around a leader. If listened to carefully, they can become a leader's best teachers.

One leader might describe the experience of leadership as doing battle, while another may describe it as an improvisational dance. Each metaphor indicates vastly different subterranean personal mythologies, and each is likely to result in wholly different actions, experiences, and consequences for the leaders and those they influence. Leaders know if and when their outward actions are consistent with their inner lives. Congruence between a leader's implicitly held personal mythologies and explicitly expressed metaphors of embodiment and his or her outward actions allows a subjective experience of well-being to occur within the leader (Dasborough & Ashkanasy, 2005, pp. 265–266). The opposite is experienced when a leader does not act in accord with his or her internally held values (Erickson, 1995, p. 124), when the story he or she tells him- or herself and others is actually a lie.

The metaphors other people use to describe a leader can also indicate whether the leader's outward manifestation of leadership is congruent with his or her privately held experience. "Speaking softly and carrying a big stick" summed up Theodore Roosevelt's presidency. This mutually agreed-upon metaphor of embodiment, by Roosevelt and the world, garnered fear and respect for the man and America throughout his tenure in political office. It seems to be a "stroke of genius" when a leader's own metaphors and stories of embodiment "coalesce, as in a dream—when, as the poet William Butler Yeats would have it, we cannot tell the dancer from the dance" (Gardner, 1995, p. 37). When there are no disparities between the metaphors leaders use to describe themselves and those that others use, an interconnectedness, or "synching up," between leader and self and leader and follower occurs.

Heroic Journeys, Toads, and Monsters

We often first encounter metaphor as children through fairy tales and myths. A really good metaphorical story draws us right into the narrative. We become engaged on every level of human experience: emotional, intellectual, imaginal, and physical. Our imaginations allow us to become one with the story's characters. Outrage, fear, shock, joy, and grief are experienced in our very bodies, viscerally, as we become one with the flow of the story's events.

The oldest myth is the heroic *monomyth* (Campbell, 1949/2008). In this story, a hero or heroine travels to a land of once-upon-a-time and far-away. In this liminal time and place, the hero or heroine does battle with monsters, solves tricky riddles, and/or completes a series of monumental tasks. These challenges necessitate the mustering up of extraordinary, internally held powers by the main character. Heretofore unaware of their existence, the hero or heroine is able to access superhuman powers by penetrating the "causal zones" of the "psyche's interior" where, of course, the *real difficulties reside*" (Campbell, 1949/2008, p. 12, italics added).

Masquerading as metaphorical monsters, from unseemly little toads to the truly horrific, the real difficulties for the protagonist rest in the inability to reconcile his or her personal mythology with the outward performance of self. A disconnect exists between the authentic hero or heroine within and the imposter that is disclosed to the world. The discrepancy has to do with the hero or heroine's dysfunctional personal relationship with his or her personal mythology. Perhaps the story has been inadvertently or purposely repressed. Perhaps the protagonist sees little value in unearthing trauma or sadness that occurred years before. Perhaps basic self-knowledge is nonexistent. Regardless, deeply disturbed by subjective feelings of being unfaithful to the true self, the hero or heroine understands at some level that the essential self has been violated (Erickson, 1995).

The heroic journey, then, is really about embracing the authentic self, toads and all. Taming monsters, solving riddles, and completing Herculean tasks trigger the process of transformation within the protagonist and compel the main character to come into his or her own. The monomyth, then, is really a story about becoming comfortable in one's own skin, about increasing the capacity for self-love, and about moving on. The myth ends with the hero or heroine returning to a waiting community where he or she proceeds to "teach the lessons" of a "life renewed" (Campbell, 1949/2008, pp. 15, 30), often as the new leader (Pearson, 1998, p. 4).

The Big Lie: Hero as Leader

A society makes leaders out of its heroes because they are perceived to "actually embody the qualities" (McLennan, 1994, p. 113) most revered by the society and with which the society most wants to be identified. Deeply embedded in humankind's collective story across all cultures (Campbell, 1949/2008; Lakoff & Johnson, 1980), our society's cultural, historical, and emotional investment in the leader-as-hero myth is significant. And therein lies the rub: leaders are heir to and culturally invested in precisely the same cultural mythologies as those they lead. Our contemporary leader-heroes regularly appear in electronic form and often hail from the arenas of entertainment, sports, politics, and big business (Bennis, 2003; McClennan, 1994). Leader-as-hero misperceptions are "formed by myths and fallacies about how a person becomes a leader" promulgated by the media (Martinek, Schilling, & Hellison, 2006, p. 142). Combined with "egocentric self-aggrandizement" (Campbell, 1949/2008, p. 10) and other psychological gratification needs of many contemporary leaders (Kets de Vries, 2003; Stech, 2004), some individuals will attain positions of leadership for the wrong reasons.

Many adolescents, for example, believe leaders must "first be good-looking, athletic, wealthy, or smart" (Martinek and others, 2006, p. 142)—in other words, be considered to be heroes or at least appear heroic—before even considering the idea of assuming a position of leadership. Equating leadership with heroism assumes that leaders will behave with others' best interests at heart. But by following an "icon of unattainable perfection" (Kerfoot, 2006, p. 116), hiding behind a façade of pretense, "inhabiting a role, [or] playing a part that imprisons them," leaders move away from their best selves and "what they are inwardly experiencing," and their subsequent suffering can be "devastating" (Ackerman & Maslin-Ostrowski, 2002, p. 19).

The Posturing Imposter

When leaders drive themselves to be something they are not, they can "set into motion entire operations founded on distorted perceptions, with serious consequences" (Kets de Vries, 2003, p. 11) for themselves, the organization, and society. Rather than attending to the "requirements of the task at hand" or to the good of the communities they serve, the "vast majority of persons" already in or seeking positions of leadership do so to fulfill their own personal gratification (Stech, 2004). Manfred Kets de Vries (2003) called these leaders "imposters." A self-identified imposter's own words provide a good example: "I have another characteristic, something that I feel inside me, some kind of insecurity in my abilities or in who I am. . . . All the time I try to prove more and more. . . . I live with this dilemma, how people perceive me and my lack of confidence that says, why do they look at me so highly, when I am . . . less than that, I live with this . . . gap" (Shamir & Eilam, 2005, p. 406).

Leaders dealing with fragile self-esteem "are especially caught up in how they feel about themselves and will take [any] variety of measures to bolster, maintain, and enhance" (Kernis, 2003, p. 3) feelings of self-worth. Fear, combined with the fact that "so much of the language of leadership is doing and action," causes leaders to worry that taking the time for deep personal reflection might appear to others as incompetence or indecisiveness (Ackerman & Maslin-Ostrowski, 2002, p. 110). When given a choice between donning a mask of competency and performing leadership transparently and vulnerably as a "deep expression" (p. 19) of oneself, it is easy to understand why a leader might choose the former over the latter. Masked leaders, though, become irrational and neurotic (Kets de Vries, 2003). The wrong move, the wrong word, will reveal deeply held feelings of undeservedness, fraudulence, and worthlessness that all the posturing and accoutrements of success disguise. The never-ending internal drama and heavy, privately held anxiety of being found out by followers (Kets de Vries, 2003, p. 116) is nightmarish.

The warning, that the "emotional and spiritual underdevelopment" of our leaders would eventually become a problem not only for organizations, but for society as a whole (Maccoby, 1976, p. 108), has been borne out in past decades and recently. We are no longer shocked or surprised to read of corporate scandals; personal, political, and fiduciary indiscretions; or environmental calamities visited upon the Earth by spiritually bankrupt leaders. Future leaders, Michael Maccoby predicted, would not "possess the moral strength to know right from wrong, [or] the courage to act on those convictions" when given a choice between the two (p. 108).

Plunging into the Psyche

More and more, though, leaders are being held accountable for their actions. They have been asked to unmask and reveal their innermost selves by being consciously "transparent with their intentions" so others can recognize that "a seamless link" (Luthans & Avolio, 2003, p. 242) exists between who they say they are and what they actually do. Leaders would be wise to take the inner, psychic journey, particularly if they wish to retain their positions of influence and authority. On the way, they will surely come upon those nasty little toads and horrific demons that every hero or heroine who undertakes the psychic journey encounters. They will be compelled to solve difficult riddles and undertake Herculean tasks that must be completed before they restore themselves to their most authentic, essential selves.

When an individual rejects the story of his or her past as irrelevant, the rejection makes self-transcendence impossible.

It causes a "self-stultifying travesty" (Taylor, 1991, p. 22) from which the true self cannot emerge. The contribution that our past histories make toward the living of our lives is significant: "We can never liberate ourselves completely" from those persons and events that "shaped us early in life" (p. 34). So we strive to make sense of our life stories. The "afflictions of our lives" permit access to our very souls, and the heroic journey takes us "step by step into [our] own undiscovered reality" (Moore, 2004, p. 26). The journey opens the way to self-knowledge and permits self-transcendence. The journey itself is not transcending; rather, it is how we respond to the monsters and how we allow them to teach us that cause self-transcendence.

The heroic journey allows us to slip-slide in and through the realms of the embodied, affective, and analytic. It permits self-transcendent experiences, those "episodes, insights, dreams, and visions that have a numinous quality" and that seem to "expand our comprehension" (Feinstein & Krippner, 1988, p. 185) of self. Even the darkest personal mythology can be instrumental in revealing our "best" selves, selves that we often unwittingly move away from during the course of our lives.

It is truly "difficult to look directly into dark and difficult terrain" (Halprin, 2003, p. 177) of our deepest selves, but there is no way out of our inner lives (Palmer, 2000, p. 80). We must take the downward and inner psychic journey and listen to the wisdom of our bodies if we are to find out who we truly are, how we might come into our own, and how we might best serve others. While the journey toward self-knowledge is a spiritual one, "it is *not* a transcendental movement upward toward the light and an ecstatic union with all of creation" (Plotkin, 2003, p. 10, italics in original): "In the deeps are the violence and terror of which psychology has warned us. But if you ride these monsters deeper down, if you drop with them farther over the world's rim, you will find what our sciences cannot name or locate . . . the unified field, our inexplicable caring for each other, and for our life together here. This is a given. It is not learned" (Dillard, 1988, p. 19).

Transcendent work of this sort is directed primarily by the body. To ignore the self-referential metaphors of embodiment that reveal our personal mythologies is to neglect a most basic tool a leader has at his or her disposal for developing self-awareness and self-knowledge. Granted, embodiedness is not the only means by which the intricacies of leadership can be understood, but to discount the body as an essential resource gives credence to the notion that leadership is a purely intellectual activity, that heart and guts, for example, play no part in its expression. It really is true that how we live in "our body is how we live in the world" (Strgar, 2012, para. 4). When we peremptorily dismiss the role the body plays in leadership, we risk making decisions based only on intellectual processes—things like the bottom line, corporate expansion, or increasing stock value—rather than what is best for ourselves, the community, and the environment.

Countering the Postmodern Megamyth

British Petroleum, Halliburton, Goldman Sachs, ExxonMobil, Walmart, and Monsanto, among some of our most powerful corporations, have each contributed to the idea that corporations are, or soon will be, running the world (Korton, 2001), that the individual is but a tiny cog in their machinations. A new and ominous societally held megamyth has arisen in this postmodern era. This myth "supports material progress and the control of nature, rather than attunement and participation with natural cycles" (Feinstein & Krippner, 1988, p. 6) and service to the community that characterized the monomyth (Campbell, 1949/2008). Phrases like "corporate greed," "environmental catastrophe," and "capitalist imperialism" are at the heart of this megamyth. Greed and scarcity, terrorism and war, eroding markets, and environmental collapse are the monsters that populate the megamyth. As individuals, we cannot escape the "distinctive mark" (Feinstein & Krippner, 1988, p. 5) that it has exercised upon our own personal mythologies. Nor can it be denied that some leaders' actions reflect this new megamyth "in microcosm" (p. 5). To some extent, each personal mythology incorporates a culture's collective mythology. As individuals, we have become as adroit at building personal mythologies founded on fear, scarcity, war, and eroding markets as multinationals and conglomerates.

We can succumb to the tyranny of the new megamyth, or we can begin to question how we ourselves are contributing to it simply because we have neglected to take our own heroic, psychical journeys. It takes real courage to drop off the edge of the known world and venture into the underbelly of one's own shadow. It takes steely nerves to seek out, ride, and tame one's demons, to deliberately puncture the "well-constructed façade of ego" (Halprin, 2003, p. 177). But even though they may have been put out of mind, our privately held toads and monsters cannot be put out of body. Leaders' worldviews, relationships, and physical and emotional expression are adversely affected when they consciously or unconsciously arrange their lives around their woundedness, when they "armor" themselves, or assume "compensatory behavior" (p. 180). This is what Parker Palmer (2000) meant when he asserted that a leader must take "special responsibility for what's going on inside him- or herself," so that a leader brings more good than harm to the world (p. 5). It is what Shirley Baugher (2005) referred to when she stated that a leader's internal incongruence can easily manifest as "anger, depression, withdrawal, inaccessibility, controlling, and/or reactive defensive behavior" (p. 15).

The journey, then, requires each of us to claim ownership for the expression of our own internal and external lives, to bring that which is unconsciously directing our lives into consciousness, and then to do something about it. It requires that a leader's "outer self" be in full compliance with the leader's inner, highest, most real self (Lakoff & Johnson, 1999, p. 282). The global need for egoless leaders who "do not fake their leadership" and who are not consumed with "developing an image or persona of a leader" (Shamir & Eilam, 2005, p. 382) is critical.

The "transformational power of being deeply understood" by others as well as by one's own self is remarkably "underestimated" in our society (Rogers, 1993, p. 7). Yet people in many organizations are seldom rewarded for possessing self-knowledge. They are, rather, rewarded "for proving themselves" (Bennis, 2003, p. 24). As such, they often are unable to "fully deploy" themselves as authentic leaders of character and vision (p. 24). When leaders shy away from the "quest to journey inward, [they] experience non-life and, accordingly, call forth less life in the culture" (Pearson, 1998, p. 4). This "is the experience of the wasteland" (p. 4). The postmodern megamyth will most certainly take us to a collective wasteland. Our own unexamined personal mythologies will deliver us into our own private hells.

The journey, though, does not require leaders to become something bigger than they already are; rather, it requires a willingness to restore themselves to their most authentic selves and to grow from there. Leaders cannot be expected to "solve the great political, social, and philosophical problems of our time" (Pearson, 1998, p. xii) until they have examined their own personal mythologies and appropriately released the monsters that populate them.

Many leadership development programs, intended to bring about positive growth and change in individuals, focus on the "acquisition of concepts, skills, and behaviors" (Shamir & Eilam, 2005, p. 409) rather than positive growth and profound personal change. The delightful fact remains that the body already has all the tools it needs to solve the problems facing us today—problems that have come about largely because of humankind's almost exclusive use of the intellectual domain, our choice to ignore the urgings and wisdom of the body, and our misguided disregard of what is going on below the neck.

The human body cannot tell a lie. Those sometimes startling self-referential metaphors of embodiment are not slips of the tongue. They are the wisdom of the body speaking out loud. When we listen to the words our bodies speak, we can interrogate the personal mythologies the words reveal. Attending to our embodiedness and self-referential metaphors of embodiment has the potential to remove us from the postmodern megamyth of narcissism, ego gratification, and greed. Our bodies can lead us to life-affirming leadership that will restore us one leader at a time to a collective ethic of service.

References

Ackerman, D. (1991). *A natural history of the senses.* New York, NY: Vintage Books.

Ackerman, R. H., & Maslin-Ostrowski, P. (2002). *The wounded leader: How real leadership emerges in times of crisis.* San Francisco, CA: Jossey-Bass.

Baugher, S. L. (2005). Learning how to lead: A lifetime journey. *Journal of Family and Consumer Sciences, 97*(3), 15–16.

Bennis, W. G. (2003). *On becoming a leader.* New York, NY: Basic Books.

Campbell, J. (1949/2008). *The hero with a thousand faces* (3rd ed.). Novato, CA: New World Library.

Dasborough, M. T., & Ashkanasy, N. M. (2005). Follower emotional reactions to authentic and inauthentic leadership influence. In W. L. Gardner, B. J. Avolio, & F. O. Walumbwa, (Eds.), *Authentic leadership theory and practice: Origins, effects and development* (Vol. 3, pp. 254–280). San Diego, CA: Elsevier.

Dillard, A. (1988). *Teaching a stone to talk* (4th ed.). New York, NY: Harper.

Erickson, R. J. (1995). The importance of authenticity for self and society. *Symbolic Interaction, 18*(2), 121–144. doi:10.1525/si.1995.18.2.121

Feinstein, D., & Krippner, S. (1988). *Personal mythology: The psychology of your evolving self.* Los Angeles, CA: Tarcher.

Fraleigh, S. (2000). Consciousness matters. *Dance Research Journal, 32*(1), 54–62.

Gardner, H. (1995). *Leading minds: An anatomy of leadership.* New York, NY: Basic Books.

Geary, J. (2011, April 11). *Metaphors in mind.* http://www.macmillandictionaryblog.com/metaphors-in-mind

Gross, C. G. (1995). Aristotle on the brain. *Neuroscientist, 1*(4), 145–250. doi:10.1177/107385849500100408

Halprin, D. (2003). *The expressive body in life, art, and therapy: Working with movement, metaphor and meaning.* London, UK: Jessica Kingsley.

Hanna, J. L. (1987). *To dance is human* (Rev. ed.). Chicago, IL: University of Chicago Press.

Johnson, M. (2007). *The meaning of the body: Aesthetics of human understanding.* Chicago, IL: University of Chicago Press.

Kerfoot, K. (2006). Authentic leadership. *Nursing Economics, 24*(2), 116–117.

Kernis, M. H. (2003). Toward a conceptualization of optimal self-esteem. *Psychological Inquiry, 14*(1), 1–26.

Kets de Vries, M.F.R. (2003). *Leaders, fools, and imposters: Essays on the psychology of leadership* (Rev. ed.). San Francisco, CA: Jossey-Bass.

Korton, D. C. (2001). *When corporations rule the world* (2nd ed.). San Francisco, CA: Berrett-Koehler.

Lakoff, G., & Johnson, M. (1980). *Metaphors we live by.* Chicago, IL: University of Chicago Press.

Lakoff, G., & Johnson, M. (1999). *Philosophy in the flesh: The embodied mind and its challenge to Western thought.* New York, NY: Basic Books.

Luthans, F., & Avolio, B. J. (2003). Authentic leadership development. In K. S. Cameron, J. E. Dutton, & R. E. Quinn (Eds.), *Positive organizational scholarship: Foundations of a new discipline* (pp. 241–261). San Francisco, CA: Berrett-Koehler.

Maccoby, M. (1976, December). The corporate climber has to find his heart. *Fortune,* pp. 98–108.

Martinek, T., Schilling, T., & Hellison, D. (2006). The development of compassionate and caring leadership among adolescents. *Physical Education and Sport Pedagogy, 11*(2), 141–157. doi:10.1080/17408980600708346

McLennan, D. B. (1994). Cultural mythology and the modern hero. In S. Drucker & R. Cathcart (Eds.), *American heroes in a media age* (pp. 111–133). Cresskill, NJ: Hampton Press.

Moore, T. (2004). *Dark nights of the soul: A guide to finding your way through life's ordeals.* New York, NY: Penguin.

Palmer, P. (2000). *Let your life speak: Listening for the voice of vocation.* San Francisco, CA: Jossey-Bass.

Pearson, C. S. (1998). *The hero within: Six archetypes we live by* (3rd ed.). San Francisco, CA: HarperCollins.

Pert, C. B. (1997). *Molecules of emotion: Why you feel the way you feel.* New York, NY: Simon & Schuster.

Plotkin, B. (2003). *Soulcraft: Crossing into the mysteries of nature and psyche.* Novato, CA: New World Library.

Rogers, N. (1993). *The creative connection: Expressive arts as healing.* Palo Alto, CA: Science & Behavior Books, Inc.

Shamir, B., & Eilam, G. (2005). "What's your story?" A life-stories approach to authentic leadership development. *The Leadership Quarterly, 16*(3), 395–417.

Stech, E. L. (2004). *The transformed leader*. Victoria, BC, Canada: Trafford.

Strgar, W. (2012, January 12). *Gratefully in a body*. http://www.huffingtonpost .com/wendy-strgar/senses_b_1190298.html

Taylor, C. (1991). *The ethics of authenticity*. Cambridge, MA: Harvard University Press.

Wolinsky, S. (1991). *Trances people live: Healing approaches in quantum psychology*. Las Vegas, NV: The Bramble Company.

Chapter Two

Dramatic Leadership

Dorothy Heathcote's *Autopoietic*, or Embodied, Leadership Model

Kate Katafiasz

This chapter examines the work of the late British drama educator and transformational leader Dorothy Heathcote. Transformational leaders are sometimes thought to have a mysterious persona or presence that is difficult to define and even more challenging to replicate. Heathcote herself was undoubtedly charismatic; but her Drama in Education conventions are increasingly used in UK schools and seem to enable many interested teachers to become transformational leaders themselves. The chapter offers some of these thirty-three conventions for dramatic action to leadership theorists and practitioners in an attempt to pinpoint what it is that drama and transformational leadership share: namely, the ability to challenge the status quo and encourage creativity. Heathcote's conventions may shed light on how this can be accomplished, because they seem to guide us into the heart of the creative process itself.

Heathcote was an actor-turned-teacher who developed her leadership model by applying what she knew about acting to the usually purely discursive practices of learning environments. She generated a powerful hybrid, which this chapter explores in some detail and which she described:

Coming from the theatre, I got to thinking it would be important to suit the word and the gesture; and the relationship with the furniture and the book; and indeed anything which at the moment assisted in the total picture becoming available to be "read." (Heathcote, 1991, p. 160)

For Heathcote, suiting the word and the gesture did not mean that languages and bodies are sutured or stuck together, with physicality merely reinforcing the meaning of the word; for her, suiting the word and gesture meant deliberately generating an exciting, dramatic disparity between them: a gap between intellect and corporeality. This chapter proposes that both drama and transformational leadership share a capacity to dispute the connections a culture routinely makes between bodies and languages; that these customary associations form the very habits and prejudices that inhibit personal and social development; and that challenging them gives people the space to question their assumptions, and so the potential to transform themselves and their situations.

The ancient Athenians were possibly the first to exploit the dramatic gap between intellect and physicality to which we refer. According to Greek scholar Reginald Winnington-Ingram (1999), the Athenian practice of Tragedy had become highly serious by 472 BC (p. 5). Drama was arguably a key component of the unusually creative culture that Thucydides described some three decades later:

The Athenians are addicted to innovation, and their designs are characterised by a swiftness alike in conception and execution; you (the Lacedaemonians) have a genius for keeping what you have got, accompanied by a total want of invention, and when forced to act, you never go far enough. (as cited in Castoriadis, 1987, p. 208)

Thucydides described a state of embodied cognition or *autopoiesis* in which the conception and execution of ideas are never far apart. To understand how to achieve this desired state of intellectual and physical coherence or flow, we need first, perhaps, to investigate the processes that disrupt it. I use the ideas of French cultural theorists Jacques Lacan and Louis Althusser, whose work has influenced American gender theorist Judith Butler and others, to investigate the ways in which culture might impose itself on individual identity, causing us to behave according to the expectations of others. I then put forward ways to subvert these systems taken from ancient Greek drama and from the transformational leadership practice of Dorothy Heathcote.

Understanding Disembodiment, or *Allopoiesis*

Judith Butler (1993) and Louis Althusser (2001) put forward theories of disembodiment, or *allopoiesis*, that are rooted in Lacan's notion that the price we pay for subjectivity is loss of embodiment. According to Lacan, languages and bodies undergo a striking reversal at what he terms the "Mirror Stage"; this occurs when we identify with our body image to establish an ego or identity that is founded upon how we imagine we are seen by others. The process may be usefully described by the ancient story of Narcissus, who famously confused a reflected or iconic image of himself with the captivating presence of another person. The crux of the Mirror Stage error is the mistaking of a substituting linguistic sign (an icon or symbol) for physicality (indexicality). After the Mirror Stage we suffer a state of confusion between what is social (languages) and what is personal (bodies) because we have mistaken icons that make meaning by substituting for objects, for indices that make meaning by being contiguous with objects. This is easier than it sounds, because iconic meaning is located in mimicry; an icon must echo its original enough to recall it in the mind of the onlooker. Icons, which may be visual and auditory, are quintessentially mimetic; an icon looks or sounds like, and may therefore be easily mistaken for, its object.

Pavlov's work on conditioned reflexes exploits the misleading associations made at the Mirror Stage. Pavlov famously trained dogs by making the sound of a bell contiguous with food, and then using the bell alone to induce the dogs' salivation. The bell starts out as an index to food and then substitutes for it symbolically; in doing this, the bell-symbol recalls food by virtue of habit and association, without even resembling it in any way. Both icons and symbols are linguistic signs that substitute for their objects. It may seem easier to confuse an icon with its object, because icons at least resemble their objects, but the habitual associations we make between symbolic signs and their objects can hijack bodies just as powerfully, as the dogs' salivation illustrates.

At the Mirror Stage, the associations we make among sounds, images, and things, between signifiers and objects, forge neural pathways in the brain; this is how we learn language and enter culture, but it is also how language and culture, in a very physical sense, enter us. Icons and symbols manifest themselves in auditory, visual, and (*passé* Helen Keller) haptic patterns, whose repetition or performance, freighted with significance, demand recognition by the subject. It is at the Mirror Stage that this recognition takes place, and it has an extraordinarily transformative effect upon the subject. Louis Althusser described this ideological enculturation in terms of the hail, in response to which the subject accepts and reproduces what is socially expected of him or her (Althusser, 2001). The subject, unaware of the other's presence, is seen by the other, recognised in some way, and addressed vocally. The subject responds to this hail by recognising something of himself or herself in the words or tone of the other's voice, and is compelled to turn around. Althusser termed this process "interpellation," and it is characterised by the subject's reception and reflection of the gaze and voice of the other. That is to say, in the act of imagining how we are seen through the eyes of the other, we become an icon of the other's gaze, mimicking, as icons do, the expectations, that is, the desire, of the other. In this spatial reversal, which Lacan termed "extimacy" (1992, p. 139), the signifier seems to change places with, and so command, the body. Because the structure of all signs is pattern, and the structure of pattern is repetition, we see a strange temporal as well as a spatial reversal taking place; repetition sets up expectations of a future predicated on past experience, trapping us like Narcissus and Pavlov's dogs in an addictive, conservative, dominant performative discourse.

This is not good news for human agency per se, let alone for transformational leaders who seek to challenge prevailing discourse. Lacan's (2006) reworking of Descartes's *cogito* makes the problem clear: "I think where I am not so I am not where I think" (p. 430); bodies and languages are separate. This is clearly at odds with what Thucydides had to say about Athenian society in which conception and execution (intellect and physicality) are clearly closely connected: movement from one to the other is swift.

Understanding the Body as a Site of Knowledge, or Autopoiesis

So how may we reverse the disembodying Mirror Stage to arrive at this desired Athenian state of embodied cognition? Lacan used the ancient tale of Zeuxis and Parrhasios to illustrate extimacy and its reversal. These competing painters exemplify different approaches to their audience that illustrate disembodying and embodying artistic methods respectively. Zeuxis had painted grapes that the birds fly down to peck at: "The stress is placed not on the fact that these grapes were in any way perfect grapes, but on the fact that the eye of the birds was taken in by them" (Lacan, 1998, p. 103). In semiotic terms, the grapes are icons or substitutions, which in a *trompe l'oeil*, the birds mistake or misrecognise as indices, objects with which they are bodily contiguous. The birds' eye is enslaved by the gaze of the painter; just as Narcissus's eye is enslaved by his own gaze, and as Althusser's addressee is enslaved by the tone of the hail.

We see Parrhasios triumph, however, "for having painted a veil so lifelike that Zeuxis, turning towards him said, '*well and now show us what you have painted behind it*'" (Lacan, 1998, p. 103). While Zeuxis has painted a *trompe l'oeil*, Parrhasios has painted "something that incites him to ask what is behind it" (p. 112). Parrhasios takes us beyond appearances, beyond the iconic image, into a gap between intellect and corporeality. This puts a temporal and spatial gap between us and our expectations: if we want to check them out, we have to move ourselves bodily, and when we do, we may find our expectations to be flawed and we are confronted with lack. As Lacan puts it:

> What is it that attracts and satisfies us in *trompe l'oeil*? When is it that it captures our attention and delights us? At the moment when, by a mere shift of our gaze, we are able to realize that the representation does not move with the gaze and that it is merely a *trompe l'oeil*. (p. 112)

The *aporia*, or gap, introduces inconsistencies between pattern and sensation, exactly in the manner experienced by Freud's patients on the couch. Freud deliberately positioned himself behind the couch so that his patients had to sit up if they wanted to see him, staging a confrontation between expectation and reality. This gap shifts us back from icon to index, in Lacan's terms, from the eye's misrecognitions, its past experiences, to the body and its contiguities; from pattern to sensation. When we stand on the cusp of the *trompe l'oeil* where Freud and Parrhasios (and as we shall see, Heathcote) place us, we are able to differentiate between iconicity and indexicality, culture and physicality, transposing the switch between semblance and proximity we made at the Mirror Stage.

The ancient theatre carefully choreographed both vocal and visual *aporia* that persist in traditional theatre practice today: an audience may address the stage with its gaze, but not with words; actors may speak, but not interpellate audiences with their gaze. The signifying aspects of voice and gaze are shared in the theatre, so that each experiences "play," a state of flexibility in which each projects and introjects different aspects of its interiority and exteriority, experiencing states of authority over, and exposure to, the other. We may characterise this transaction in the terms of Lacanian philosopher Jacques Rancière (2004) as "democratic" political subjectivisation, which disturbs the "aesthetic coordinates of perception, thought and action" (p. 83). Theatre masks and the *skene*, a wooden structure behind the acting space, provided the ancients with spaces behind the actor's face and the stage itself; connections between signifier and object can be stretched by such spaces, to involve audiences in different intensities of metonymic engagement. "Violent death characteristically occurs within, that is, inside the *skene*, and has its dramatic impact through the death cries of the victim and the controlled passion of the messenger speech" (Gould, 1999, p. 13); the strategy introduces play between signs that generate meaning by means of condensation or association, and those that displace; between the messenger's words and the raw, unmediated voice of a death cry. The conditions for *autopoiesis*, or self-creation, are generated by helping the onlooker differentiate between substitution and contiguity, semblance and proximity. The drama separates culture and physicality by breaking Mirror Stage associations; the gaps or *aporia* of the ancient stage interrupt the illusion of a seamless articulation, or "suture" as Lacan puts it, between bodies and languages.

Dorothy Heathcote's Autopoietic Leadership Model

In her article "Signs (and Portents?)" Dorothy Heathcote (1991) set out thirty-three conventions for dramatic action as a guide for leaders and educators who wish to generate play, the flexibility between bodies and languages that produces agency. To achieve this, the conventions all structure subtly different ways for the class to interact with fictional or historic characters, or "others." In this way, Heathcote managed a variety of strategies for the class to engage with the social gaze. These strategies fall into two basic time states: "now time," in which the role (and so the social gaze) is present; and "imminent time," in which the role (and so the social gaze) is absent. In imminent time the role is represented by attractive visual or auditory signifiers, whose object we feel exists just beyond our sight or hearing. This state of the role being "presently absent" in imminent time is exciting, because signifiers and objects are in flux; the role might reappear, might come back to life, or might notice us eavesdropping. Imminent time also gives the class the enormous benefit of being able to observe and discuss the role, in some cases blatantly and in others more subtly, protected from the gaze of the other in much the same way as the traditional theatre audience. Compare this state of affairs with the more conventional classroom in which we habitually have to submit ourselves to the interpellating words *and* gaze of the teacher. If we characterise seeing and speaking as embodied or *autopoietic* activities, while being seen and spoken to are *allopoietic* or disembodied, then we can begin to grasp how imminent time positions classes to be active rather than passive with signifiers, not mimetically repeating social structure but confronting it enactively in the Athenian manner, in a process that *autopoietic* theorists term "embodied cognition" (Magalhäes & Sanchez, 2009, p. 38).

But as well as managing the dynamics of seeing and being seen, the conventions also disturb the audiovisual synchrony, characterised by "lip-sync," to which we have become so accustomed from watching film and television. Heathcote's conventions regularly position us in the same way that the ancient

Athenians positioned their audiences and Freud positioned his patients on the couch. That is to say, they prevent us from seeing and hearing the same thing at the same time; a disruption that, as we have seen, seems to shift us from a state of *allopoietic* receptivity into a state of *autopoietic* activity. The eye and ear are not knitted up for us as they were when movies became talkies; to make them work together we must become physically involved ourselves, putting us in the state of active in-between-ness, or tension, characterised as "Dionysian vitality" by Rollo May in his discussion of creativity (1994, pp. 115, 50).

All of Heathcote's conventions are characterised by such intermediality. The first fifteen mostly position us between iconic and indexical signifiers, so that we are concerned with the role's visual and auditory appearance and spatial whereabouts. The second sixteen create a tension between symbolic and indexical signifiers, so that we become concerned with the words used by the role, focusing on when, why, and how they may have been written or spoken, and how they relate to the present moment. As we explore the thirty-three conventions, we note their capacity to generate an extraordinarily intense engagement in learners; because the conventions reverse the Mirror Stage merger of pattern and sensation, and instead make them distinct from each other, nothing is habitual or can be taken for granted. May (1994) termed this state of creativity the "encounter of the intensively conscious human being with his or her world" (p. 54). That transformative affects and skills can be deliberately generated by intermedial configurations of sign may be of significant interest for leadership theorists and practitioners.

In the first convention, the role is "actually present, naturalistic, yet significantly behaving, giving and accepting responses" (Heathcote, 1991, p. 166). The second is "the same, except framed as film. That is, people have permission to stare but not intrude. 'Film' can be stopped and restarted, or re-run." In the third convention, the role is "present as in 'effigy.' Can be talked about, walked around, and even sculpted afresh if so framed." The fourth convention is "the same, but with the convention that the effigy can be brought into life-like response and then returned to effigy" (p. 166). When the role shares now time with the class as in the first convention, the *allopoietic* pressure of the eye of the other, or gaze, is upon them; when the role is in imminent time, as with the examples of film or effigy, the class is released from that pressure. When, as in convention 4, the role shifts from imminent time absence into now time presence and back again, the class shifts from being exclusively active in relation to auditory and visual signifiers to being active and passive; from seeing, talking, and touching, to being seen, spoken to, and potentially even touched. In addition to this, when something we took to be inanimate becomes animated, we may experience a momentary uncanny confusion between signifier and object. And when the role returns to effigy, the process is uncannily reversed; something we took to be animate becomes inanimate; we regain our power over the signifier, but often with a sense of having lost something in the process.

Leaders may note from these first four conventions that in addition to the emotional affects outlined, important skills may be generated by our intermedial position between icons and indices. When the role is animate, we are constrained because we see and are seen; we are heard and hear; we may touch the role, but it may also touch us. When the role is iconic, as it is when represented as film, we may see without being seen in return, giving us the power of the voyeur who may watch but not intrude. When the role is represented by an effigy, we acquire the transformational power of the sculptor to reshape the signifier; a power swiftly lost when the effigy comes to life, and regained but probably modified when the effigy returns to inertia. These conventions seem to provide a useful focus for observation skills; classes may look more and more actively until they seem to look with their whole bodies, as sculptors do.

In convention 6, the "role as portrait or effigy is activated *to hear* what the class is saying. This causes selective language" (Heathcote, 1991, p. 166). Convention 7 is "the role as above, but activated to speak only, and not be capable of movement" (p. 166). Again the portrait or effigy crosses over from absence, or imminent time, into presence in now time, but only partially, so that we may see the physical impact of our words in 6 and may ourselves be physically affected by the words of the otherwise physically inert "other" in 7. Leaders may note that we are placed in an intermedial position between languages and bodies here; this is a position that focuses attention on linguistic authority. When words are used upon bodies that may not use words in response, such as words used by parents, teachers, actors, or figures of authority, their extraordinary power to sculpt, or transform, bodies may be observed.

Convention 9 combines the two dimensions of an iconic drawing with the three dimensions of being handled or played with, by representing the role in a "drawing seen in the making, of someone important to the action, as on a blackboard" (Heathcote, 1991, p. 166). Convention 10 involves the "stylised depiction of someone. For example, an identikit picture made by the class, who are framed as detectives, gives us a two-dimensional image that emerges before our eyes in a different way" (p. 166). Convention 11, "the same, except made beforehand, so it is a *fait accompli*" (p. 166), may confound expectations even more strongly, by making its entrance fully formed; it may be unveiled or revealed to the class in a *coup de théâtre*. In these conventions, we are prevented in some way from seeing the image, or we have to wait before we see; this play of time and space puts us in a gap between pattern and sensation. Eventually we observe or infer a connection between signifier and object, but we must wait to do so in a state of expectation. These conventions are the visual equivalent of the rattle, a sound whose cause we cannot identify; these are images we cannot immediately identify, which interpellate, or "see us" before we see them; signifiers that direct attention to their objects indexically, by "blind compulsion" (Chandler, 2002, p. 41), and therefore hold the class in their thrall. Leaders may observe the curatorial principle that withholding access to images makes them become quite literally captivating.

Convention 14 presents us with empty clothes, that is, "clothing of persons cast off in disarray. For example, the remains of a tramp's presence, or a murder, or an escape as in a highwayman situation" (Heathcote, 1991, p. 166). Drawings, photographs, and clothes that were once contiguous with the person who drew the image, was photographed, or wore the clothes generate the same sense of loss we experienced when the role returns to effigy in convention 4; the indexical signifier has been "torn away from the object" (Chandler, 2002, p. 41). The dramatic principle made available to leaders by this convention is the tragic power of lack, or absence. We might argue that this generates the *autopoietic* care for and responsibility toward the other that tragedy gave the ancient Athenians.

While the first fifteen conventions compose mainly visual *aporia*, the second sixteen direct attention largely to the auditory. Just as in the first fifteen we engaged in imminent time with the remnants of a lost physicality, with aspects of a body that frequently lay behind or beyond representation, in the second sixteen conventions we engage with similarly elusive aspects of voice. In these latter conventions the role is most directly present through his or her own words, that is, through speaking, through reading his or her work aloud, and through things that he or she has written. Then, at one remove, the role's spoken words have been written and are voiced by others; his or her written words are spoken by others; and at another remove the role is simply written and spoken about by others in their words.

When we are in touch with the role via words that have ostensibly been written by the role, as in conventions 31, 32, and 33, we engage with the role through the "finding of a cryptic code message. For example 'tramps' or 'spies,'" or through "the signature of a person found. For example, a half burned paper"; or through the "sign of a particular person discovered. For example, the special mark of the Scarlet Pimpernel" (Heathcote, 1991, p. 167). In each case we use our eyes rather than our ears in relation to the symbol, sign, or mark; each visual clue marks contiguity with the role, which may be far distant or long gone: his or her secret concerns, his or her name, his or her hand. Guy Fawkes's signed confession to conspiring to blow up the British Houses of Parliament in 1605 indexes his shaky hand following days of torture in the Tower of London; it is a case in point. Leaders may notice that when signifiers are "torn away from the object" (Chandler, 2002, p. 41), the object or role still seems to haunt the signifier; now time presence haunts the aporia in imminent time. As Freud (1919/2003) observed, objects from the past seem to stalk signifiers of the present: "You cannot walk over a dried up pond without constantly feeling the water might reappear" (p. 129). Because these signs are present, the role, though absent, becomes almost tangibly imminent, as though speaking to us silently through time; as Jacques Rancière (2004) put it, "Meaning is inscribed like hieroglyphics on the body of things and waits to be deciphered" (p. 82).

In other conventions, the role is in touch with the class through reading their writings. In convention 18 we have "an account written by the person who reads it to others, for example a policeman giving evidence or a confession. The role is present in this case but in contact through their writing as an author might well be" (Heathcote, 1991, p. 167). In convention 22 a letter is "read in the voice of the writer. This is an emanation of a specific presence, not just any voice, communicating the words" (p. 167). In both the former more formal case, and the latter more personal case, we may both see and hear the role. Yet seeing and hearing are not seamlessly connected; the tone of voice and visual signifiers belong to now time, the role is present, but the words themselves belong to the time when they were written. Because of the co-presence of the written word and voice, we may focus our attention on the facts the words convey and their emotional impact on the speaker; on the past in the light of the present, and the present in the light of the past. In both cases, the contrast between present and past that is contained in the reading voice, the temporal separation of word and voice, mean that although we may look at the role, we are more likely to be scrutinising how he or she sounds. Leaders may observe that just as we turned to conventions 1 to 4 to encourage visual scrutiny, we may use conventions 18 and 22 to encourage careful listening.

Interestingly, the conventions that deal with the role speaking—25, 26, and 27—also discourage (but do not prevent) us from looking at the role. These are "voice of a person overheard talking to another in informal language, that is using a naturalistic tone"; "the same, but in formal language"; and "a conversation overheard, the people are not seen. Deliberate eavesdropping as in spying" (Heathcote, 1991, p. 167). If we eavesdrop or overhear something, we may not be seen to be focusing our attention on it, or we accidentally become aware of it whilst our attention is focused on something else. So the implication of these conventions is that while we may see the role, we are looking—or pretending to look—at something else. While word and voice are both in now time (the role is present), auditory and visual signifiers are split; we may not see what we hear, or hear what we see. Intriguingly, in convention 27 the constraint on the visual intensifies, and we may neither see nor, as "spies," be seen. The creative tension generated here, which may interest leaders, is between words and voices; informal speech suggests an accent on vocal tone, while formal speech foregrounds the constative import of the words themselves.

In conventions 28, 29, and 30, the role is absent, so we are in imminent time; but others have made written note of things they have said. These conventions show the appropriation of the voice: "a report of a conversation, written and spoken by another"; "a reported conversation with two people reading the respective 'parts'"; and "a private reading of conversations, reported as overheard" (Heathcote, 1991, p. 167). Conversations overheard in the presence of the role are reported in imminent time in the role's absence; this in a voice or voices that may or may not be sympathetic to the original speakers. These voices may undermine or distort the original meaning, subtly as in mimicry, or more overtly as in satire or pastiche. The readers reading the respective parts may focus on emphasising or concealing their attitudes to the original, making the distinction between past and present harder or easier for the observer to make. In the former two conventions we may see as well as hear the readers, so both auditory and visual signifiers operate in the role's absence; we have to work harder to imagine how the originals may have looked and sounded. These conventions give the class the extraordinary transformational power, the capacity to take over a role, that is usually possessed by the actor. A private reading of the conversations, as in convention 30, is less intrusive, however, because the voice is not used; the physicality of the original speaker is not adopted, even though the conversation is overheard and the words themselves have been appropriated.

The vocal appropriation of the written word seems less intrusive than the appropriation of the voice, because although diaries and letters are private documents, the act of writing is more deliberate and less physically intimate than the act of speaking. Indeed, the flavour of these conventions is quite different. Convention 17 is "an account of a person written as if from that person, but read by someone else. For example, a diary"; convention 23 is a letter "read by another with no attempt to portray the person who wrote it, but still expressing a feeling"; convention 24, a "letter read without feeling. For example as evidence, or accusation in a formal situation" (Heathcote, 1991, p. 167). Because the role has written his or her own words in these instances, rather than having them noted down by an eavesdropper, the physicality and purpose of the writer seem more solidly behind them. The first brings words written by the role into the imminent time of the learning environment via the voice of the other, in a way that allows the reader to impose any inflection, or none. The second emphasises the emotionality of the reader's voice, so that the significance of the words to the class in imminent time is emphasised. In the third, the constative significance of the words to the person who wrote them is brought forcibly into imminent time, because the tonality of the reading voice is restricted. The transformative power of the voice to alter the impact of the word, as used by barristers in courts of law, is brought to the fore for leaders here.

These vocal appropriations of the written and spoken word all open an intermedial gap between the word and voice, between languages and bodies, between absence and presence, generating Rollo May's (1994) creative tension. It may be of interest to note that revoicing the spoken words of the role gives the class the power to focus on their own interests, while voicing the role's written words seems to embody, or dramatise, the role's concerns, bringing them to the fore. When signifiers are "torn away from their object" (Chandler, 2002, p. 41), the loss of the object may be powerfully felt as in classical Tragedy, which generates compassion in the class, or the signifier may be appropriated for the purposes of the class in imminent time, which generates potentially comic authority. These conventions generate a potentially vast range of affects, accessed by the ancients in their comic and tragic dramas.

In convention 19 we have "an account written by someone, of someone else and read by yet another"; convention 21 is "a report of an event but formalised by authority or ritual. For example, an account of bravery in battle on an occasion of the presenting of posthumous medals" (Heathcote, 1991, p. 167). In these conventions the role is absent, written about, and the accounts or reports read aloud. In the former, less formal convention, we have many layers to contend with: the person, the word, and the voice are all separated, so the connections between role, writer, and reader cannot be observed and have to be inferred, making the convention curiously involving for the class. The words are freighted with the absence of two people, and so potentially poignant; the third party reading the words may be disconnected emotionally, injecting a note of irony to the already complex palimpsest. In the latter convention, the reader's authority, or the formality of the reader's situation, gives the words prominence over the reading voice, taking away one of the layers and making the reading more apparently factual.

In the final category, the role is absent and is spoken about by another. Convention 16 gives "an account of a person by another person in naturalistic fashion. For example, 'Well when last I saw him he seemed alright. I never dreamed anything was wrong'" (Heathcote, 1991, p. 167). Convention 20 is a "story told of another in order to bring that person close to the action. For example, 'I saw him open a safe once. It was an incredible performance. I'm not sure if he'd assist us though'" (p. 167). In both cases, we look at the speaker, so auditory and visual signifiers are not split; the words are not read, so there is no gap between voice and word. But although we both see and hear the speaker, we neither see nor hear the person of whom he or she speaks, so these signifiers may be operating quite independently of their object; we are dependent on the powers of observation of the other, and also on his or her truthfulness. Because we can see the speaker, visual and auditory signifiers operate in synchrony, verifying each other, so we may be inclined to trust them. These conventions have the considerable power of gossip to characterise and interpellate or conjure the role, in terms that suit the speaker.

Conclusion

This chapter offers Heathcote's conventions for dramatic action to leadership theorists and practitioners because they seem to generate Rollo May's (1994) "Dionysian vitality" (pp. 115, 50), the mysterious creative flow described by Thucydides that transforms both situations and identities. This creativity, we propose, is rooted in a dramatic intervention, so that the apparently seamless connections between bodies and languages that are forged at Lacan's Mirror Stage are disrupted. Heathcote's conventions provide us with thirty-three nuanced ways to introduce "play," the formal Derridean (2000) flexibility between culture and physicality. We argue that these conventions create the intense, involving, and ultimately transformative encounters with the world that Rollo May claimed are experienced by artists.

Conventions 1 to 15, for instance, offer classes different ways of engaging with the role in the visual field. The various configurations of iconic and indexical signifiers place classes on a dramatic "cusp" or borderline between looking and being seen, between what we may term "embodied" and "disembodied" seeing. Classes experience the dynamics of interacting with the living other; observing moving two-dimensional images as a film editor might; configuring the three-dimensional image physically as a sculptor; being aware of effects their words might have on the physicality of the silent other as an actor might be; being physically affected by words as audiences are. Classes encounter carefully curated images as in an art gallery or museum, and face a tinge of tragic loss when their expectations are confronted with lack.

Conventions 16 to 33 put us in touch with the role through the written or spoken word in the symbolic mode; again, the role hovers between presence and absence so that the class is placed among voices and words, experiencing embodied and disembodied speaking, on a cusp between making meaning from contiguities (handwriting and voices) and substituting signs (words). The class encounters words as an anthropologist might, as hieroglyphic signs, key to unlocking cultural secrets of the past; listening as a detective or a spy listens, alert to any incongruity between word and voice; speaking as an actor, barrister, or gossip might, choosing to inflect a word with a certain emotional tone to change its meaning. Discrepancies between pattern and sensation can decenter, engage, and generate the transformative affects leaders seek. As May (1994) remarked, "People can more accurately observe precisely when they are emotionally involved—that is, reason works better when emotions are present; the person sees sharper and more accurately when his [sic] emotions are engaged" (p. 49).

We can understand play, in this Derridean sense, as a pleasurably liminal state in which learners may personally mediate between linguistic pattern and prelinguistic sensation. According to Lacan (1998), such intermediality both "attracts and satisfies us" (p. 112). Play transforms situations and identities because it gives us opportunities to engage dynamically with signifiers. *Allopoietic* learning implies a certain passivity or receptivity in relation to signifiers; like the industrial assembly line, *allopoietic* systems are "subordinated to the production of something different from themselves, they are not autonomous" (Maturana & Varela, 1980, p. 80). When we are active with signifiers, however, we are engaging with culture, not simply reproducing it. Play is *autopoietic* and transformational because it puts us in a position to define, as well as be defined by, culture.

Implications for Further Study and Research

The UK website www.mantleoftheexpert.com is a resource for educators who wish to use Heathcote's strategies; it contains digital footage of Heathcote and other practitioners using the conventions, as well as many free articles relating to the theory and practice of the work. Grimley and Holt Primary School in Worcester and Woodrow First School in Redditch in the British

West Midlands are notable for using Heathcote's dramatic learning systems to deliver their entire curriculum. Their work demonstrates the principles outlined in this chapter and is at present unresearched.

References

Althusser, L. (2001). Essays on ideology. In C. Counsell & L. Wolf (Eds.), *Performance analysis* (pp. 32–42). London, UK: Routledge.

Butler, J. (1993). *Bodies that matter: On the discursive limits of "sex."* London, UK: Routledge.

Castoriadis, C. (1987). *The imaginary institution of society*. Cambridge, MA: MIT Press.

Chandler, D. (2002). *Semiotics: The basics*. London, UK: Routledge.

Derrida, J. (2000). Structure, sign, and play in the discourse of the human sciences. In D. Lodge (Ed.), *Modern criticism and theory* (pp. 88–103). London, UK: Longman.

Freud, S. (2003). *The uncanny*. Harmondsworth, UK: Penguin. (Original work published 1919)

Gould, J. (1999). Tragedy in performance. In P. Easterling & B. Knox (Eds.), *Greek drama* (pp. 6–29). Cambridge, UK: Cambridge University Press.

Heathcote, D. (1991). *Collected writings on education and drama*. Evanston, IL: Northwestern University Press.

Lacan, J. (1992). *The seminar of Jacques Lacan, Book VII: The ethics of psychoanalysis*. New York, NY: Norton.

Lacan, J. (1998). *The seminar of Jacques Lacan, Book XI: The four fundamental concepts of psychoanalysis*. London, UK: Norton.

Lacan, J. (2006). *Ecrits*. London, UK: Norton.

Magalhäes, R., & Sanchez, R. (2009). *Autopoiesis in organisation theory and practice*. Bingley, UK: Emerald Group.

Maturana, H., & Varela, F. (1980). *Autopoiesis and cognition: The realization of the living*. London, UK: Reidel.

May, R. (1994). *The courage to create*. London, UK: Norton.

Rancière, J. (2004). *The politics of aesthetics*. London, UK: Continuum.

Winnington-Ingram, R. P. (1999). The origins of tragedy. In P. Easterling & B. Knox (Eds.), *Greek drama* (pp. 1–6). Cambridge, UK: Cambridge University Press.

Chapter Three

Leadership in the Time of Liminality

A Framework for Leadership in an Era of Deep Transformation

David Holzmer

> Today, many things indicate that we are going
> through a transitional period, when it seems that
> something is on the way out and something else
> is painfully being born. It is as if something were
> crumbling, decaying, and exhausting itself—while
> something else, still indistinct, were arising from
> the rubble.
>
> *Vaclav Havel (1994)*

As economic destabilization, political turmoil, and global crises continue to breed uncertainty and, at times, alarm among those inside and outside of organizations, a growing consensus has formed that our society has entered into an era of unprecedented transition (Acemoglu & Robinson, 2012; Acemoglu, Robinson, & Verdier, 2012; Reinhart & Rogoff, 2011; Rifkin, 2009, 2011). While some may conclude that events such as the lingering global financial meltdown and the planet's climate crisis signal oncoming collapse (Heinberg, 2011; Martenson, 2011), there are others (Gilding, 2011; Hala & Marien, 2011) who believe that these systemic disruptions are fortuitous indicators of the emergence of a more stable and resilient social order. However, even if concern over either of these contrasting scenarios seems overstated, it is clear that organizations and their leaders are now forced to contend with challenges that were quite unprecedented just a generation ago. Indeed, today many leaders are struggling to make sense of confounding conditions and circumstances that no longer conform to traditional models and social norms. More and more the thought is emerging that uncertain conditions *inside* organizations reflect broader cultural transitions taking place *outside* organizations, and these transitions are prompting reconsideration of what leadership means and how it is practiced. Wilfred Drath (2001), for example, acknowledged this linkage when asserting that "leadership is in fact changing in ways determined by changes in our way of life, in our ways of understanding, and especially in our ways of interrelating" (p. xiv).

A New Mind-Set Needed to Address Unprecedented Demands

The idea that new models and practices are needed to replace long-familiar ones has been raised by many (Collinson, 2012; Heifetz, Grashow, & Linsky, 2009; Hughes, Thompson, & Terrell, 2009; Mabey & Morrell, 2011; Nye, 2008). Lichtenstein, Uhl-Bien, Marion, Seers, Orton, and Schreiber (2006) have raised concerns that conventional models of leadership, particularly those based on hierarchical power structures, "are less and less useful given the complexities of our modern world" (p. 2); however, the transition toward new, more fitting leadership practices summons both scholars and practitioners to cultivate a new kind of thinking and discourse on the subject. Along such lines a number of leadership and organizational thinkers (Beech, 2011; Collinson, 2012; Drath, McCauley, Palus, Van Velsor, O'Connor, & McGuire, 2008; McCauley, Drath, Palus, O'Connor, & Baker, 2006; Uhl-Bien, Marion, & McKelvey, 2007) have argued that it is not new tools and techniques but more sophisticated worldviews that are needed to address the challenges leadership now faces. McGonagill and Dörffer (2010), for example, pointed out that "all the tools in the world will not change anything if the mindset does not allow and support change" (p. 3).

This chapter proposes a three-part framework to enable both scholars and practitioners to develop such mind-sets by cultivating their own thinking about leadership in an era when industrial age practices and principles no longer apply as they once did. The intent of the framework is to create what Harding (1998) called a "thinking space" where "new kinds of questions are asked" (p. 17). The framework describes three interrelated conceptual domains—liminality, performance, and dialogue—that get to the heart of flux and uncertainty while simultaneously grounding scholars and practitioners in perspectives that help in the development of tools and mind-sets for moving ahead. Liminality, performance, and dialogue serve as important and integrated moorings or reference points to help leaders better respond to their own and others' experience of disruptive transformation. This framework will be useful in helping leaders address such fundamental issues as how leadership can remain relevant, how leaders can effectively engage with those around them, and what methods can best help leaders accomplish these objectives.

Introducing the Framework

This chapter outlines a general overview of the three-part conceptual framework, including a discussion of the rationale informing its structure and purpose. This is followed by three sections, each covering one of the three conceptual domains of liminality, performance, and dialogue. This conceptual design supports practice and scholarship that are congruent with the dynamics of disruptive change. It also supports leaders in the further development of their own self-concepts that are evolving as a result of upheaval and transition. The objectives could therefore be said to follow Cooper and Law's (1995) call, based on their observations of change and its impact upon personal ontology, for a "sociology of becoming" (p. 238).

The framework provides an interdisciplinary foundation for reflective inquiry through which leaders may work with those around them (compare Drath, 2001; Goldstein, Hazy, & Lichtenstein, 2010; Küpers & Weibler, 2008; Shaw, 2002) and move beyond the identified limitations of models that cast them (leaders) as all-knowing heroic exemplars (Crevani, Lindgren, & Packendorff, 2007; Grint, 2010; Roth, 1994; Yukl, 1999). This framework is intended to help move beyond the fragmentation and constraint associated with industrial era command-and-control approaches (Crevani and others, 2007; Drath, 2001; Grint, 2010) to change and toward more integrative views.

Many of the framework's central features look beyond the primary epistemological foundation of leadership studies. The central features have been drawn from several complementary disciplines, including anthropology, performance studies, psychology, and feminist social theory.

Instead of simply providing a new set of tools or "fresh" takes that essentially repackage long-held assumptions in order to address current challenges, the framework aims to question leadership's long-standing reliance upon the positivist ideals of heroic rationality (Hosking, 2007; Küpers & Weibler, 2008; Western, 2008). Instead, by adopting a broader vision that aims to look beyond the limitations of positivist models (Argyris, 2000; Drath, 2001; Murrell, 1997), this framework offers a set of core concepts intended to support the continual cultivation of more complex and inclusive (Kegan, 1994) ways of understanding the world.

This move toward more complex and inclusive forms and practices of leadership follows thinking advanced by a number of scholars, including McGonagill and Dörffer (2010), who reported that a "new leadership paradigm seems to be emerging that is marked by an inexorable shift away from one-way, hierarchical, organization-centric communication toward two-way, network-centric, participatory and collaborative leadership styles" (p. 3). Marion (1999) likewise offered a useful rationale for this new, more fluid mind-set when writing that

> if environments are stable, unchanging, and predictable, then leaders can put together a rather simple organizational structure, one run by a handful of straightforward rules and with minimal supervision. If the environment is unstable, however, organizational structure must be flexible, i.e., leaders and workers must be able to adapt on the fly and to make ad hoc decisions. Such environments are far too complex to be dealt with by a simple organizational structure. (p. 84)

As Marion (1999) asserted, in some settings, fixed rules and solid structures may work well to ensure reliable outcomes. However, more and more (Petrie, 2011), organizations are struggling when confronting turbulence, at least partly because of leaders' reliance upon approaches more suited to a time when stability and predictable growth could be expected.

For this reason, the framework's three core conceptual domains of liminality, performance, and dialogue can help leaders transition from the traditional ideals of prediction, rationality, and control toward more adaptive perspectives (Drath, 2001; Heifetz, 1994; Murrell, 1997) based on process (Shaw, 2002; Tsoukas & Chia, 2002); embodiment (Stacey, 2005, 2010); and relationality (Gergen & Thatchenkery, 2004; Hosking, 2007; Uhl-Bien & Ospina, 2012). Liminality supports this move by familiarizing leaders with the ideas of perpetual flux and disruption. Performance contributes to this by helping leaders develop a coherent sense of identity in the face of their many, sometimes divergent, roles, all of which appear influenced by the underlying tension between stability and flux that Marion (1999) described. Dialogue offers leaders a means of grounding the theoretical aspects of this framework in material practice.

The framework is intended to help leaders better understand the collective scripting of new and future mental models. For this reason it is instructive to briefly review how traditional models of leadership—those based upon narratives of heroic leaders (Grint, 2010; Hosking, 2007) and the ongoing reaffirmation of their image and actions (Meindl, Ehrlich, & Dukerich, 1985) as revered exemplars—came into being.

In their examination of the socially constructed nature of organizational life, Gergen and Thatchenkery (2004) pointed out that much of what is popularly understood today about organizations and leadership came into vogue in the first quarter of the twentieth century. At this time, Enlightenment-era thinking about progress and the nature of individuality was still dominant. As they noted, "It is this eighteenth-century valorization of the individual mind that came to serve as the major rationalizing device for the twentieth-century beginnings of organizational science" (p. 230). The authors pointed out that this link between the individual and rationality has, over time, become a deeply entrenched social script wherein individuals designated as "leaders" are revered as the exemplars of rational thought and actions. Hosking (2007) made the case that the organization is subsequently considered to be the material manifestation of the leader's thinking and actions.

The three interdependent conceptual domains of the framework I offer serve as a foundation upon which leaders can individually and collaboratively construct alternative mental models predicated on the notion that change emerges from within the system itself, not outside of it. In fact, change should be considered an inherent characteristic (Tsoukas & Chia, 2002) of the organization, woven deeply into the fabric of its being. As I discuss, by understanding organizations as sites of liminality, members will be better equipped to recognize and engage with the turbulence and disruptive change through communicative acts (Ford, 1999; Shaw, 2002).

A Three-Part Conceptual Framework

Conceptual Domain 1: Liminality

Central to this framework is the notion of liminality, a disorienting and disruptive period of transition that anthropologist Victor Turner (1971) has referred to as "the betwixt and between" (p. 4). While the term is now most often used metaphorically, Turner (1977a) explained that liminality, an idea taken from anthropological accounts detailing structured rites of passage in indigenous societies, served as a "vehicle of transition from one sociocultural state and status to another" (p. 466). Turner (1971, 1977b, 1986a, 1986b), for example, pointed out that the idea of liminality remains valuable for describing a tumultuous reorientation, where future conditions, which ultimately offer greater opportunities and empowerment based upon a more encompassing and complex worldview, can no longer be ascertained via once-reliable tools of prediction.

When applied as a conceptual grounding for further discussion, the notion of liminality is a valuable heuristic for understanding conditions marked by pervasive uncertainty and ambiguity. For leaders, this proves important in a world that is increasingly complex, interdependent, contextualized, and unwilling to succumb to the traditional demands for unequivocal formulas and forecasting. Beech (2011), who recognized the mismatch between current challenges and traditional remedies, argued—paradoxically, perhaps—that for leaders faced with unrelenting turbulence, the idea of liminality offers a stabilizing and generative influence amid "instabilities in the social context, the ongoing ambiguity and multiplicity of meanings, [as well as] the lack of resolution" (p. 288).

Liminality, while acknowledging disruption and upheaval, derives strength and relevance by helping to focus individuals toward their own and their society's inherent undercurrents of renewal and realignment (Beech, 2011; Turner, 1971). For leaders attempting to navigate conditions of flux or ambiguity, liminality helps to support the transition away from fixed hierarchical arrangements toward new forms and practices rooted in more resilient and collaborative structures (McGonagill & Dörffer, 2010) that constructively respond to change and disorientation. Such change is then not experienced as periodic disruptions but as the new norm (Tsoukas & Chia, 2002).

Leaders, then, must approach liminality as an important and necessary condition in a disruptive and systemic process unfolding on cultural, political, economic, and organizational scales. However, this same understanding of liminality is equally valuable when approaching disruption on a much smaller scale. In addition to addressing systemwide macro-disruptions, liminality is also a valuable reference point for individuals confronting their own mental, emotional, and relational disorientation as a result of undergoing life-changing conditions on a broader scale. For such individuals, particularly those in positions of leadership, familiarity with the idea of liminality also helps them to acquire more complex and inclusive worldviews and identities as a way to make sense of disruptions during times of great change.

In this way, leaders can make use of liminal spaces to construct new narratives that, as Turner (1977b) noted, are based upon "potency and potentiality" (p. 46) while affording effective opportunities for more collaborative action (Gergen & Thatchenkery, 2004) rather than seeing them as unwelcome times of loss or upheaval needing to be overcome or endured.

Awareness of divergent norms and the tension they generate is critical for leaders wishing to leverage disruption and take advantage of liminality as an archway toward the creation of new processes and forms. Tension arising from the interaction of diverse elements (Gregory, 1999; Page, 2007; Thomas & Gregory, 1995), whether they be individuals from divergent cultures or ideas derived from divergent paradigms, can act as a potent catalyst (Goldstein and others, 2010; Uhl-Bien and others, 2007) for creative problem solving and of collaborative innovation. By exploring this tension and utilizing its generative potential, leaders can more fully develop the rich reservoir of generative energies (Beech, 2011; Patterson, 2009; Turner, 1971, 1977b) contained within liminal experiences. However, such attunement also calls for an awareness of how organizational members are often caught in the gap between historical norms and rapidly shifting, highly ambiguous demands. In addition, for leaders, awareness of the inability of past models to adequately address present problems can help them be more "present" (Santorelli, 2011) with themselves and others while being better able to facilitate outcomes during times of uncertainty and upheaval. Such presence can alert them to the fact that they may experience a broad range of emotions, some quite uncomfortable, when trying to balance the outmoded notion (Manz & Sims, 1989) of the heroic leader (Grint, 2010; Meindl and others, 1985) with the complex demands of liminal transitions (compare Shaw, 2002). With this awareness, leaders may be better situated to address their work from a perspective that includes a broader pallet of sense-making modalities. These new options are the result of a new mind-set that calls into question leadership's long-standing and unquestioning reliance upon perspectives wrought from Cartesian thinking. Such a mind-set requires a wholesale reconsideration of the very mental models upon which our assumptions about leadership and organizations rest.

Yet, the effectiveness of such rethinking depends on expanding leaders' awareness of liminality and how liminality intersects with organizational life on a micro and a macro scale. With an understanding of liminality, members can begin to appreciate the shifting and contingent nature of their own thought processes. For members, this, in turn, can open the door to the realization that one's entire frame for organizing and engaging with reality is, likewise, capable of change and development (Kegan, 1982, 1994) depending upon contextual demands. As Torbert's (2004) research showed, such recognition can offer the individual an opportunity to develop a meaning-making system more aligned with the shifting and ambiguous nature of his or her experience within the organization.

The notion that the ebb and flow of members' relational dynamics continually influence an organization's awareness of its own identity is congruent with the work of scholars (Drath, 2001; Hosking & McNamee, 2006) who approach leadership and organizations as socially constructed processes. As Drath pointed out, "In trying to make leadership happen while working together, people construct one another" (p. xvi). Moreover, by beginning to work *with* relational dynamics—and specifically with the tension between traditional role expectations and the psychoemotional demands of bodies interacting within a shared space—leaders have an opportunity to support others in the process of broadening their own perspectives of organizational life (Corman & Poole, 2000; Hosking & McNamee, 2006; Kegan, 1982). Such development can, in turn, help to expand the individual's psychosocial awareness and help individuals integrate more complex and inclusive meaning-making systems (Kegan, 1982, 1994; Torbert, 2004). As Rooke and Torbert (1998) have shown, this evolution of individuals' cognitive capacity also positively affects the problem-solving capacity of the organization as a whole.

Conceptual Domain 2: Performance

If the notion of liminality is introduced to help leaders understand the shifting environment and contingent contexts in which they lead, then the idea of performance is important to help leaders better understand their own evolving roles and identity within these settings. Goffman (1959) was one of the first critical thinkers to explore the notion of performance as a sociological construct. His approach holds to the idea that performance is simply a process through which one individual acts in a manner intended to elicit a predetermined response from others. As Goffman framed it, performance encompasses "all the activity of a given [individual] on a given occasion which serves to influence in any way another" (p. 15).

A clearer understanding of performance's relationship to leadership emerges from Judith Butler's (1988) notion of "sedimented acts." Developed in her work on performance and gender, the term is one Butler used to describe the "deeply entrenched or sedimented expectations" (p. 524) that an individual unconsciously acts out in order to influence others' behavior so as to adhere to society's deeply held presumptions about power and authority.

Considering leadership's long association with hierarchical structures and control practices (Eisler & Carter, 2010; Evans, 2011), Butler's idea of sedimented acts helps to illustrate how traditional notions of leadership practice depend upon the repetition of culturally inscribed routines of authority and domination. Viewed from this perspective, a new awareness emerges where traditional leadership practices are now understood to be based upon the performance of sedimented acts for the purpose of control and domination.

Control and Embodiment. The idea that leadership is informed by an impulse to engage in performances of control is underscored by leadership's long-standing tendency (Ladkin, 2011) to separate the mind from the body. For centuries, this view has asserted the notion that leadership is a process that resides not in the body or the emotions but in the realm of symbolic abstraction (Lord & Shondrick, 2011). This separates leadership from the human body while also denying its basis in corporeal experience. As Ladkin noted, this separation can be traced back to the Enlightenment's quest for "ultimate truths." In large measure this quest, which has influenced many of the structures and paradigms that continue to inform Western society, is underscored by the belief that the one "true" reality can only be apprehended through the mind, and that sense perception, at best, is only capable of delivering inconsistent and unreliable information.

This idea of disconnection from the body is supported by Hansen, Ropo, and Sauer (2007), who pointed to the influence of the seventeenth-century thinker René Descartes (1596–1650) and asserted that "Cartesian thinking did not so much separate the mind/body as simply ditch the body" (p. 546).

Ladkin (2011) pointed out how in today's leadership environment, Descartes's pursuit of "ultimate truths" clearly undermines the experience of embodiment because, with Cartesian thought, "the cognitively based, transcendent aspects of being human have been privileged over the immanent, corporeal ones" (p. 58). A similar idea is suggested by Ropo and Parviainen (2001), who pointed out that the traditional approaches to leadership and organizational theory "tend to ignore the body . . . or treat it as an object and nothing else" (p. 1).

Yet this tradition of separating bodily experience from cognitive engagement runs counter to what is now being proposed by others (Hansen and others, 2007; Harquail & King, 2010; Ladkin, 2011; Uhl-Bien, 2006). Stacey's (2010) work, for example, on leadership and embodiment identified the latter as a highly practical approach to leading in conditions of complexity. In support, Stacey makes the case that "it is the body rather than consciousness that understands the world" (p. 128).

O'Malley, Ritchie, Lord, Gregory, and Young (2009) provided an explanation of why leaders must be aware of the influence of embodiment in leadership practice: "The physical states, perceptual structures, and motor systems that accompany knowledge creation are incorporated into knowledge itself" (p. 154). For leaders, this idea that knowledge extends beyond what can be perceived and processed by the intellect alone unsettles the very foundation of traditional models by challenging the idea of cognition as a process based exclusively on symbols and abstractions (Lord & Shondrick, 2011) that are capable of conveying the "full range of individuals' organizational experience" (Harquail & King, 2010, p. 1622).

An approach that incorporates embodied perspectives will support leaders' becoming more conscious of the multifaceted nature (Cook-Greuter, 2005; Kegan, 1982, 1994) of their own identity, how that identity is performed, and what that identity represents to others in an organizational setting (Fairhurst & Grant, 2010). This consciousness can help them become more aware of the tensions and incongruities that occur when traditional role identities fail to help leaders cope with the psychoemotional impact of complex and shifting demands. However, in such situations, leaders can reflexively strive to balance (Bohm & Factor, 1995) their own culturally prescribed roles with their embodied experience. This can help members leverage the generative potential of liminality by understanding how meaning itself is continually being rescripted and how this rescripting continually redefines the organization anew (Goldstein and others, 2010; Tsoukas & Chia, 2002).

Performance, Embodiment, and Generative Tension. Viewed through the lens of liminality, where the so-called ultimate truths underscoring the very idea of leadership begin to be seen as fluid, contestable, and, by extension, socially constructed, the assumptions underscoring heroic leadership performances begin to seem less absolute. This, in turn, affords scholars and practitioners the opportunity to look toward a more conscious and embodied approach to leadership practice. Traditional images of leadership reflect fixed, absolutist values and characterizations. By contrast, the notion of liminality helps to further a vision of leadership as an ongoing dialectic between two related but frequently divergent processes: the leader's enactment, or performance, of reified social norms, and the leader's own embodied experience of that performance.

Put another way, in addition to undertaking the enactment of culturally sanctioned performances, the leader is also a body in performance with other bodies, having the experience that Donna Ladkin (2011) refered to as "a visceral, felt response" (p. 153).

Thus, instead of enforcing control and compliance, leaders, who can never fully escape the performative aspects of their role, can begin to approach their performance more consciously. In this way, sedimented acts can be utilized for the purpose of providing the structure and feedback needed to encourage the divergent thinking (Csikszentmihalyi, 1996) and the generative tension (Gregory, 1999; Page, 2007; Thomas & Gregory, 1995) needed for the emergence (Goldstein and others, 2010) of more complex models of problem solving and innovation.

By introducing an embodied approach, the framework helps scholars and practitioners recognize that tension ensuing between the experience of performance and that of embodiment can be a valuable resource. Moreover, by approaching leadership as an embodied performance through which hierarchical norms are openly acknowledged and appropriately utilized, such performances can, over time, promote a vision of leadership as collaborative social process in which bodies are engaged in the moment-by-moment rescripting of meaning and objectives.

Three Goals of Embodied Performances. Performance as a conceptual domain achieves three crucial goals: (1) acknowledges both the reified and the embodied aspects of performance; (2) treats them as equally important, refusing to privilege one over the other; (3) allows leaders to explore the creative dynamics that emerge through the generative tensions that result from the interplay of reified and embodied aspects of performance. The framework's third domain shows that these tensions and their associated creative forces are experienced through the process of dialogue.

Liminality has traditionally offered rebirth through a disruption in established routines and relationships. Stacey (2005) alluded to the body's capacity for supporting regenerative social processes when he pointed out that "human interaction is basically responsive communication between human bodies where each is conscious and self-conscious, and so capable of reflection, reflexivity, imagination and fantasy" (p. 26). Stacey's notion of engaged, mindful communication is critical, for it not only gets to the heart of what liminality offers, it also points the way toward the practical application of the abstract principles discussed in this chapter through the practice of dialogue.

Conceptual Domain 3: Dialogue

Unlike traditional anthropological accounts of liminal passages (Van Gennep, 1960) in which the individual is only able to reconsider his or her identity by being separated from his or her primary community, contemporary accounts (Beech, 2011) indicate that those in the midst of the liminal experience need direct engagement with their community in order to experience the rebirth of their identity. Leadership theorists from complexity science (Goldstein and others, 2010; Hazy & Silberstang, 2009; Shaw, 2002) and the social sciences (Drath, 2001; Fairhurst & Grant, 2010; Hosking & McNamee, 2006) are in agreement that transformation is a social process that occurs through collaborative engagement, or as Gergen (2009) called it, "the confluence." Gergen explained that "we exist within a confluence—an array of mutually defining relationships with each other and our surrounds" (p. 56). As Goldstein and others (2010) pointed out, "The true catalysts of innovation are the web of relationship— in the nexus of interactions" (p. 2). For these and other authors, the dynamic center of this web is the communicative process; or, put another way, the dialectical space "between" people where meaning is fluid and contestable.

Because the communicative space between people is so crucial for the emergence of new ideas and awareness, the process of dialogue is the third component in the framework for leadership in this era of liminality.

Dialogue as a Transformative Process. Scholars (Bohm, 1996; Ford, 1999; Isaacs, 1999) increasingly recognize dialogue for its ability to shift mind-sets within collaborative settings and establish new frames of meaning that accommodate more complex forms of sense-making. Theoretical physicist David Bohm (1996) was one of the first to closely examine the power of dialogue as a catalyst for transformation. As a result of his exploration, Bohm determined that "dialogue is really aimed at going to the whole thought process and changing the way the thought process occurs collectively" (p. 10). Shaw (2002) also found this in her examination of dialogue as the primary tool for shifting organizational identity. She writes that "in the movement of our everyday communicative activity, we are creating who we are and what we can do together within shifting constraints of a material, technological and social nature" (p. 30).

While it is beyond the scope of this chapter to offer a road map for using dialogue in this way, it is clear that in this time of liminality, more effective forms of leadership and sense-making will not depend on heroic leaders or oppressive power dynamics; such advancement lies in the ability to speak to one another openly and with a clear sense of purpose about the confounding nature of all that is before us.

Thoughts for Practice and Future Consideration

This chapter explores leadership through a three-part conceptual framework. In so doing, I suggest that new perspectives emerge through the dynamic tension between reified leadership routines and the mental, emotional, and physical response patterns that arise through bodies in relationship with other bodies. However, new perspectives only come to full fruition when organizational tensions are brought into focus through a process of dialogue through which individuals have the opportunity to explore new ideas and identities through collective sense-making.

The chapter is intended as a conceptual tool to aid scholars and leadership practitioners in the development of new forms of leadership practice and new ways to think about leadership. Torbert (2004) found that leaders required advanced psychological development to develop and use more complex and inclusive worldviews, and that this development is only possible if leaders surrender traditional worldviews and deeply reflect upon their beliefs about both leadership and themselves. Such introspection, he found, leads to a shift toward new, more complex ways of thinking that, in turn, support more inclusive and multiperspectival worldviews.

Given the disruptive conditions leaders now face, research into potential correlations between awareness of liminality and cognitive development could prove important for helping scholars and practitioners better understand how disruptive dynamics might support the acquisition of more complex ways of seeing the world. Such research could also open the way toward new approaches to leadership that frame disruption and upheaval as harbingers of new systems of thought based upon higher-stage cognitive development. Research aimed at the development of such mind-sets could also lead to the discovery of new models of leadership practice based on the revelation of heretofore unimagined ways of creating meaning and coherence amid extreme conditions of upheaval and uncertainty.

References

Acemoglu, D., & Robinson, J. A. (2012). *Why nations fail: The origins of power, prosperity and poverty*. New York, NY: Crown Publishers.

Acemoglu, D., Robinson, J. A., & Verdier, T. (2012). *Can't we all be more like Scandinavians? Asymmetric growth and institutions in an interdependent world*. London, UK: Centre for Economic Policy Research.

Argyris, C. (2000). *Flawed advice and the management trap: How managers can know when they're getting good advice and when they're not*. New York, NY: Oxford University Press.

Beech, N. (2011). Liminality and the practices of identity reconstruction. *Human Relations*, 64(2), 285–302. doi:10.1177/0018726710371235

Bohm, D. (1996). *On dialogue*. London, UK: Routledge.

Bohm, D., & Factor, D. (1995). *Unfolding meaning: A weekend of dialogue with David Bohm*. New York, NY: Routledge.

Butler, J. (1988). Performative acts and gender constitution: An essay in phenomenology and feminist theory. *Theatre Journal, 40*(4), 519–531.

Collinson, D. (2012). Prozac leadership and the limits of positive thinking. *Leadership, 8*(2), 87–107.

Cook-Greuter, S. R. (2005). *Ego development: Nine levels of increasing embrace*. http://panendeism.web.officelive.com/Documents/9%20levels%20increasing%20embrace%20update%202007.pdf

Cooper, R., & Law, J. (1995). Organization: Distal and proximal views. *Research in the Sociology of Organizations, 13*, 237–274.

Corman, S. R., & Poole, M. S. (2000). *Perspectives on organizational communication: Finding common ground*. New York, NY: Guilford Press.

Crevani, L., Lindgren, M., & Packendorff, J. (2007). Shared leadership: A postheroic perspective on leadership as a collective construction. *International Journal of Leadership Studies, 3*(1), 40–67.

Csikszentmihalyi, M. (1996). *Creativity: Flow and the psychology of discovery and invention*. New York, NY: HarperCollins.

Drath, W. H. (2001). *The deep blue sea: Rethinking the source of leadership*. San Francisco, CA: Jossey-Bass.

Drath, W. H., McCauley, C. D., Palus, C. J., Van Velsor. E., O'Connor, P.M.G., & McGuire, J. B. (2008). Direction, alignment, commitment: Toward a more integrative ontology of leadership. *The Leadership Quarterly, 19*(6), 635–653. doi:10.1016/j.leaqua.2008.09.003

Eisler, R., & Carter, S. (2010). Transformative leadership: From domination to partnership. *Revision, 30*(3–4), 98–106. doi:10.4298/REVN.30.3.4.98-106

Evans, T. (2011, March). Leadership without domination? Toward restoring the human and natural world. *Journal of Sustainability Education, 2*. http://www.jsedimensions.org/wordpress/wp-content/uploads/2011/03/Evans2011.pdf

Fairhurst, G., & Grant, D. (2010). The social construction of leadership: A sailing guide. *Management Communication Quarterly, 24*(2), 171–210. doi:10.1177/0893318909359697

Ford, J. D. (1999). Organizational change as shifting conversations. *Journal of Organizational Change Management, 12*(6), 480–500. doi:10.1108/09534819910300855

Gergen, K. J. (2009). *Relational being: Beyond self and community*. Oxford, UK: Oxford University Press.

Gergen, K. J., & Thatchenkery, T. J. (2004). Organization science as social construction: Postmodern potentials. *Journal of Applied Behavioral Science, 40*(2), 228–249. doi:10.1177/0021886304263860

Gilding, P. (2011). *The great disruption: Why the climate crisis will bring on the end of shopping and the birth of a new world*. New York, NY: Bloomsbury.

Goffman, E. (1959). *The presentation of self in everyday life*. Garden City, NY: Doubleday.

Goldstein, J., Hazy, J. K., & Lichtenstein, B. B. (2010). *Complexity and the nexus of leadership: Leveraging nonlinear science to create ecologies of innovation*. New York, NY: Palgrave Macmillan.

Gregory, T. A. (1999). Beyond winners and losers: Diversity as a learning phenomenon. In P. Senge, A. Kleiner, C. Roberts, R. Ross, G. Roth, & B. Smith (Eds.), *The dance of change: The challenges to sustaining momentum in learning organizations* (pp. 274–279). New York, NY: Doubleday Currency.

Grint, K. (2010). The sacred in leadership: Separation, sacrifice and silence. *Organization Studies, 31*(1), 89–107. doi:10.1177/0170840609347054

Hala, W., & Marien, M. (2011). Global megacrisis: A survey of four scenarios on a pessimism-optimism axis. *Journal of Futures Studies, 16*(2), 65–84.

Hansen, H., Ropo, A., & Sauer, E. (2007). Aesthetic leadership. *The Leadership Quarterly, 18*(6), 544–560. doi:10.1016/j.leaqua.2007.09.003

Harding, S. (1998). *Is science multicultural?* Bloomington, IN: Indiana University Press.

Harquail, C. V., & King, A. (2010). Construing organizational identity: The role of embodied cognition. *Organization Studies, 31*(12), 1619–1648. doi:10.1177/0170840610376143

Havel, V. (1994, July). The need for transcendence in a postmodern world. Liberty Medal acceptance speech at Independence Hall, Philadelphia, PA.

Hazy, J. K., & Silberstang, J. (2009). Leadership within emergent events in complex systems: Micro-enactments and the mechanisms of organisational learning and change. *International Journal of Learning and Change, 3*(3), 230–247. doi:10.1504/IJLC.2009.02469

Heifetz, R. A. (1994). *Leadership without easy answers*. Cambridge, MA: Belknap Press of Harvard University Press.

Heifetz, R., Grashow, A., & Linsky, M. (2009, July 1). Leadership in a (permanent) crisis. *Harvard Business Review*, p. 62.

Heinberg, R. (2011). *The end of growth: Adapting to our new economic reality*. Gabriola Island, BC, Canada: New Society Publishers.

Hosking, D. M. (2007). Not leaders, not followers: A post-modern discourse of leadership processes. In B. Shamir, R. Pillai, M. Bligh, & M. Uhl-Bien (Eds.), *Follower-centered perspectives on leadership: A tribute to the memory of James R. Meindl*. Greenwich, CT: Information Age.

Hosking, D. M., & McNamee, S. (2006). *The social construction of organization*. Malmö, Denmark: Liber & Copenhagen Business School Press.

Hughes, M., Thompson, H. L., & Terrell, J. B. (2009). *Handbook for developing emotional and social intelligence: Best practices, case studies, and strategies*. San Francisco, CA: Pfeiffer.

Isaacs, W. (1999). *Dialogue and the art of thinking together: A pioneering approach to communicating in business and in life*. New York, NY: Currency.

Kegan, R. (1982). *The evolving self: Problem and process in human development.* Cambridge, MA: Harvard University Press.

Kegan, R. (1994). *In over our heads: The mental demands of modern life.* Cambridge, MA: Harvard University Press.

Küpers, W., & Weibler, J. (2008). Inter-leadership: Why and how should we think of leadership and followership integrally? *Leadership, 4*(4), 443–475. doi:10.1177/1742715008095190

Ladkin, D. (2011). *Rethinking leadership: A new look at old leadership questions.* North Hampton, MA: Elgar.

Lichtenstein, B. B., Uhl-Bien, M., Marion, R., Seers, A., Orton, J. D., & Schreiber, C. (2006). Complexity leadership theory: An interactive perspective on leading in complex adaptive systems. *Emergence: Complexity and Organization, 8*(4), 2–12.

Lord, R. G., & Shondrick, S. J. (2011). Leadership and knowledge: Symbolic, connectionist, and embodied perspectives. *The Leadership Quarterly, 22*(1), 207–222. doi:10.1016/j.leaqua.2010.12.016

Mabey, C., & Morrell, K. (2011). Leadership in crisis: "Events, my dear boy, events." *Leadership, 7*(2), 105–117. doi:10.1177/1742715010394732

Manz, C. C., & Sims, H. P. (1989). *Superleadership: Leading others to lead themselves.* New York, NY: Prentice Hall.

Marion, R. (1999). *The edge of organization: Chaos and complexity theories of formal social systems.* Thousand Oaks, CA: Sage.

Martenson, C. (2011). *The crash course: The unsustainable future of our economy, energy, and environment.* Hoboken, NJ: Wiley.

McCauley, C. D., Drath, W. H., Palus, C. J., O'Connor, P.M.G., & Baker, B. A. (2006). The use of constructive-developmental theory to advance the understanding of leadership. *The Leadership Quarterly, 17*(6), 634–653. doi:10.1016/j.leaqua.2006.10.006

McGonagill, G., & Dörffer, T. (2010). *Leadership and Web 2.0: The leadership implications of the evolving Web.* Gütersloh, Germany: Bertelsmann-Stiftung.

Meindl, J. R., Ehrlich, S. B., & Dukerich, J. M. (1985). The romance of leadership. *Administrative Science Quarterly, 30*(1), 78–102.

Murrell, K. L. (1997). Emergent theories of leadership for the next century: Towards relational concepts. *Organization Development Journal, 15*(3), 35–42.

Nye, J. S. (2008). Recovering American leadership. *Survival, 50*(1), 55–68.

O'Malley, A. L., Ritchie, S. A., Lord, R. G., Gregory, J. B., & Young, C. (2009). Incorporating embodied cognition into sensemaking theory: A theoretical integration of embodied processes in a leadership context. *Current Topics in Management, 14*, 151–182.

Page, S. E. (2007). *The difference: How the power of diversity creates better groups, firms, schools, and societies.* Princeton, NJ: Princeton University Press.

Patterson, J. A. (2009). Organisational learning and leadership: On metaphor, meaning making, liminality and intercultural communication. *International Journal of Learning and Change, 3*(4), 382–393. doi:10.1504/IJLC.2009.02622

Petrie, N. (2011). *Future trends in leadership*. Greensboro, NC: Center for Creative Leadership.

Reinhart, C. M., & Rogoff, K. S. (2011). *This time is different: Eight centuries of financial folly*. Princeton, NJ: Princeton University Press.

Rifkin, J. (2009). *The empathic civilization: The race to global consciousness in a world in crisis*. New York, NY: Jeremy P. Tarcher/Penguin.

Rifkin, J. (2011). *The third industrial revolution: How lateral power is transforming energy, the economy, and the world*. New York, NY: Palgrave Macmillan.

Rooke, D., & Torbert, W. R. (1998). Organizational transformation as a function of CEO's developmental stage. *Organization Development Journal, 16*(1), 11–28.

Ropo, A., & Parviainen, J. (2001). Leadership and bodily knowledge in expert organizations: Epistemological rethinking. *Scandinavian Journal of Management, 17*(1), 1–18. doi:10.1016/S0956-5221(00)00030-0

Roth, T. (1994). How the post-heroic leader scores. *Management Development Review, 7*(6), 4–6. doi:10.1108/09622519410771736

Santorelli, S. (2011). "Enjoy your death": Leadership lessons forged in the crucible of organizational death and rebirth infused with mindfulness and mastery. *Contemporary Buddhism, 12*(1), 199–217.

Shaw, P. (2002). *Changing conversations in organizations: A complexity approach to change*. London, UK: Taylor & Francis.

Stacey, R. D. (2005). *Experiencing emergence in organizations: Local interaction and the emergence of global pattern*. London, UK: Routledge.

Stacey, R. D. (2010). *Complexity and organizational reality: Uncertainty and the need to rethink management after the collapse of investment capitalism*. London, UK: Routledge.

Thomas, R. R., & Gregory, T. A. (1995). Managing diversity: A new perspective on managing conflict. *AIMD Research Notes, 2*(8/9), 1–3.

Torbert, W. R. (2004). *Action inquiry: The secret of timely and transforming leadership*. San Francisco, CA: Berrett-Koehler.

Tsoukas, H., & Chia, R. (2002). On organizational becoming: Rethinking organizational change. *Organizational Science, 13*(5), 567–582. doi:10.1287/orsc.13.5.567.7810

Turner, V. W. (1971). Betwixt and between: The liminal period in *rites de passage*. In J. Helm (Ed.), *Symposium on New Approaches to the Study of Religion: Proceedings of the 1964 Annual Spring Meeting of the American Ethnological Society* (pp. 4–20). Seattle, WA: University of Washington Press.

Turner, V. W. (1977a). Frame, flow and reflection: Ritual and drama as public liminality. In M. Benamou & C. Caramello (Eds.), *Performance in postmodern culture* (pp. 33–58). Milwaukee, WI: University of Wisconsin–Milwaukee, Center for Twentieth Century Studies.

Turner. V. W. (1977b). Variations on a theme of liminality. In S. F. Moore & B. G. Myerhoff (Eds.), *Secular ritual* (pp. 36–52). Assen, Netherlands: Van Gorcum.

Turner, V. W. (1986a). *The anthropology of performance*. New York, NY: PAJ Publications.

Turner, V. W. (1986b). Dewey, Dilthey, and drama: An essay in the anthropology of experience. In V. W. Turner, E. M. Bruner, & C. Geertz (Eds.), *The anthropology of experience* (pp. 33–44). Urbana, IL: University of Illinois Press.

Uhl-Bien, M. (2006). Relational leadership theory: Exploring the social processes of leadership and organizing. *The Leadership Quarterly, 17*(6), 654–676.

Uhl-Bien, M., Marion, R., & McKelvey, B. (2007). Complexity leadership theory: Shifting leadership from the industrial age to the knowledge era. *The Leadership Quarterly, 18*(4), 298–318. doi:10.1016/j.leaqua.2007.04.002x

Uhl-Bien, M., & Ospina, S. (2012). *Advancing relational leadership research: A dialogue among perspectives*. Charlotte, NC: Information Age.

Van Gennep, A. (1960). *The rites of passage*. Chicago, IL: University of Chicago Press.

Western, S. (2008). *Leadership: A critical text*. Thousand Oaks, CA: Sage.

Yukl, G. (1999). An evaluative essay on current conceptions of effective leadership. *European Journal of Work and Organizational Psychology, 8*(1), 33–48. doi:10.1080/135943299398429

Chapter Four

Seeking Alignment in the World Body

The Art of Embodiment

Skye Burn

> Art embodies. Art is unique in that it unifies
> the material with the spiritual. There is no way
> to perceive the spiritual without the material;
> conversely, without spirit the forms yield no lasting
> truth. Art's form is material, yet it deals with inner
> reality. It is embodiment.
>
> *Karen Stone (2003, p. 29)*

As humanity ventures further into the twenty-first century, globalization, mass media, and the Internet are weaving a web of connections. The consciousness of separation is yielding to the awareness that we are one body. What happens in Burundi or Brazil trembles the entire web. Images of the tsunami in Japan broadcast horror onto the shores of distant hearts. Secondhand smoke from coal burning in China pollutes our communal living space. The U.S. recession destabilized the global economy. The sight of abject poverty or violence in one part of the world depletes our communal sense of well-being, while evidence of noble human nature increases our collective sense of well-being. Gradually we are acknowledging that all parts of the world body are interconnected and interdependent and no part can experience itself as a separate entity isolated from the whole.

At the same time, as we are drawn into the consciousness of oneness, humanity is undergoing an excruciating process of differentiation and dismemberment, a sense of being torn apart by social, political, economic, and cultural adversity. As the world population grows, we are learning to live in closer quarters and closer contact with one another, forcing us into a deeper familiarity and deeper knowing. In struggling to access this deeper knowing, we are confronting our differences. Ironically, as we become more acutely conscious of what sets us apart, we face the need to discover and strengthen what holds us together.

The world body is to humanity what my body is to me. Just as my ankle bone is connected to my leg bone, South America is connected to North America, Asia is connected to Europe, and Africa is connected through the plasma of oceans to the whole. I think of different parts of my body as separate—my fingers, my legs, my head, my torso—but when I need to act, the parts of my body work together.

Today, humanity is facing situations that threaten our communal safety, including economic instability, climate change, environmental degradation, resource depletion, food and water shortages, terror, violence. To resolve these situations, all parts of the world body must work together and act as one, with a sense of common purpose. Yet many parts resist integration. Ethnic, religious, economic, political, and ideological factions pursue their separate agendas and refuse to join in working for the common good. Overall, humanity's resistance to unification, personified and embodied in diverse parts of the world body, has a debilitating effect on our collective ability to resolve the challenges we face in the world today. On the collective level, where these matters must be resolved, the world body is unable to "get its act together."

As a whole, humanity is suffering from psychological conditions associated with the lack of integration on the individual level (Jung, 1960, 1954/1966; Kernberg & Michels, 2009; Weill Medical College of Cornell University, 2012), including anxiety, depression, terror, extremism, impaired agency, and oscillations in relationships with self and others. While the symptoms associated with the lack of integration are apparent worldwide, for examples we need look no further than the United States. The U.S. Congress is so polarized and split into factions that the governing body (representing our communal agency) is unable to act with clear intent to resolve issues vital to our communal well-being, such as health care and pollution. In addition, according to statistics issued in 2012 by the Institute of Mental Health, 18 percent of U.S. adults and 25.1 percent of youth ages 13–18 have anxiety disorder, and 6.7 percent of adults suffer from depression yearly. The level of terror in the United States has reached such proportions that fear consumes vast amounts of our energy and resources. As allocations for fighting terrorism, securing borders, and shoring up defenses skyrocket, budgets for human services, education, and the arts diminish.

"Splitting," a condition associated in individuals with borderline disorder, extremist thinking, other-directed mood swings, and oscillations in the experience and appraisal of the self, is evident in the world body in extremist views of America, Iran, North Korea, Russia, corporations, and/or the government as the embodiment of good or evil (*we* are good, *they* are evil) and oscillations between self-congratulation (humans are the apex of evolution) and self-flagellation (we have mucked up in creating the world). The world body is manifesting, and humanity is embodying, the symptoms of splitting and severe dissociation because of the lack of integration in the collective psyche.

The Challenge for Leaders

For the world body to function effectively we must find ways to integrate the diverse parts of humanity into a cohesive whole, and we must find the right balance between humanity's various roles and interests. Just as inner conflict stymies an individual's effectiveness, the world body cannot function effectively when parts of humanity are "at war" with other parts.

Psychologists address the need for integration on the individual level. In treating individuals, psychologists work to integrate all parts of the person into a cohesive whole so they function with a unified sense of purpose, and so every part is fairly represented in the actions of the whole and no part is squelched, denied, or repressed.

Leaders address the same need on the collective level. In the field of leadership, integration is called "alignment." Leaders work to attain alignment in developing organizations, communities, and teams or work groups. *Alignment* means all members of a group are working cohesively with a sense of common purpose toward a common goal (Bodaken & Fritz, 2006; Jaworski, 1998; Sawyer, 2007; Senge, Scharmer, Jaworski, & Flowers, 2004). With alignment, work flows. Alignment "is the magical moment" when a "group is in sync and the performers seem to be thinking with one mind" (Sawyer, p. 50). Without alignment people work at cross-purposes and "pull in different directions" (Bodaken & Fritz, p. 147).

Today, the primary challenge for leaders is to attain alignment in the world body and the global community. In *Cultivating Peace*, James O'Dea (2012) observed, "Our evolving story as a species seems to want us to learn how we can integrate our unique individual and collective identities" (p. 214), and he offered pointers for dispelling the resistances to integration. When every part of humanity is boldly in sync, and we collectively act as one, humanity will be freed from the conditions associated with splitting and dissociation and the world body will come alive in ways it never has before.

The Primary Task for Leaders

James Kouzes and Barry Posner (2002) observed that two primary leadership tasks are to "model the way" and "inspire a shared vision" (p. 13). I add that leaders must also correctly interpret the want or need being expressed by the world body. As James MacGregor Burns (2003) noted, "Summoned forth by human wants, the task of leadership is to accomplish some change in the world that responds to those wants" (p. 2).

Interpreting the Situation

An accurate interpretation of the world situation is necessary for effective execution. In creating communities, organizations, and the world, as in creating works of art, "it is the conflict of these two principles—execution and interpretation—that is at the root of all the errors, all the sins, all the misunderstandings that interpose themselves" between the work and the audience (Stravinsky, 1942/1970, p. 122). When world leaders fail to understand what a situation is calling for, the world situation will worsen until their interventions hit the mark.

Listening to the world body, hearing the disenchantment, anxiety, depression, terror, and violent emotions being expressed (physically embodied) in situations around the world, tells us the current interpretations are missing the mark. The lack of success may be due in part to the fact that world leaders are prescribing economic, political, and military interventions in situations where the underlying cause is a lack of alignment, which calls for integrative measures and a commitment to making something beautiful and magical happen.

Modeling the Way

Modeling the way requires leaders to embody (to be a manifestation of) the integration they are leading others toward. Kouzes and Posner (2002) noted, "Words and deeds must be consistent. Exemplary leaders go first. They go first by setting the example through daily actions" (p. 14). To exemplify alignment, leaders must do the work necessary to ensure their own personalities are integrated, well balanced, and coherent, and they are not projecting unresolved aspects of themselves onto others. For each leader, the task of embodying alignment is a personal journey undertaken on his or her own.

Inspiring a Shared Vision

In contrast, inspiring a shared vision is a communal task undertaken with others. To originate a shared vision requires input and feedback from every sector of the world body, proffered by people who understand and respond to different dimensions of the world situation, including the spiritual, material, and cosmic dimensions. The diverse stakeholders contribute different lenses, sensitivities, fields of knowledge, and areas of expertise. Ultimately, sourcing a shared vision requires seeing behind the guises of otherness to discern the deepest nexus of connection: our common identity, common purpose, and common goal.

Seeds of a Shared Vision

In my understanding, sourcing a shared vision requires (1) discovering what resonates with the world body, (2) changing the contextual framing of our communal work, and (3) seeing and understanding our common goal.

Discovering What Resonates

To discover what resonates requires listening to the world body and paying attention to feedback. As a baseline leaders need to ask, Do all parts of the world body identify with the vision? Does the vision work? Does it inspire all parts of the world body to work together with a sense of common purpose? Do some parts resist and thwart the vision? Feedback from the world body tells us whether the vision is working or whether it needs to be modified or scrapped.

Changing the Contextual Framing

By *contextual framing* I mean how we collectively perceive and experience the meaning, purpose, and goal of human activity worldwide; how we explain to future generations what we are doing and have done in the past; in other words, how we "understand our *mission*" and the direction we are headed (DePree, 1987, p. 33).

In organizations, Bodaken and Fritz (2006) observed, "It is not the actual individuals who limit the team's ability to function well. Rather, it is the organizational context in which they work. If we can change the context, we can change the team's performance" (p. 126). Thus, it is not the separate parts of humanity (humanists, progressives, conservatives, Christians, Muslims, atheists, terrorists, politicians) that limit our collective ability to work together cohesively; rather, it is the lack of a contextual framing that allows all parts of the world body to see the purpose of our communal activity and understand how we are collectively working in diverse ways toward a common goal and honor the gifts "each of us as individuals bring to the group effort" (DePree, 1987, p. 77).

None of the current contextual framings available to humanity supports alignment on a deep enough level to integrate all parts of humanity into a cohesive whole. To illustrate the situation, consider two large-scale contextual framings: evolution and creationism. In 1859, the publication of Charles Darwin's *On the Origin of Species* reframed human experience, notably in the West. From the beginning, Darwin's vision has resonated strongly with scientists while it has elicited strong resistance from Christian parts of the world body. The resistance is not to the vision per se. The resistance derives from what the vision could mean in terms of the potential loss of identity, life purpose, and role in the world body. Certain Christians resist the vision of evolution because adopting it would mean losing their identity (we are created in the image of God and ultimately are one with the Creator) and sense of purpose (we have a creative purpose beyond survival of the fittest). Likewise, for scientists to adopt the vision of creationism without empirical evidence would mean forfeiting their identity, purpose, and role. While the contextual framings of evolution and creationism support alignment in separate sectors of the world body (for example, scientists generally are aligned in support of evolution, and some Christian groups are united in their opposition), neither framing supports alignment on a level that allows scientists and Christian parts of the world body to see and understand how they are working in diverse ways toward a common goal.

Inherently, the new contextual framing must be so inclusive and true to the meaning and nature of our communal work that it becomes not only a lens of self-reflection but also "lived form-in-the-making" (Sheets, 1966, p. 148). In *The Phenomenology of Dance*, Maxine Sheets observed, "The reflected-upon body is always an externally related system of parts and never a totality which is lived" (p. 27). Any contextual framing must not distract from the life of the work. She explains that the "dance does not come alive until the dancer passes beyond a mastery of structure, and comes to realize the dynamic flow inherent in the total piece" (p. 109).

Proposal for a Shared Vision

I propose art making offers a contextual framing in which all parts of humanity can find their belonging and realize the dynamic flow inherent in creating the world. Art is universal in scope and offers a framing that transcends separate individuals and cultures. Further, looking through the lens of art provides a fresh perspective that can free humanity from habitual ways of thinking and can open the door to world renewal.

I submit that we are collectively engaged in a creative process. All parts of humanity are creating the world and have been through the ages. All parts of the world body contribute in diverse ways to the communal work of world making, and in this context can be found our common identity, common goal, and common purpose.

If the world is a work of art, and humanity is the artist creating the world, our common identity is the artist or creator. Looking through the lens of art, our common goal is to create a world that truly is a work of art, a timeless masterpiece, alive in its essence and alive with meaning. Our purpose is to create a world that embodies the essence we seek to reveal.

To clarify, as I have noted elsewhere (Burn, 2012), in creating the world humanity works with the medium of nature (matter, natural resources). The world is not the Earth, per se, any more than Michelangelo's *Pietà* is the marble from which it is hewn or Picasso's *Guernica* is the paint from which it is made. The world is a human creation. The world is everything on Earth that shows evidence of human touch. Martin Heidegger remarked, "World and earth are essentially different from one another and yet are never separated. The world grounds itself on the earth, and earth juts through the world" (Heidegger, 1994, p. 267).

Creating a World That Truly Is a Work of Art

The artist has four objectives in creating works of art, two that reside in the work and two that reside in the artist. The first two are (1) create a form that fully embodies the essence and (2) get to the place where "it works." The second two objectives are (3) attain the flow state and (4) achieve mastery.

Objective 1: Embodying Essence

The word *art* stems from the root *ar*, which means to join together. Artistic practice involves the union of form and essence, as spiritual practice involves the union of soul and body. Artists create tangible forms that capture, embody, and reveal intangible essences, as a painting captures the spirit of someone or something; a poem reveals meaning; a dance embodies feeling; and a symphony embodies the soul of music. In art making, the purpose of creating the form is to reveal the essence. Poet Denise Levertov (1973) noted, "Form is never more than a *revelation* of content" (p. 13). In the world of art, the essence decides what form is fitting. Unfitting forms fall by the wayside of human memory. True works of art are treasured and endure.

Implications for Leadership. From an artistic perspective, humanity seeks to create a world that fully embodies and reveals the essence of what it means to be human. We seek to create a world that embodies the essence of peace and the spirit of unity. Our ultimate objective is to unify the intangible essence realm (heaven) and tangible form realm (Earth, the material realm).

To create a world that fully embodies and reveals the essence of what it means to be human we cannot disown, deny, squelch, or repress any part of humanity. For leaders, it is misleading to incite some parts of the world body to silence or demean other parts of the world body. The result of silencing the self is depression and violence (Gilligan, 2010, xiii). To create a world that embodies the spirit of unity we must get to the place where all parts of the world body act as one in meeting the challenges of our times. David Bohm noted, "The most important thing going forward is to break the boundaries between people so we can operate as a single intelligence" (cited in Senge and others, 2004, p. 195). For the world to embody the essence of peace we must get to the place where we collectively feel at peace with the world we have created, which means listening to feedback from the world body and listening to conscience.

Objective 2: Getting to the Place Where "It Works"

Artists often use the phrase "it works." In *Experimental Drawing*, in his chapter "Organization/Structure: Making Things 'Work

Together,'" Robert Kaupelis (1992) explained what artists mean by this phrase:

> If you have ever listened to artists talking about particular works of art, a phrase that you have no doubt heard over and over again is that "it works" or, conversely, "it doesn't work." . . . If you were to ask these artists what they mean, they would probably come up with such terms or phrases as: it's composed; it has structure; it makes a statement; it's unified; it's well-organized; it's harmonious throughout; it's well-designed; there's a total integration of parts; nothing is superfluous; everything holds together. In more detailed terms, what they mean is that the organization of a drawing creates an expressive form in which all of the parts, as well as the artist's intentions, are related to one another and to the total form in a unique and distinctive way. (p. 39)

Clearly, judging by the feedback from the world body (expressed in forms of violence, criticism, disenchantment, depression, terror), humanity has not yet gotten to the place where "it works" in creating the world. Although there are plentiful indications that the world as a work of art is coming together, the work is muddled. The world does not make a clear statement; it is not unified; the parts are not integrated; everything does not hold together; it is not harmonious throughout; there is considerable waste or superfluity; and humanity's intentions are unclear and show little relationship to the total form.

Implications for Leadership. The meaning of the phrase "it works" in the field of art is analogous to the concepts of alignment and integration in the fields of leadership and psychology, respectively. Thus, there is a strong and direct correlation between the state of the world and the psychological integration of the artist (humanity).

Again, the challenge is to achieve integration and alignment in the world body. From a leadership perspective, many members of the global community are still pursuing their own goals and separate agendas without considering or being recognized and honored for their contributions to our communal work. As Ben Hecht, Claire Dias Ortiz, and Steve Downs (2012) observed in their webinar, *Leading in a Hyperconnected World*, "While today it is conventional wisdom that major issues are far too complex and interconnected for any one entity to solve alone, many leaders and organizations continue to pursue their own agendas with isolated impact."

From an artistic perspective, the world is a work in progress. The creative process began when humanity began seeking to control nature (the medium of life) to serve human creative purposes. Today, the evidence suggests we have reached the stage at which the work is *coming together*. Despite the evidence of dissociation, fragmentation, and splitting reflected in the patterns of culture, we are seeing an emerging realization of wholeness, in systems thinking, globalization, the Internet, and the symbolism of the World Wide Web. Since the 1960s, while humanity has been experiencing wrenching disintegration and dismemberment of social norms and institutions, we have also experienced movement toward integration in the world body and the world.

Through the civil rights movement in the United States and elsewhere, and the worldwide women's movement, black and white and feminine and masculine components of the world body have become integrated, and formerly repressed parts of humanity are more fully represented in humanity's world-making activities. As a consequence, the world more fully embodies the essence of what it means to be human.

Richard Nixon's trip to China in 1974 and, later, the lifting of the Iron Curtain opened the way for cultural exchange between the East and West, to the extent that our economies are now inextricably connected and we have developed a taste for each other's foods. Likewise, since the 1970s the world body has focused considerable energy on integrating the spiritual and material dimensions of human lived experience, with attention also given to resolving the science/religion conflict. Overall, this process of integration is a classic configuration of the archetypal union of opposites (Jung, 1963/1977) on a global scale.

In other areas as well, our communal work is coming together. Educational institutions are encouraging interdisciplinary studies to integrate previously siloed fields of knowledge. Businesses are integrating environmental considerations into their bottom lines. And, as noted previously, travel, immigration, mass media, and the Internet are precipitating exposure to otherness and weaving a World Wide Web of virtual and on-the-ground connections.

Ironically, the terrorist attacks on September 11, 2001, which tore apart our hearts, also instilled a greater awareness of wholeness. On December 10, 2001, in his speech at the Nobel Prize ceremony, United Nations Secretary General Kofi Annan (2001) spoke of the deepening awareness of our common bond.

> We have entered the third millennium through a gate of fire. If today, after the horror of 11 September, we see better, and we see further—we will realize that humanity is indivisible. New threats make no distinction between races, nations or regions. A new insecurity has entered every mind, regardless of wealth or status. A deeper awareness of the bonds that bind us all—in pain as in prosperity—has gripped young and old. (para. 6)

The evidence of increasing integration is offsetting the evidence of polarization, dissociation, and splitting, and leaders need to decide where they want to focus their energies in creating the world. Do they want to serve the process of integration and embodiment or continue perpetuating the social ills that plague humanity?

Objective 3: Attaining the Flow State

The artistic concept of flow also corresponds to alignment and integration. *Flow* is a state of being and state of consciousness.

The flow state is attained when all parts of a person or all members of a group work together and operate as a single intelligence.

Imagine a group of musicians creating music. As the musicians start playing together, they seek alignment around the archetypal patterns forming elements of music: rhythm, harmony, pitch, melody, and timbre. Listening closely, as the musicians play together, one hears them making progress toward the moment when the music "works," that is, the moment when the performance comes together and the music comes alive. The music works when the musicians attain the flow state. In the flow state there are no impediments or blocks to the life of the music. The soul of the music is fully embodied in the created sounds, and the musicians and audience are transported to another world, the timeless world where music lives.

For humanity to attain the flow state in creating the world, all parts of the world body must be aligned with the *"propriate strivings* or life *themes"* of the whole (Csikszentmihalyi, 1990, p. 230). If some parts of the world body are not aligned, humanity as a whole will not attain the flow state. By analogy, if one musician "does his own thing" without consideration for the whole, playing in a different key, with a different rhythm, or with a different melody, the music will not come alive. It will not work.

Implications for Leadership. From a leadership perspective, "having people in the organization who are not aligned with the dream" or vision results in "deep incoherence in the organization" (Jaworski, 1998, p. 127).

If humanity's goal in creating the world is to produce a timeless work of art, attaining the flow state is vital to our success. Timeless works are created in the flow state. Researchers who study flow agree that being in the flow state confers a sense of timelessness (Csikszentmihalyi, 1990; Jaworski, 1998; Sawyer, 2007). While a work in progress is directed toward a goal in the future, the flow state entails being fully present. In *The Forgotten*

Power of Rhythm, percussionist Reinhard Flatischler (1992) noted, "Everyone knows, consciously or unconsciously, this 'other sense of time.' Some describe it as a wave standing still while all around it the water flows on. Others simply refer to this state as the experience of the present moment" (p. 89). For leaders, part of the challenge is helping humanity transition from working to make progress to living fully in the present.

Objective 4: Achieving Mastery

Mastery is attained in the delicate balance between control and surrender. On the one hand, artists learn to control the medium. On the other hand, they need to let go and surrender control so the essence can move without impediment into form and action (Bogart, 2001; Herrigel, 1953; Murphy, 1992).

Imagine a pianist. Her performance is technically flawless, but unfortunately the music has no life. She has mastered control of the medium, but she has not let go and surrendered to the life of the work. She has not let herself become an instrument or conduit through whom the music flows and manifests in the world. Her work is mechanical and soulless. She has not attained mastery.

The key to creating a work that is alive in its essence is to "bring forth the emerging reality *as it desires*" (Jaworski, 2012, p. 181). Artists listen to the work. They pay attention and go where "it wants to go." They surrender their images, ideas, beliefs, and expectations of what the work should look like or be like. They surrender their attachment to outcome and let the essence dictate what form the work takes. They trust the process.

Implications for Leadership. Changes in the field of leadership reflect humanity's movement toward mastery in creating the world.

The field of leadership began to integrate principles of artistic mastery into leadership practice in the 1970s with the advent of "servant leadership." Before the 1970s, leaders operated primarily in the command-and-control mode. Leaders sought to control situations, control events, control how people behave, and control what form the world takes. Robert Greenleaf, partly in response to the massive social movements of the '60s and '70s, turned the focus of leadership to serving what wants to emerge. Greenleaf (1977) emphasized the importance of listening: "A natural servant automatically responds to any problem by listening *first*." He added that one becomes a servant leader through a "long arduous discipline of learning to listen" (p. 31). By listening to the world body and listening to the world, Greenleaf said, leaders sense "the *unknowable* and are able to *foresee the unforeseeable*." By listening, leaders sense what is not yet tangible. They "know some things and foresee some things that those presuming to lead do not know or foresee as clearly" (p. 35). They sense what wants to emerge and help it find its true form of expression in the world. In *Theory U*, Otto Scharmer (2007) expanded the concept of "leading into the emerging future" (p. 163).

Beyond listening, mastery entails letting go and trusting the process. If leaders (like artists) listen closely and go where the work leads, if they surrender their egos and let go of ideas, images, and expectations of where the work should lead or what it should look like, if they go where "it wants to go," they experience the mystery and magic of co-creation. The universe or creation supports their work.

In *Trust the Process: An Artist's Guide to Letting Go*, Shaun McNiff (1998) explained, "The creative process is an intelligence that knows where it has to go. Somehow it always finds the way to the place where I need to be, and it is always a destination that never could have been known by me in advance" (p. 31). In the field of leadership, Jaworski (1998) echoed McNiff: "Our journey is guided by invisible hands with infinitely greater accuracy than is possible through our unaided conscious will" (p. 119). Master artists and leaders alike surrender to that intelligence and trust those invisible hands to lead them accurately. They trust life.

Finally, mastery confers a sense of effortlessness. Leaders and artists prize the moment when the work develops a life of its own, when the work becomes rhythmic. At that moment the onus of leadership lifts and the work becomes a dance, a call and response to a cosmic pulsation. One is carried by the rhythm of the work. Flatischler (1992) noted, "When we physically sense the supportive power of a pulsation, it creates within us the psychological qualities associated with being carried: a feeling of effortlessness and safety, and the inner knowledge that life has the power to carry us, if we allow it" (p. 88).

Creative work has a rhythm, consisting of a pattern of beats and off-beats. In music, "when musicians allow themselves to be carried by the silent pulse, the listener will connect consciously or unconsciously to the feeling of being carried" (Flatischler, 1992, p. 89) or transported. The silent pulse is the off-beat, or "ghost beat," as it is sometimes called. In creating the world, actions and events constitute the beat. The off-beat or silent pulse is the space between events sensed as a readiness, an opening, a "teachable moment" in the world body (Burn, 2005). On the one hand, when leaders are tuned to the off-beat in creating the world and their interventions are impeccably timed to coincide with conditions of readiness in the world body, things come together and fall into place effortlessly, magically. Then we are operating in the flow mode. On the other hand, when our timing is off, and we are not in the flow mode, "the effortless nature of the enterprise disappears, and everything becomes struggle and strain and hard work" (Jaworski, 1998, p. 129).

Currently the world body is still caught in the struggle of creating the world. The work is not yet effortless. For leadership, the challenge is how to bring the world body to the place where we collectively operate in the flow mode, where magic happens in the mystery of co-creation.

References

Annan, K. (2001). Nobel Prize acceptance speech. Oslo, Norway: Norwegian Nobel Committee. http://www.nobelprize.org/nobel_prizes/peace/laureates/2001/annan-lecture.html

Bodaken, B., & Fritz, R. (2006). *The managerial moment of truth: The essential step in helping people improve performance.* New York, NY: Free Press.

Bogart, A. (2001). *A director prepares: Seven essays on art and theatre.* New York, NY: Routledge.

Burn, S. (2005). The readiness factor: Optimal conditions for a change of heart and mind. *International Readings on Theory, History and Philosophy of Culture, 21,* 279–292.

Burn, S. (2012, February). The leadership response: Developing an artistic take on the world situation. Paper presented at Tobias Leadership Conference, Colorado Springs, CO.

Burns, J. M. (2003). *Transforming leadership: A new pursuit of happiness.* New York, NY: Atlantic Monthly Press.

Csikszentmihalyi, M. (1990). *Flow: The psychology of optimal experience.* New York, NY: HarperCollins.

DePree, M. (1987). *Leadership is an art.* East Lansing: Michigan State University Press.

Flatischler, R. (1992). *The forgotten power of rhythm.* Mendocino, CA: LifeRhythm.

Gilligan, C. (2010). Preface. In D. Jack & A. Ali (Eds.), *Silencing the self across cultures: Depression and gender in the social world* (p. xiii). New York, NY: Oxford University Press.

Greenleaf, R. (1977). *Servant leadership: A journey into the nature of legitimate power and greatness.* New York, NY: Paulist Press.

Hecht, B., Ortiz, C. D., & Downs, S. (2012, May 30). *Leading in a hyperconnected world: Driving innovation & impact with digital media* [Webinar]. Stanford, CA: Stanford Social Innovation Review.

Heidegger, M. (1994). The origin of the work of art. In S. D. Ross (Ed.), *Art and its significance: An anthology of aesthetic theory* (pp. 254–280). Albany, NY: State University of New York Press.

Herrigel, E. (1953). *Zen in the art of archery.* New York, NY: Pantheon.

Jaworski, J. (1998). *Synchronicity: The inner path of leadership.* San Francisco, CA: Berrett-Koehler.

Jaworski, J. (2012). *Source: The inner path of knowledge creation.* San Francisco, CA: Berrett-Koehler.

Jung, C. G. (1960). *The structure and dynamics of the psyche* (R.F.C. Hull, Trans.). New York, NY: Bollingen Foundation, Pantheon.

Jung, C. G. (1966). *The practice of psychotherapy: Essays on the psychology of the transference and other subjects* (R.F.C. Hull, Trans.). New York,

NY: Bollingen Foundation, Princeton University Press. (Original work published 1954)

Jung, C. G. (1977). *Mysterium coniunctionis: An inquiry into the separation and synthesis of psychic opposites in alchemy* (R.F.C. Hull, Trans.). New York, NY: Bollingen Foundation, Princeton University Press. (Original work published 1963)

Kaupelis, R. (1992). *Experimental drawing.* New York, NY: Watson-Guptill.

Kernberg, O. F., & Michels, R. (2009). Borderline personality disorder. *American Journal of Psychiatry, 166*(5), 505–508. doi:10.1176/appi .ajp.2009.09020263

Kouzes, J., & Posner, B. (2002). *The leadership challenge.* San Francisco, CA: Jossey-Bass.

Levertov, D. (1973). *The poet in the world.* New York, NY: New Directions.

McNiff, S. (1998). *Trust the process: An artist's guide to letting go.* Boston, MA: Shambhala.

Murphy, M. (1992). *The future of the body: Explorations into the future of evolution.* New York, NY: Jeremy P. Tarcher.

O'Dea, J. (2012). *Cultivating peace: Becoming a 21st-century peace ambassador.* San Rafael, CA: Shift Books.

Sawyer, K. (2007). *Group genius: The creative power of collaboration.* New York, NY: Basic Books.

Scharmer, O. (2007). *Theory U: Leading from the future as it emerges.* Cambridge, MA: Society for Organizational Learning.

Senge, P., Scharmer, O., Jaworski, J., & Flowers, B. S. (2004). *Presence: Human purpose and the field of the future.* Cambridge, MA: Society for Organizational Learning.

Sheets, M. (1966). *The phenomenology of dance.* Milwaukee, WI: University of Wisconsin Press.

Stone, K. (2003). *Image and spirit: Finding meaning in visual art.* Minneapolis, MN: Augsburg.

Stravinsky, I. (1970). *Poetics of music: In the form of six lessons.* Cambridge, MA: Harvard University Press. (Original work published 1942)

Weill Medical College of Cornell University. (2012). *Description of transference-focused psychotherapy for borderline personality disorder.* Ithaca, NY: Personality Disorders Institute. http://www.borderlinedisorders.com/ transference-focused-psychotherapy.php

Part Two

Leaders Are Their Bodies

Lena Lid Falkman

How can leadership be understood as something done by and through bodies? How can leadership be acted out as bodily expressions and experiences? How can leadership be lived as, and translated through, embodied experiences? As Lois Ruskai Melina pointed out in the introduction, in this volume we are not only dealing with ways to conceptualize relationships between leadership and the body, we are also searching for ways to articulate and translate the embodied knowledge of leadership.

In Part Two the contributions all describe and analyze leadership as embodied expressions. These bodily expressions are not limited to body language. Bodily expressions are here widely and inclusively understood as the body as living, experiencing, and showing leadership. Bodies are shown to be restraints and resources, but also media through which leadership is created, experienced, and understood. By seeing leadership as something involving the body of the leader, there are insights to be found on issues of self-awareness and identity as well as areas of rhetorical and authentic leadership.

Maylon Hanold shows how the leadership area lacks insight about the influence and the importance of the socially constructed body. In the changing global world, there is a need to understand, and break out of, the gendered and contextual settings. Hanold focuses on the leadership practice of self-awareness. With a Foucauldian approach, she articulates the place of the body in self-awareness. Further, by acknowledging the importance of the body as a social construction, Hanold presents a diverse and inclusive way of expressing leadership and being a leader.

The next chapter also deals with self-awareness. Kimberly Yost describes how self-awareness through art can be used for transformative personal leadership. The exercise of creating a symbol of self in the form of a crafted doll, and then reflecting about the doll and the process, leads to insights on assumptions of leadership and to an exploration in authentic leadership. The women introduced in this chapter created bodily symbols of themselves, and this led to embodied understanding of their leadership and their own identities.

Nora Méndez and Fernando Mora show how identity can be—or rather, is—embodied. We follow three female pastors and learn how they form themselves as leaders, acting in male-dominated organizations, taking on positions traditionally held by men. The story becomes one of embodied leadership identity created through power struggle and resistance. Specifically, acts of resistance are shown to be important in the embodiment of identity.

In her chapter, Elizabeth D. Wilhoit uses enacted, critical rhetoric to show how the body can be a medium for authentic leadership. She demonstrates how the inclusion of the body can enrich the understanding and practice of authentic leadership, that is, to use, act, show, and live your message as a leader through your own body. The case study is that of Michelle Obama, who, through the initiative "Let's Move," wants to influence American children to adopt healthier lifestyles. One

important aspect of authentic leadership in this case is the identification between audience and sender of message, expressed by
and through the body.

The purpose of this volume is to explore how leadership is
embodied. This part displays this in concrete ways. The findings
indicate how the area of leadership can be enriched if only the
body is accepted and included as a way of expressing and understanding the processes and relations of leadership.

Chapter Five

(De/Re)Constructing Leading Bodies

Developing Critical Attitudes and Somaesthetic Practices

Maylon Hanold

Reconsideration of what constitutes effective and more inclusive leadership requires not only an embodied view of leadership but also one that at its core remains critically based. Given the growing concern that today's leaders need new ways of thinking and being to keep pace with an increasingly diverse world, new attitudes have been promoted in the leadership literature. Despite these theoretical calls for more feminine, inclusive forms of leadership, masculine forms of leadership are dominant, resulting in continued discrimination based on perceived lack of fit (Heilman, 2001) and role incongruity (Eagly & Chin, 2010; Eagly & Karau, 2002). Eagly and Chin (2010) believed that these discriminatory practices occur in subtle and unconscious ways.

Within the leadership literature, the process of uncovering deeply held beliefs has been described as self-awareness (Avolio & Gardner, 2005; Avolio, Walumbwa, & Weber, 2010; Boyatzis & McKee, 2006; Walumbwa, Avolio, Gardner, Wernsing, & Peterson, 2008). The development of self-awareness is understood as a process through which leaders can discover inner truths and values, allowing them to become authentic. Although a few scholars (Goleman, 1995; Ladkin & Taylor, 2010) have noted that the body plays a role in this process, I argue that these current understandings of the body's role in leadership are limited. It is not that the self-awareness practices encouraged by these scholars are of no use; rather, I claim that these understandings are insufficient for developing a self-awareness that can lead to more inclusive forms of leadership.

Primarily, I argue that current views of the body in the leadership literature are based in naturalist and essentialist notions and that a social constructionist view of the body is needed for development of a deeper, more accurate self-awareness. The current views are limited in that they assume the body is (1) adequately understood as a biological phenomenon and (2) uniquely the site of a "true self." While social constructionist views differ with respect to just how much the body is a social product, all of them reject the naturalist and essentialist approaches as adequate for understanding how we experience our bodies (Shilling, 2003).

Desires and experiences of our bodies are influenced by socially dominant ideologies. For example, bodily feelings of discomfort when in the company of people markedly different from oneself are the result of socially constructed views. Negative body feelings often emerge despite rational views of others. I propose that embracing a social constructionist view of the body allows us to develop a critical attitude toward these "natural" feelings and ultimately empowers us to make substantive changes. This critical view brings us closer to realizing the full potential of self-awareness as an important activity of leadership effectiveness. I take the view that a complex understanding of the body as simultaneously biological and socially constructed is needed to become a more inclusive leader.

In light of these aims, I first turn to Foucault to develop a critique of the body's current place in self-awareness. Drawing on Foucault's notions of power, discipline, and discourse, I show how the body has become shaped by dominant leadership ideology. How we want to be as leaders and how we think about self-awareness as leaders extend from unchallenged discourses about leadership. Then, I employ Foucault's concept of *problematization* to challenge and reconceptualize the self-aware, embodied leader. Here, the essential problematization is recognizing that leadership discourses have ignored the socially constructed body. I show how this omission results in unchallenged prejudices that negatively affect how we lead. Reconceptualization of the self-aware leader involves incorporating an understanding of the socially constructed body and developing a critical attitude in order to recognize these biases. Finally, through insights from somaesthetic philosophy, I provide a practical agenda for how leaders might go about cultivating a more thoughtful, critical self-awareness that ultimately leads to more inclusive leadership.

Contemporary Leadership: Promises and Problems

Contemporary leadership imperatives stem from postmodern sensibilities that "uncertainty, movement, multiplicity of meaning, fragmentation and indeterminacy" (Hatcher, 2003, p. 392) characterize the world in which people lead. As globalization proceeds, there is a growing number of women and minorities in leadership positions as well as a significantly growing diverse followership that "challenges all leaders to take into account the perspectives of people representing backgrounds, beliefs, and mores different from their own" (Eagly & Chin, 2010, p. 216).

Due to these demands, leadership scholars have called for a wider range of skills, including those qualities often associated with feminine styles of leadership (Billing & Alvesson, 2000; Hatcher, 2003). While the "softer" skills of empathy (Goleman & Boyatzis, 2008); kindness (Mortimer, 2009); and participatory, relational styles (Billing & Alvesson, 2000; Lipman-Blumen, 1996) have made their way into discussions about what it means to be an effective, inclusive leader, practically it appears that leadership positions remain populated by white males and that leadership is ıinantly tied to masculine attributes (Eagly & Chin, 2010; Fondas, 1997; Guthey, 2001; Hearn, 1993, 2000).

Although "masculine" leadership shows some decrease in recent years (Koenig, Mitchell, Eagly, & Ristikari, 2011), the "softer" skills of empathy and kindness seem to hold little validity with aspiring leaders (Holt & Marques, 2012). The "masculine" attributes most associated with leadership include being self-sufficient, competent, decisive, action oriented, and competitive (Eagly & Chin, 2010; Powell, Butterfield, & Parent, 2002). There are two noted problems that stem from the mismatch of expected leader behavior and calls for "softer," "feminine" approaches. First, the labeling of softer skills as "feminine" reinforce dominant ideas about masculine/feminine qualities and reproduce the inequalities of the binary, making it difficult for both men and women to embrace these aspects of leadership (Billing & Alvesson, 2000). Second, the inequalities produced by the binary privilege male, white, heterosexuals and subordinate female, nonwhite, nonheterosexuals. Thus, these minorities are viewed as unfit for leader responsibilities (Eagly & Chin, 2010). This "lack-of-fit" (Heilman, 2001) and "role incongruity" (Eagly & Chin, 2010; Eagly & Karau, 2002; Heilman & Eagly, 2008) have been proposed as explanations for continued discrimination against women and minorities.

While it is beyond the scope of this chapter to explore in depth the phenomenon of underrepresentation of women and minorities in leadership roles, Eagly and Chin (2010) summarized the phenomenon well:

> The activation of cultural stereotypes inconsistent with widely accepted ideals of leadership thus can undermine leadership opportunity not only by eliciting doubts about stereotyped individuals' leadership abilities but also by making them personally anxious about confirming these doubts and therefore wary about taking on leadership roles. (p. 218)

Thus, moving into leadership positions for minorities is problematic based on the biases in hiring practices as well as self-imposed limits created by those potentially being hired. More notably, they remarked that despite minority job applicants' having equivalent qualifications to those of white, male counterparts, discrimination "continues to proceed in covert, subtle, and unintentional forms . . . by means of 'mindless' processes that operate beyond their conscious attentional focus, all the while thinking that they are merely choosing the best person for the job or otherwise acting in an unbiased manner" (p. 217).

What remains relatively unexplored is the body's involvement in these "mindless processes." If discrimination is not necessarily of the mind, then how is the body implicated in the reproduction of privileged attributes of leadership, presumably occurring at the unconscious level? Furthermore, how might we rethink the contemporary leadership strategy of developing self-awareness from an embodied perspective that takes into consideration "unintentional forms" of prejudice?

Leadership: Discourse and "Docile" Bodies

Through his observations of the military and prisons, Foucault (1977a) showed how bodies become "docile" through desire rather than coercion. In other words, instead of power being something that one exerts over another in the form of coercion or oppression, Foucault (1977b) noted, "Power would be a fragile thing if its only function were to repress. If, on the contrary, power is strong this is because, as we are beginning to realize, it produces effects at the level of desire" (p. 59). Furthermore, desire is produced through discursive constructions, which "produce the objects of our knowledge. They govern the way that a topic can be meaningfully talked about and reasoned about. They also influence how ideas are put into practice and used to regulate the conduct of others" (Hall, 1997, p. 44).

Thus, discursive constructions are not simply textual, but permeate the physical (Foucault, 1977a, 1977b, 1983).

Discourse and Docile Leader Bodies

Discourses are detected by the regularity with which they emerge over a long period of time (Foucault, 1970). Specifically, Foucault (1972) examined how scientific discourse sets in motion particular ways of talking about the body. These categorizations generate a sense of "normal." It is from this sense of "normal" that the individual is compelled (through desire) to self-regulate and align his or her identity with dominating or accepted discourses (Foucault, 1983). More precisely, discourse has significant effects on the body because the power–knowledge nexus "turns it [the body] into an 'aptitude,' a 'capacity,' which it seeks to increase" (Foucault, 1977a, p. 138). Dominant discourses become embodied through the reciprocal relationship between docility and utility in which the more useful a body becomes, the more "docile," disciplined, and obedient it becomes.

As noted earlier, leadership discourse remains firmly grounded in "masculine" attributes despite the fact that contemporary leadership theory offers alternate discursive constructions of leadership. Following Foucault, it is important to examine how these discursive constructions become *physical*. While there remains a paucity of theoretical consideration of the body in leadership, an examination of body practices acknowledged in the self-awareness discourse shows that these articulations serve to constrain how leader bodies can be and move. For example, Trichas and Schyns (2011) showed that facial expressions determine whether or not people perceive leadership qualities or not. In particular, when participants observed facial expressions associated with being tough but positive, the actors were perceived as being good leaders. In contrast, when facial expressions were deemed more "soft" and sensitive, the actors were viewed as being less leaderlike. There is scientific evidence to suggest that a smile understood as warmth does imbue more positive associations with good leadership (Gorman, 2011; Trichas & Schyns, 2011), but softer expressions still yield a lower perception of leader competency, although perceptions are contextually dependent as well (Eagly, 2005; Trichas & Schyns, 2011). Trichas and Schyns suggested that leadership training should involve self-awareness about and development of leaderlike expressions to increase leader effectiveness.

What constitutes effective leadership expressions becomes more complex when considering context. For instance, as long as leadership is deemed to require warmth and relational expertise, body actions and dispositions aligned with these aspects are viewed as appropriate, and women (and other minorities) find little issue assuming these types of leadership positions (Eagly, 2005; Eagly & Chin, 2010). However, when women try to fit into leadership positions viewed as requiring more masculine, traditional leadership qualities, expectations about their physicality shifts, and female leaders respond accordingly. Eagly (2005) noted that "women have changed over time, to incorporate more masculinity in both their behavior and their self-concepts" (p. 470) without lessening their leadership credibility by being too masculine or appearing incongruent with their femininity.

Examples of female leaders changing body behaviors to appear more "leaderly" are common. For instance, a female symphony conductor changed the pitch of her voice and other mannerisms in order to become more leaderly (Cheng, 1998). This included lowering her voice and assuming more controlled behaviors. Also, McBroom (1986) recounted one female leader's adoption of more masculine behaviors while balancing the feminine: "I learned that you had to be slightly less warm, slightly less good-natured, slightly less laughing, carefree, and happy. You have to put on a more serious demeanor, to establish credibility more quickly. I don't advocate trying to be nasty, but you stop trying to be warm, wonderful, and nice. It works better" (p. 73).

These women acknowledged that changing attitudes requires development of self-awareness in order to change an aspect *of the body*. Moreover, these women desired these behaviors because they realized that "it works better" (McBroom, 1986, p. 73). They have actualized a capacity that they feel compelled to continue. In doing so, they become docile and "obedient" bodies through desire. It is important to note that these constraints regarding the body apply equally to men (Billing & Alvesson, 2000; Hatcher, 2003). Normalized expectations about male and female physicality combined with the dominant views of leadership serve to constrain the way we view competent leadership in specific contexts, limiting the ways leader bodies can move and be in each of these contexts, setting in motion very limited views about who qualifies as a legitimately leading body.

The Problem of Self-Awareness

Further examining the notions of self-awareness and "leaderly" conduct reveals additional complexities regarding leaders' bodies. Developing self-awareness has been acknowledged as a way for leaders to be more effective by making sure their leaderly conduct is aligned with follower expectations (Gardner, Avolio, Luthans, May, & Walumbwa, 2005; Ladkin & Taylor, 2010). A notable example demonstrates how this type of self-awareness resulted in a leader body that maintained effective leadership but reproduced prejudice. In an effort to align with follower expectations of leaderly conduct, an Australian female police commissioner decided to refrain from attending a Gay Rights March because of severe public criticism, although she fully supported gay rights (Sinclair, 2004). The commissioner's bodily absence was discussed as an effective leadership practice because of the congruence between leader behavior and public expectations

(Ladkin & Taylor, 2010). Although it was acknowledged that the commissioner was able to support gay rights in other ways, the complicit support of heteronormative biases through an absent body defined as leaderly conduct makes this particular way of bringing the body into leadership literature antithetical to more inclusive forms of leadership. In this instance, the desire to be a leaderly body subsumed the desire to be a "just" body. Thus, it appears that dominant discourses of leader effectiveness shape leading bodies in profound ways. This observation warrants further examination.

Silencing of the Social/Cultural Body

In addition to the articulation of knowledge, Foucault (1978) also thought that disciplinary discursive productions could be detected by trying "to discover how the related facts of interdiction or concealment are distributed" (p. 73). In short, by revealing "things said and those concealed, the enunciations required and those forbidden" (p. 100), it is possible to observe the full effects of the power–knowledge nexus and understand how discourse serves to "authorize particular voices and silence others" (Laurendeau & Adams, 2010, p. 433). What remains unsaid or concealed about the body in the concept of leader self-awareness is that the body is socially constructed. By focusing self-awareness strategies on natural and biological views of the body, the *social/cultural* body is effectively silenced. Such silencing is problematic. If only natural and biological views of the body are acknowledged, it limits how we understand not only the practices of self-awareness but also the purposes of self-awareness.

As noted earlier, a social constructionist view of the body brings in the possibility of understanding the body as shaped by the biases and prejudices of socially dominant views. I argue that this silence authorizes leading bodies to be primarily concerned with effectiveness and not necessarily justice. Furthermore, the unacknowledged social/cultural body means that self-awareness strategies that could potentially work to uncover biases and prejudices of the body have not been seriously explored.

To illustrate how leadership theory uses the body to enhance effectiveness and simultaneously subordinates justice and inclusivity, I focus on the following two ways the body is viewed in the concept of self-awareness that serve to silence the social/cultural body: (1) the body is a powerful site of the "true" unmediated and pure self, and (2) maladaptive emotions, like all emotions, are held deeply within our bodies. I argue that while these views produce some useful ideas about how to lead more effectively, they reproduce dominant forms of leadership and subvert attempts to rethink more inclusive leadership practices.

First, the body has been perceived as a site for the true self. The assumption is that the body can serve as grounding for leader behavior, which is perceived as a path toward more authentic leadership. Ladkin and Taylor (2010) posited that "the leader's body, and the way he or she uses it to express their 'true self'" (p. 65) mediates whether or not a leader is perceived to be authentic or not. Their position that followers are able to perceive subconscious, subtle bodily movements as powerful signals about leaders' deeper convictions and feelings is a significant and valuable insight. Recent findings in neuroscience showing that we mirror the feelings and emotions of those around us (Goleman & Boyatzis, 2008) lend strong support to the idea that no matter what leaders verbally express, there is an underlying communication happening that is equally as important. Thus, in order to be authentic and more effective as leaders, it is important for leaders to develop self-awareness about their feelings and align outward enunciations and actions with these inner emotions and feelings (Goleman & Boyatzis, 2008; Ladkin & Taylor, 2010).

While such alignment appears essential to effective leadership, this focus obscures the social/cultural body. The body is positioned as a reliable, unmediated source (Ladkin & Taylor,

2010), although it simultaneously harbors biases and prejudices (Goleman, 1995; Shusterman, 2008) that ultimately work
against rational statements of inclusivity. From a theoretical
standpoint, alignment of the inner and outer selves may be a
leadership imperative. However, this current approach to self-
awareness serves to uphold the inviolability of the body, silencing the body's less just tendencies.

Second, maladaptive emotions are of the body. Emotional
intelligence has emerged as an important leadership self-
aware technique aimed at raising awareness of these emotions
(Avolio & Gardner, 2005; Goleman, Boyatzis, & McKee, 2004;
Walumbwa and others, 2008). Goleman (1995) showed that
understanding one's own emotions as well as detecting others' emotions allow leaders (people) to work more effectively
together. The assumption underlying much of Goleman's work is
that biases and prejudices are deeply held emotions that are practically impossible to change. Goleman noted that while "racial
attitudes of American whites toward blacks have become increasingly more tolerant, more subtle forms of bias persist: people dis-
avow racist attitudes while still acting with covert bias" (p. 157).
He acknowledged the social/cultural body when he said, "Since
prejudices are a variety of emotional learning, relearning is [ital-
ics in the original] possible" (p. 159). Still, privileging effectiveness, Goleman suggested, "It is more practical to try to suppress
the expression of bias rather than trying to eliminate the attitude
itself" (p. 158). While acknowledging the biased body, Goleman's
focus on practicality serves to silence the social/cultural body. In
doing so, biases of the body remain unchallenged, and the expectations of leadership practices stay focused on effectiveness.

Reconceptualizing the Self-Aware Leader

Later in his life, Foucault became less interested in how bodies
are disciplined and more concerned with the notion of critique

that can help us "separate out, from the contingency that has made us what we are, the possibility of no longer being, doing, or thinking what we are, do, or think" (Foucault, 1984, p. 46). For Foucault, self-awareness was not about searching for the deepest, inner "true" self. Instead, self-awareness relied on the intellectual act of problematization, that is, "to render alien modes of thought and behavior that we accept as normal and everyday" (Lloyd, 1996, p. 244).

note

The key to Foucault's approach is that the body could function as a source of those problematizations. He observed that once power exerts an effect over the body, "there inevitably emerge the responding claims and affirmations of one's own body against power" (Foucault, 1977b, p. 56). Foucault said that when the body goes through a "limit experience," it is possible to recognize that the "distinctions central to the play of true and false are pliable, uncertain, contingent" (as cited in Miller, 1993, p. 30). From this realization, Foucault argued that individuals are then "free" to choose from a wider range of discursive constructions to "transform themselves in order to attain a certain state of happiness, purity, wisdom, perfection or immortality" (Foucault, 1988, p. 18).

Such a view allows a reframing of the self-awareness process in resonant leadership (McKee & Boyatzis, 2006). Here, self-awareness involves noting significant signs from the body that "power stress" is occurring. Power stress is a body experience through which one realizes that he or she has reached a limit. In fact, McKee and Boyatzis remarked that the body is not suited to daily stresses that leaders face in today's dynamic world. They argued that leaders tend to sacrifice for organizations, and in doing so, they move into states of "dissonance" characterized by exhaustion or physical ailments. Once at these limits, self-awareness involves detecting these significant body signs of fatigue, lack of clarity, or emotional distress.

Through a process called "mindfulness," the authors showed how leaders can recuperate their bodies through exercise, take notice of their strengths and weaknesses, and observe how their actions make others wary, nervous, or frustrated. Deeply rooted in body sensations, the strategy is to become aware of these deeper feelings, letting oneself become vulnerable and open to self-critique. The next step is to imagine an "ideal self" by searching for the "real" self at the deepest level. In the search for the "real" self in resonant leadership, the absence of the social/cultural body becomes apparent once more, despite some level of critique.

Acknowledging the Social/Cultural Body

Through a Foucauldian lens, a more nuanced, social/cultural body becomes observable. Namely, Foucault believed the body is not only a site where "willing, and feeling and thinking all take root [but] . . . also a place of obscure wounds, baffling torments, and uncertain instincts . . . palpable in a welter of contradictory inclinations and aversions" (as cited in Miller, 1993, p. 182). It is the latter aspect of the body that remains elusive in the self-awareness constructs described thus far.

To achieve more inclusive forms of leadership, uncovering and challenging the embodied biases and prejudices need to be part of self-awareness development. As Shusterman (2008) noted, "Much ethnic and racial hostility is not the product of logical thought but of deep prejudices that are somatically expressed or embodied in vague but disagreeable feelings that typically lie beneath the level of explicit consciousness" (p. 25). Our aversions to people occur at a visceral level and often go unnoticed because they confirm what we may have been socialized to believe.

What is needed is a critique not only of when the body *fails* leaders, but also of when it *supports* leaders in ways that allow them to continue discriminatory practices. Such is the impetus of Foucault, to question that which appears normal, that which may be framed as not the right "fit," that which might ultimately contradict a leader's publicly acknowledged intentions to work toward tolerance and acceptance of diversity. Foucault's notion of problematization takes self-awareness beyond recognizing when leaders are failing in "leaderly" conduct, are exhausted, dissonant, or lacking judgment, and moves us toward a more ethical purpose; however, it seems clear that "limit experiences" should not be relied upon to detect subtle forms of aversions and discomfort that may be limiting our views of legitimate leading bodies.

Somaesthetics: Becoming a Self-Aware, Inclusive Leader

Given that somaesthetics is "powerfully present in Foucault" (Shusterman, 2008, p. 23), my present aim is to show how somaesthetic practice can serve as an important strategy of developing self-awareness. With the aim of recognizing the biased body, I suggest that somaesthetics offers a way to develop *critical*, *bodily* self-awareness, which is the act of bringing to consciousness and problematizing subtle forms of hostility, fear, and discomfort that occur unconsciously through our daily interactions with people different from us. In other words, somaesthetic practice can help leaders gain a "clearer awareness of one's somatic reactions [so that] one can also improve one's behavior toward others in much wider social and political contexts" (Shusterman, 2008, p. 25), helping leaders and those hiring into leadership positions to loosen and ultimately sever the "visceral grip of the prejudice" (p. 25).

The process of developing a critical, bodily self-awareness is achieved through focusing on the three fundamental branches of somaesthetics: analytic somaesthetics, pragmatic somaesthetics, and practical somaesthetics (Shusterman, 2008). Analytic somaesthetics explains how our bodies are essential to perception and how body practices shape and are shaped by our knowledge of

the world. As described earlier, Foucault's notion of "docile" bodies offers a way for leaders to describe and understand the visceral
quality of biases and prejudices. Pragmatic somaesthetics align with
Foucault's notion of problematizations in which body experiences
can serve as transforming experiences. Pragmatic somaesthetics
promotes conscious body scans in order to detect those feelings of
discomfort and aversion toward those different from ourselves or
different from our leader expectations. In other words, the first step
to "expunging them [biases] is to develop the somatic awareness to
recognize them in ourselves" (Shusterman, 2008, p. 26).

While difficult, pragmatic somaesthetics combines the
intentionality of body scans with critical awareness of bodily
held prejudices and makes this work possible. Finally, practical somaesthetics asserts that analysis and critical, bodily self-
awareness are insufficient. Ultimately, "actually pursuing such
care through intelligently disciplined practice aimed at somatic
self-improvement" (Shusterman, 2008, p. 29) is the only way to
change somatic responses so that they align with professed anti-
racist, antisexist, antihomophobic claims. Refashioning bodily
feelings is done by imagining how one might feel differently in
the presence of "others," then practicing this at every opportunity.

Conclusion

The aim of this chapter has been to rethink the ways the body
has been conceptualized within leadership self-awareness. A
Foucauldian approach has allowed us "to detach from established knowledge, ask fresh questions, make new connections,
and understand why it is important to do so" (Cole, Giardina, &
Andrews, 2004, p. 207). Globalizing efforts have created an
increasingly diverse workforce and leadership. Despite these significant changes, leader attributes remain gendered and contextual. Such thinking reproduces body practices accepted as leader
appropriate. Although contextually dependent, dominant discursive

constructions of the leader as decisive and action oriented have produced body practices that align with masculine attributes understood as leaderlike.

Furthermore, discursive constructions of the body as the site of a true self have also shaped leader body practices. Through Foucault's concept of "docile" bodies it has been possible to break from this established knowledge and see how limiting these views of the body are within the discourse of self-awareness. Such a view has encouraged asking "fresh questions" about the body's role in self-awareness. Such questions revolve around the body's role in reproducing biases and prejudices at the subconscious level as well as the body's potential role in problematizing visceral biases.

By combining Foucault's notion of embodied discourse, problematization, and the aims of somaesthetics, it is possible to reconceptualize what self-awareness entails and move self-awareness toward an ethical aim of inclusivity and acceptance of diverse leading bodies. Discovering and refashioning the subconscious connections between the body and biases become a new kind of work for the leader aiming to be self-aware. Such work is important for leaders working with a diverse workforce. More important, however, critical, bodily self-awareness opens avenues for actualizing more diverse leadership as well as reconceptualizing more diverse ways of being leaders.

References

Avolio, B., & Gardner, W. L. (2005). Authentic leadership development: Getting to the root of positive forms of leadership. *The Leadership Quarterly, 16*(3), 315–338. doi:10.1016/j.leaqua.2005.03.001

Avolio, B. J., Walumbwa, F., & Weber, T. (2010). Leadership: Current theories, research, and future directions. *Annual Review of Psychology, 60*, 421–449. doi:10.1146/annurev.psych.60.110707.163621

Billing, Y. D., & Alvesson, M. (2000). Questioning the notion of feminine leadership: A critical perspective on the gender labelling of leadership. *Gender, Work & Organization, 7*(3), 144–157. doi:10.1111/1468-0432.00103

Boyatzis, R., & McKee, A. (2006). Intentional change. *Journal of Organizational Excellence, 25*(3), 49–60. doi:10.1002/joe.20100

Cheng, M. N. (1998). Women conductors: Has the train left the station? *Harmony, 6*, 81–90.

Cole, C. L., Giardina, M. D., & Andrews, D. L. (2004). Michel Foucault: Studies of power and sport. In R. Guilianotti (Ed.), *Sport and modern social theorists* (pp. 207–223). New York, NY: Palgrave Macmillan.

Eagly, A. H. (2005). Achieving relational authenticity in leadership: Does gender matter? *The Leadership Quarterly, 16*(3), 459–474. doi:10.1016/j.leaqua.2005.03.007

Eagly, A. H., & Chin, J. (2010). Diversity and leadership in a changing world. *American Psychologist, 65*(3), 216–224. doi:10.1037/a0018957

Eagly, A. H., & Karau, S. J. (2002). Role congruity theory of prejudice toward female leaders. *Psychological Review, 109*(3), 573–598. doi:10.1037/0033-295X.109.3.573

Fondas, N. (1997). Feminization unveiled: Management qualities in contemporary writings. *Academy of Management Review, 22*(1), 257–282. doi:10.5465/AMR.1997.9707180266

Foucault, M. (1970). *The order of things: An archeology of the human sciences.* New York, NY: Vintage Books.

Foucault, M. (1972). *The archeology of knowledge and discourse on language.* New York, NY: Pantheon.

Foucault, M. (1977a). *Discipline and punish: The birth of the prison* (2nd ed.). London, UK: Penguin Books.

Foucault, M. (1977b). *Power/knowledge: Selected interviews and other writings 1972–1977.* New York, NY: Pantheon.

Foucault, M. (1978). *The history of sexuality: An introduction.* New York, NY: Vintage Books.

Foucault, M. (1983). The subject and power. In H. L. Dreyfus & P. Rainbow (Eds.), *Michel Foucault: Beyond structuralism and hermeneutics* (2nd ed.). Chicago, IL: University of Chicago Press.

Foucault, M. (1984). What is enlightenment? In P. Rainbow (Ed.), *Foucault reader* (pp. 32–50). New York, NY: Pantheon.

Foucault, M. (1988). Technologies of the self. In L. H. Martin, H. Gutman, & P. H. Hutton (Eds.), *Technologies of the self: A seminar with Michel Foucault.* Amherst, MA: University of Massachusetts Press.

Gardner, W. L., Avolio, B. J., Luthans, F., May, D. R., & Walumbwa, F. (2005). "Can you see the real me?" A self-based model of authentic leader and follower development. *The Leadership Quarterly, 16*(3), 343–372. doi:10.1016/j.leaqua.2005.03.003

Goleman, D. (1995). *Emotional intelligence.* New York, NY: Bantam Books.

Goleman, D., & Boyatzis, R. (2008, September). Social intelligence and the biology of leadership. *Harvard Business Review*, pp. 74–81.

Goleman, D., Boyatzis, R., & McKee, A. (2004). *Primal leadership: Learning to lead with emotional intelligence*. Cambridge, MA: Harvard Business Review Press.

Gorman, C. K. (2011). Avoiding mixed messages: Understand the impact of body language. *Strategic Communication Management, 15*(4), 32–35.

Guthey, E. (2001). Ted Turner's corporate cross-dressing and the shifting images of American business leadership. *International Journal of Business History, 2*(1), 111–142. doi:10.1093/es/2.1.111

Hall, S. (Ed.). (1997). *Representation: Cultural representations and signifying practices*. Thousand Oaks, CA: Sage.

Hatcher, C. (2003). Refashioning a passionate manager: Gender at work. *Gender, Work and Organization, 10*(4), 391–412. doi:10.1111/1468-0432.00203

Hearn, J. (1993). Emotive subjects: Organizational men, organizational masculinities and the (de)construction of 'emotions.' In S. Fineman (Ed.), *Emotion in organizations* (pp. 142–166). London, UK: Sage.

Hearn, J. (2000). On the complexity of feminist intervention in organization. *Organization, 7*(4), 609–624.

Heilman, M. E. (2001). Description and prescription: How gender stereotypes prevent women's ascent up the organizational ladder. *Journal of Social Issues, 57*, 657–674. doi:10.1111/0022-4537.00234

Heilman, M. E., & Eagly, A. H. (2008). Gender stereotypes are alive, well, and busy producing workplace discrimination. *Industrial and Organizational Psychology, 1*(4), 393–398. doi:10.1111/j.1754-9434.2008.00072

Holt, S., & Marques, J. (2012). Empathy in leadership: Appropriate or misplaced? An empirical study on a topic that is asking for attention. *Journal of Business Ethics, 105*(1), 95–105. doi:10.1007/s10551-011-0951-5

Koenig, A. M., Mitchell, A. A., Eagly, A. H., & Ristikari, T. (2011). Are leader stereotypes masculine? A meta-analysis of three research paradigms. *Psychological Bulletin, 137*(4), 616–642. doi:10.1037/a0023557

Ladkin, D., & Taylor, S. S. (2010). Enacting the 'true self': Towards a theory of embodied authentic leadership. *The Leadership Quarterly, 21*(1), 64–74. doi:10.1016/j.leaqua.2009.10.005

Laurendeau, J., & Adams, C. (2010). "Jumping like a girl": Discursive silences, exclusionary practices and the controversy over women's ski jumping. *Sport in Society, 13*(3), 431–447. doi:10.1080/17430431003588051

Lipman-Blumen, J. (1996). *The connective edge: Leading in an interdependent world*. San Francisco, CA: Jossey-Bass.

Lloyd, M. (1996). A feminist mapping of Foucauldian politics. In S. Hekman (Ed.), *Feminist interpretations of Michel Foucault*. University Park, PA: Pennsylvania State University Press.

McBroom, P. A. (1986). *The third sex: The new professional woman*. New York, NY: William Morrow.

McKee, A., & Boyatzis, R. E. (2006). Renewing and sustaining leadership. *Leader to Leader, 2006*(40), 30–36. doi:10.1002/ltl.175

Miller, J. (1993). *The passion of Michel Foucault.* Cambridge, MA: Harvard University Press.

Mortimer, C. (2009). Developing a new perspective on leadership theory: From a tree of knowledge to a rhizome of contingencies. *Electronic Journal of Business Research Methods, 7*(1), 55–65.

Powell, G. N., Butterfield, D. A., & Parent, J. D. (2002). Gender and managerial stereotypes: Have the times changed? *Journal of Management, 28*(2), 177–193. doi:10.1177/014920630202800203

Shilling, C. (2003). *The body and social theory* (2nd ed.). Thousand Oaks, CA: Sage.

Shusterman, R. (2008). *Body consciousness: A philosophy of mindfulness and somaesthetics.* New York, NY: Cambridge University Press.

Sinclair, A. (2004). Journey around leadership. *Discourse: Studies in the Cultural Politics of Education, 25*(1), 7–19. doi:10.1080/0159630042000178455

Trichas, S., & Schyns, B. (2011). The face of leadership: Perceiving leaders from facial expression. *The Leadership Quarterly, 23*(3), 545–566. doi:10.1016/j.leaqua.2011.12.007

Walumbwa, F., Avolio, B. J., Gardner, W. L., Wernsing, T., & Peterson, S. (2008). Authentic leadership: Development and validation of a theory-based measure. *Journal of Management, 34*(1), 89–126. doi:10.1177/0149206307308913

Chapter Six

Dollmaking as an Expression of Women's Leadership

Kimberly Yost

When I was very young, my grandmother made me a Raggedy Ann doll with lots of yellow yarn hair. When I was four, I decided to give all my dolls a haircut. A lifetime later, Raggedy Ann sits in my studio, smudged and time-worn, with her spiky yellow yarn hair, gently reminding me of my grandmother's love and my mother's horror at my hairdressing skills. My mother and grandmothers enjoyed dollmaking their entire lives. I came to dollmaking only a few years ago from an interest in exploring the divine feminine. My mother and grandmothers have now passed. Their legacy of dollmaking remains strong, though, and I discovered a way to incorporate dollmaking into my study and practice of leadership.

In the fall of 2010, I attended a strategic planning session for the leadership branch of an alumni association at a small, private midwestern college. The session discussed ways the association could meet the needs of alumni of the graduate organizational leadership program. Of particular interest to me was the expressed need for continuing education in leadership and opportunities to explore women's leadership issues. Consequently, I saw the opportunity to engage female graduates in a continuing education workshop that integrated issues surrounding women's leadership and personal transformation with arts-based learning.

Artistic learning is intuitive and releases emotional knowledge embedded in the unconscious or that defies verbalization.

Traditional learning depends on techno-rational cognitive means of understanding. Our complex world "cannot be fully understood solely by reference to scientific forms of logic and sense-making. The arts, and arts-based practices, provide different ways of both describing and relating to that complexity, thereby offering novel ways of responding to it" (Ladkin & Taylor, 2010, p. 235). In contrast, informal "artistic ways of knowing help us to experience the world in more holistic ways that deepen our understanding of self, others, and the world around us" (Lawrence, 2008, p. 67). This deep understanding is the outcome of the transformational change that can occur when we engage in artistic modes of learning and goes beyond the personal inner life to impact our ways of being within organizations and other social groups. As Mavrinac (2005) noted, "Organizations learn through individuals" (p. 394). Yet, "leaders must experience personal transformation within themselves before they can truly help to transform other people" (Tucker & Russell, 2004, p. 104).

Positing a post-heroic model of leadership opens a space for accessing and benefiting from the personal knowledge of everyone within an organization. However, the post-heroic leadership model, emphasizing personal and organizational transformation, contains qualities coded as feminine within American society (Fletcher, 2004). These feminine codes complicate the recognition of post-heroic leadership qualities as an advantage in an organizational context predominantly defined through masculine codes. Fletcher (2004) demonstrated this point by revealing language describing the traits of heroic leadership as masculine and using terms such as "individualism, control, assertiveness, and skills of advocacy and domination" (p. 650). Conversely, words associated with post-heroic leadership, such as "empathy, community, vulnerability, and skills of inquiry and collaboration" (p. 650), are typically ascribed to socially understood concepts of femininity.

The influence of this socially constructed identity could contribute to the hesitance of organizations to develop along transformational leadership paths that uphold distributive leadership, relational practice, and mutual learning (Fletcher, 2004). Additionally, race, class, gender, position in the organizational hierarchy, and other characteristics used to classify people, are strong elements that separate groups and "influence the way individuals think about themselves and others" (Nkomo, 2010, p. 75). Power is inherent within these classifications, depending upon which group may enjoy privileges within the organization or within the larger society. In organizations with dominant masculine expressions, efforts to enact feminine expressions could be met with opposition. Yet, "social power is not sufficient for social transformation unless it is yoked to structures that function in such a way as to overcome resistance to the collective project" (Reicher, Haslam, & Hopkins, 2005, p. 563). Furthermore, "the very possibility of leadership depends upon the existence (or manufacture) of a shared social identity" (p. 553). The development of a group within a larger organization that discovers a shared social identity will create emergent leaders and has the potential to transform that organization if internal structures can be put in place to overcome resistance to change.

Advocates of bringing artistic processes to organizational practice point to the desire for workplace creativity, innovation, and inspiration sought by business leaders and offer engagement with the arts as a means for accomplishing the paradigmatic shift in how individuals learn within an organization (Adler, 2006). Yet organizations seem doubtful about arts-based learning as a means for developing leadership skills. Chia and Holt (2008) contended that business schools stress representational learning (that is, theories, models, and subject–object detachment), thereby producing business professionals who lack alternative experiential learning and, thus, bring this epistemic model into the organization. Taylor and Ladkin (2009) acknowledged the dominance of rational-cognitive approaches to organizational learning, but "argue that arts-based methods can provide the means for accessing and developing this way of approaching the world, which in turn could contribute to a more holistic way of engaging with managerial contexts" (p. 56). Indeed, Adler (2006) concluded, "The time is right for the cross-fertilization of the arts and leadership" (p. 488).

Keeping in mind the expressed needs for continuing education in leadership, coupled with exploration of gender issues and the transformative potential of arts-based learning, I constructed a workshop that explored dollmaking as an expression of women's leadership. Wicks and Rippin (2010) developed a similar study in the United Kingdom using male and female second-year graduate students in organizational leadership. This leadership development was based on what Woodward and Funk (2010) termed "an aesthetically-informed hermeneutic approach to leadership ... [where] exploration of the inner self becomes essential in any artist-leader development work" (p. 301). The emergence of meaning is a process that can be activated by connecting with an object or activity that engages "our sensual territories—the embodied, emotional, sensual, symbolic elements of ourselves in our cultural environments" (Woodward & Funk, 2010, p. 302). However, Palmer (1969) explained, the "aesthetic moment" should not be regarded in terms of "sensuous pleasures" but as a form by which "the truth of being [is] manifest" (p. 245). As a *group* activity, the creation of art becomes less about individual artistic skill and restores "what is an essential element of human activity, enabling us to experience and reflect on our lives in ways less accessible through non-artistic modes" (Wicks & Rippin, 2010, p. 260). Furthermore, art making "captures the essence of the individual's sense of her own leadership . . . while the finished art object serves as [a projection] for the individual and her own leadership practices" (Taylor & Ladkin, 2009, p. 61).

Using dolls as the artwork from which to explore identity can be construed as hopelessly gendered and backward. Yet the reclamation of traditional women's crafts is gaining momentum. Chansky (2010) noted, "Certain symbols may be reclaimed as some semblance of power is gained by the minority group, upon the realization that part of their historical roots have faded in the rush to downplay differences" (p. 681). Although Chansky was discussing needle arts, my proposition is that the use of the female figure, embodied in a doll, provides a catalyst that creates a rich and deep understanding of self and future visions for leadership development.

Leadership development programs can often be intellectualized and disconnected from personal experiences. Even if reflection on personal experience is encouraged, reflection is "in the head" and lacks tangible qualities. Combining the intellectual understanding of leading as a woman with the tactile experience and visual manifestation of creating an object symbolizing the personal reflection provides an alternative means for exploration that can be quite profound. This chapter explores one such arts-based leadership development activity.

The Workshop Project

The workshop was an opportunity for continuing education in leadership studies through an arts-based learning event exploring women's leadership and gender issues by inviting participants to create dolls that embodied their current or future visions of themselves as leaders. The organizational goals included the establishment of continuing education opportunities, providing a mechanism for networking and mentoring, and advancing the mission of the alumni association for personal and professional growth, while contributing to the college's overall mission and values. Through reflection, discussion, and art making, participants were able to reach deeper into their understanding of themselves to gain a greater appreciation for who they are as women and how those qualities affect their leadership practices.

The agenda for the workshop was for participants to journal from prompted questions, discuss responses to the journal prompts in a group, and create a doll that personified each participant's current or future vision of herself as a leader. One week later, a follow-up survey was e-mailed to participants to gain their post-workshop reflections and reactions.

The participants (Deb, Cindy, and Eleanor) were all in their mid-fifties, white, and had ten to twenty years of practicing leadership within their respective organizations. As the college and master's programs are relatively small, I was acquainted with each of the participants through alumni events and in my position at the college.

Journal and Discussion Responses

Q1: Please write about a significant memory of a doll.

As each of the participants is a mother, they shared their memories of dolls and their children. Deb shared that she had been a bit of a tomboy as a girl and never played with dolls, nor did she ever receive a doll from her parents, but she wanted her daughters to play with dolls as young children. She reflected on this decision as a means for providing "role models or someone they could relate to in their pretend play."

Eleanor described herself as a "girly girl" and had a vivid memory of a particular "Toni" doll from her childhood. She doesn't recall naming the doll, but she still has all the clothes her mother made for the doll each year at Christmas. This was one of her only dolls compared to her daughters' "bins of naked Barbies." Eleanor said her reflection on her childhood doll made her "want to go and pull her out and look at all of it."

Cindy shared memories of her children's dolls, with her eldest daughter preferring stuffed animals, though she noted mostly male representations were available, like Mickey Mouse and Bert and Ernie; her second daughter "loved everything traditionally doll—baby dolls, talking dolls, and especially Barbies" until she was in her early teens; and her son loved Pooh Bears and GI Joes. She shared her realization that even boys play with dolls, but at the time she thought dolls were "too feminine" and had tried to "steer her kids clear" of them.

Responses to this question about doll memories provided insight into the differing childhood experiences each participant had with dolls. Memories of dolls were tied to family relationships— both positive and negative—and provided an interesting framework for the spoken and unspoken contradictions participants held about the social construction of playing with dolls. Dolls were clearly seen as a childhood experience and not something useful in their adult lives.

Q2: What words best describe who you are as a woman right now?

This question was deliberately designed to allow participants to "brainstorm" descriptive words as opposed to providing a prose description of who they think or feel they are as a woman. The adjectives provided by the participants were compiled and pasted into Wordle for visual analysis. Wordle is a free Internet application, described as "a toy for generating 'word clouds' from text" that "depends on core layout algorithms within a Java platform" (www.wordle.net). The clouds give greater prominence to words that appear more frequently in the source text.

The more prominent descriptive words of *evolving, change, ambitious, committed,* and *health* (used in the context of being emotionally healthy) suggest the women presently acknowledge they are in a place of transformation. Several accompanying words—*tension, baggage, stressed, boundaries, fractured*—demonstrate that transformation is not a gentle or easy process.

The discussion of this question quickly turned to the tensions between public and private selves. Deb declared that she had written down all positive adjectives, but there was "the other side." She was accustomed to labeling herself as "just a secretary" and not a leader because she did not yet possess the job title of a leader. She declared that she was "taking a vow never to say that again."

For Eleanor, the tensions were reflected in her decision not to climb the corporate ladder but to put her children first as a twice-widowed single mother. "But sometimes I look at others and wonder [why/how they got there]." She is trying to become "more comfortable in my own skin" and considers herself an emerging informal leader within the workplace.

Cindy echoed the concept of "owning who you are" and "I don't pretend to fit into my [rural] community." She sees herself in the process of evolving, which "if you don't, you're dead." This has placed pressures on her marriage, and she was firm in declaring her conscious decision to stay in her marriage as it relates to her own integrity and the general complexity of life. She is also "learning healthier ways to deal with crap ... overcome obstacles ... and work with others' strengths."

I noted how closely related womanhood and leadership were for the participants and how this relationship created tensions in their public and private spheres. Moving into the third question, I mentioned that they might find themselves repeating descriptions from question 2, but they laughed and said they had already come to that realization.

Q3: What words best describe who you are as a leader right now?

Similar to question 2, participants brainstormed words describing who they think or feel they are as leaders and pasted them into Wordle. For this question, no words were more prominent within the source text than any other words. This is not to assume each woman leads differently, but they each had unique adjectives for describing their leadership qualities.

The discussion following the journal reflection centered on experiences in their master's of organizational leadership (MOL) program. Cindy felt she had "changed drastically since the MOL," and was more "integrated," "decisive," and "fair and balanced." She stated that she is more able to "hold what's best for my company, my employees, and myself" and "comfortable saying 'I don't know.'" Deb felt the descriptive words from question 2 were all appropriate, and she would add *evolving* and *team focused* to her leadership description because of the MOL. Eleanor shared that the greatest learning from the MOL was her ability to work with a difficult person because she is "respectful now" and sees herself as more diplomatic. My sharing reflected the tensions between my desire to be seen as an emergent leader and my anxieties over how my leadership actions and ideas may be received, thus causing me to be timid and nervous in many of my leadership opportunities and "cloaking" my authenticity.

While *transformational* was used by one of the participants, the feminine coded words per Fletcher (2004) describing post-heroic transformational leadership—such as *empathy, vulnerability, collaboration*—were not specifically used. In addition, the participants used more words to describe themselves as leaders than as women. This furthers the need to question how women's leadership practices are linguistically described in general. In other words, where is the collective lexicon for succinctly expressing qualities of women's leadership? Although beyond the boundaries of this particular study, this is an area deserving greater attention and study.

Q4: If you were to create a doll that represents who you are or who you want to become as a leader, what words would you use to describe what that doll might look like? Feel free to draw or doodle your description, too.

This journal prompt was designed to get the participants (including the author) thinking or feeling about the process of dollmaking and creating a vision for their doll. There was no group discussion of this exercise. Two of the participants doodled concepts—a scale and a staircase—and brief words,

Dolls Created by Participants: Kimberly, Cindy, Eleanor, and Deb (left to right)

while two participants only included word descriptions of their vision. Participants were then invited to choose a doll blank, or make their own, and create their vision of who they are or would like to become as leaders.

Q5: Does your doll visually represent you? In what ways? How did this make you feel?

Deb wrote:

> My doll represents me as a tatter[ed] and torn woman of character who is continually emerging and evolving. One who is competent, confident, and comfortable in her own skin. I've come a long way baby.

Eleanor wrote:

> She looks happy, put together, yet has some personal touches.
>
> I like her, I like me.

Cindy wrote:

> Purple/pink represents integrated wisdom of the feminine self.
>
> Sparkles & jewels represent the true me that shines through.
>
> Purple bindings are the strength—the 2 legs I stand on.
>
> Snowflake/sparkle breasts are the happiness that I'm female.
>
> Epaulets represent leadership.
>
> Chains only on the front represent the masculine company for which I work—binding/masking/not caring about the feminine qualities that I could bring.

I wrote:

> I am flowing, varied, bright, shiny. Naked—reaching for the authentic & vulnerable.

In the discussion, Eleanor introduced her doll as "a little boring, but kind of me," which provoked protests from the other participants, who saw the doll as quite interesting. They commented on the detail of the painted red "fingernails" and the shiny gold tube beads sewn on the feet for a "pedicure." Eleanor admitted she did like the wardrobe and thought it represented how she likes to present herself in a sophisticated manner, which increases her confidence.

Deb introduced her doll by saying, "Don't take it the wrong way." She saw her doll as conservative in dress and personality, which she is "at times." Deb admitted to keeping to a clear internal vision of what she *should* look like as a leader and, through the group discussion, came to understand that her doll might not be the leader she will become if she more fully cultivates her authentic self.

I introduced my doll as an internal vision of myself as an emerging leader and remarked that the process allowed me to reflect on how my previous description of personal leadership qualities' being "cloaked" no longer represented valid feelings.

The only participant to create a two-sided doll was Cindy. We all found this intriguing, and Cindy gave a lengthy description of the doll. She introduced her doll by saying, "This wasn't what I was expecting her to turn out like," later elaborating that she had "wanted nice and neat." Each element of her doll was intentionally included and clearly demonstrated the dichotomy of her public/private self as a leader and the challenges she faces. Of particular note, the "back view" of her personal self has open eyes and a wide, smiling mouth with teeth, while the "front view" of her public self shows eyes and mouth closed. The public self is also draped in chains, which symbolize the constricting nature of her workplace leadership practice. However, she also bound the doll's legs in pink and purple ribbons, which she described as being the strength she developed over the years to withstand the challenges.

Each doll was amazingly different and reflected various solutions to an intentionally ambiguous challenge to create a doll that embodied each woman's personal understanding of who she is or wants to be as a leader.

Q6: What was your "process" in creating your doll? Did you stick to an internal vision and the descriptive words you wrote or were you more spontaneous or adaptive as you worked?

Cindy previously mentioned that her doll was not what she had expected and her initial plan was disregarded once she began the making. Her journal more fully reflects her experience: "What emerged was nothing like what was planned. In fact, there was no plan, only art. But as I worked I could feel the symbology of the leadership process emerge. This is a picture of who I am today. It confirms that I have more to offer than the company is willing to accept. . . . I've known I need to be someplace else, someplace healthier, & I think that is what emerged from this process."

Both Deb and Eleanor wrote and discussed how their process kept very close to the description they had originally reflected upon. Deb also offered that she would like to do the workshop again, but "focus more on my personality away from work, then compare the two [dolls]." She further commented, "We don't pull strengths from the outside world to the work world."

The women were clear in the perception of their "leader selves" as being a public performance, but now, through the understanding they gained from the workshop, it seemed their womanhood also had a duality for public and private performance, with the private self remaining hidden. I interpret Deb's comment as being made because of deeper understanding regarding her authentic self (as a result of this inquiry) and the desire to relax the tension between that self and the self she labels as public and portrays to others.

Post-Project Responses and Reflections

A week after the workshop, an e-mail survey was sent to participants to gain additional reflections and reactions to the experience. As a temporary community of women, the participants were highly favorable about the learning experience, mentioning how the experience highlighted the differences in how each of them enacts leadership with different strengths and that this individual approach should be honored. The opportunity for reflection was considered beneficial, and utilizing an arts-based activity allowed for the subconscious to emerge, because art has "the ability to lead us deeper into ourselves and allow to bubble to the surface those things that are deeply a part of us," as one participant observed. Indeed, the art making changed the way in which one participant views reflective practices. "Most reflective processes in which I've participated have had a deep, almost (if not actual) painful process associated with it. . . . [T]he act of making something offered a way to bring forward something positive, to complete the meditative process with something beautiful to show for it."

The participants all responded favorably to the workshop as a catalyst for personal and professional growth. Survey responses did not indicate a momentous shift in the ways in which they viewed themselves as leaders or as women. Rather, they indicated that the workshop validated, confirmed, and empowered their understandings. Cindy wrote, "I was amazed to see visually demonstrated how much of my feminine strength I hide at work to fit into . . . the masculine construct of business."

Discussion

Although this particular event privileged female MOL graduates, and participation was quite modest, the intention was for the organization, as a whole, to more fully understand the power of arts-based learning and consider subsequent continuing education programs. Fletcher (2004) noted, "Leadership depends on creating a learning environment . . . the ability to create conditions where new knowledge—collective learning—can be cocreated and implemented" (p. 649). This workshop built upon that understanding and introduced a kinesthetic-aesthetic learning style not typically associated with leadership development in higher education.

Furthermore, as current economic and personnel environments of organizations place limitations on meeting the relational support needs of employees (Parker, Hall, & Kram, 2008), the external mechanism of the dollmaking workshop was seen as a means by which women could initiate supportive relationships. As Parker and others recognized, self-knowledge leads to a greater ability in developing relationships, whereby "identity and competence are continuously reshaped and affirmed through interactions with others" (p. 489). Creating a temporary community of women engaged in an activity of self-awareness toward understanding their similarities and differences in relation to leadership practice allowed a space for (re)shaping and (re)affirming their identity in a supportive environment not readily accessible in their lives.

The use of arts-based activities furthers leadership development in ways that become personal and embedded. Indeed, one of the strengths of arts-based methods is to transform impersonal, generalized theories into personalized, connected illustrations of leadership (Taylor & Ladkin, 2009). The key is in understanding that the "truth" discovered in the experience can be different for each individual because of incorporation with her totality of experiences, knowledge, and feelings. There is the challenge of advancing the relationship between the workshop experience and the participant's public/private transformation as well as translating the outcomes to the day-to-day obstacles participants confront in their leadership roles. This project was fortunate to have participants who were self-reflective prior to their involvement, and their graduate studies prepared them to be transparent and conscious of using all their experiences to inform their leadership behaviors.

Long-term systemic change was not the primary focus of this project. As noted earlier, individuals' ability to transform themselves by becoming more self-aware and create or discover a shared identity within an organization can provide the impetus for larger organizational change. This is a "bottom-up" strategy based on the needs of individuals, which over time may evolve or disappear. Linking individual transformation to organizational transformation is not clearly seen within the boundaries of this study. Typically, transformational change within an organization can take from three to ten years (Mavrinac, 2005). What is important to note, however, is the potential for change within a variety of systems. As individuals change, they affect each social system of which they are a member. The vision for the change project was built upon the understanding that leadership skills can be developed from the inside out and personal change provides a foundation from which organizational change can occur. With this in mind, the project could prove to be dynamic in ways that are not readily quantified or observed.

An ethical consideration, which Rippin (2007) described as "bourgeois excess," occurs within this activity. The dollmaking in this instance is a leisure pastime—no matter that it is also an educational activity. The ability to schedule time for personal exploration and art making is itself a privilege of the educated middle class. Moreover, given that this is an exercise in personal growth and development, there is an implication that class identity and improvement weigh heavily on the ability of an organization to engage in change processes. Rippin (2007) saw this as a fundamental issue, stating that we should "resist the simplistic notions that by fixing leadership we can fix persistent systems of inequities without requiring any fundamental social and cultural change" (p. 220). And yet, transformational social change on a large scale cannot happen without the transformation of individuals within the social system. A first step must be taken by a few before the whole may take a leap.

Although our group was small, we all considered the experience quite profound. As this was a planned change initiative, a collaborative approach was essential (Levy, 1986). Following Heron and Reason (2001), I was mindful of the concept of conducting research "with" others rather than "on" others. While this project was not designed for full integration of the co-operative inquiry features Heron and Reason advocate, I was aware of the ethical responsibilities of engagement with the participants as opposed to "studying" them.

I was particularly struck by the insights the women had about themselves as women and as leaders—and how closely aligned their understandings were. I agree with Deb, who expressed a need for another workshop in which she would reflect upon herself as a woman outside of work and see how a doll from that perspective would compare to the doll she made for the first workshop. This is one idea for further exploration of the duality of the public/private selves and could be beneficial to deepening our understanding of women's leadership practices. More to the point, this exploration could facilitate further revelation of participants' authentic self. Through the creation of a doll symbolizing their leadership practice or vision, participants were able to move closer to their own sense of authenticity. Particularly with the example of the two-sided doll, the truth of how many women mask their authenticity in a male-dominated environment is demonstrated. With consideration for Cindy's knowledge of her authentic self in opposition to the self she presents in her workplace, exploring ways of integrating or reconciling these selves could be quite powerful. In addition, the tension between the rebel and the conformist, as in Deb's doll, becomes tangible and acknowledged in a way that underscores the need for reconciling or embracing these characteristics to become a more authentic self and leader.

This concept merges with the theoretical construct of Reflected Best Self (RBS), which "represents a fusion of the reality of lived experience . . . with the idealized sense of possibility for who one can be(come) when one fully embodies his or her best self" (Roberts, 2012, p. 5). In addition, exploring one's RBS can lead to enhanced personal expressiveness, connectedness with others, increased skills for coping with stress, and greater clarity for personal goals and possibilities (Roberts, Dutton, Spreitzer, Heaphy, & Quinn, 2005). The implication is that "individuals can begin to discover, embody, and then incorporate strengths and virtues into their work-related identities" (Dutton, Roberts, & Bednar, 2010, p. 283). For some participants, further exploration could lead to increased satisfaction and fulfillment within their current work environment. For others, the process may be a "jolt" that allows them to envision and create a new path in a different organization.

The key to further exploration of women's leadership practices and unveiling an authentic self in a public space is to create a welcoming environment for this to occur. As Cahnmann-Taylor (2008) explained, arts-based inquiries can be risky on personal, professional, and scholarly levels, and an important consideration is to advance arts-based learning with artists who are also scholars. In this way, the objections and concerns about quality and value can be mitigated. This research area is still too recent to have a substantial body of scholarship available and the inevitable criteria for quality and worth that result from critical appreciation of the methods for arts-based research. This should not deter us, however, from continuing to explore how arts-based research can be a catalyst for personal and, ultimately, organizational change.

This project confirmed the power of dollmaking as a catalyst for exploring how women view their leadership qualities and roles. The act of creating a doll—a body symbol—representing how we perceive ourselves as women leaders is a compelling exercise that deepens our understanding of self and draws out the unconscious assumptions we hold about ourselves.

References

Adler, N. J. (2006). The arts and leadership: Now that we can do anything, what will we do? *Academy of Management Learning & Education, 5*(4), 486–499.

Cahnmann-Taylor, M. (2008). Arts-based research: Histories and new directions. In M. Cahnmann-Taylor & R. Siegesmund (Eds.), *Arts-based research in education: Foundations for practice* (pp. 3–15). New York, NY: Routledge.

Chansky, R. A. (2010). A stitch in time: Third-wave feminist reclamation of needled imagery. *Journal of Popular Culture, 43*(4), 681–700. doi:10.1111/j.1540-5931.2010.00765

Chia, R., & Holt, R. (2008). The nature of knowledge in business schools. *Academy of Management Learning & Education, 7*(4), 471–486.

Dutton, J. E., Roberts, L. M., & Bednar, J. (2010). Pathways for positive identity construction at work: Four types of positive identity and the building of social resources. *Academy of Management Review, 35*(2), 265–293.

Fletcher, J. K. (2004). The paradox of postheroic leadership: An essay on gender, power, and transformational change. *The Leadership Quarterly, 15*(5), 647–661. doi:10.1016/j.leaqua.2004.07.004

Heron, J., & Reason, P. (2001). The practice of co-operative inquiry: Research "with" rather than "on" people. In P. Reason & H. Bradbury (Eds.), *Handbook of action research: Participative inquiry and practice* (pp. 179–188). Thousand Oaks, CA: Sage.

Ladkin, D., & Taylor, S. S. (2010). Leadership as art: Variations on a theme. *Leadership, 6*(3), 235–241. doi:10.1177/1742715010368765

Lawrence, R. L. (2008). Powerful feelings: Exploring the affective domain of informal and arts-based learning. *New Directions for Adult and Continuing Education, 120,* 65–77. doi:10.1002/ace.317

Levy, A. (1986). Second-order planned change: Definition and conceptualization. *Organizational Dynamics, 15*(1), 5–23.

Mavrinac, M. A. (2005). Transformational leadership: Peer mentoring as a values-based learning process. *Libraries and the Academy, 5*(3), 391–404. doi:10.1353/pla.2005.0037

Nkomo, S. M. (2010). Social identity: Understanding the in-group/out-group group phenomenon. In K. Hannum, B. B. McFeeters, & L. Booysen (Eds.), *Leading across differences* (pp. 73–79). San Francisco, CA: Pfeiffer.

Palmer, R. E. (1969). *Hermeneutics: Interpretation theory in Schleiermacher, Dilthey, Heidegger, and Gadamer.* Evanston, IL: Northwestern University Press.

Parker, P., Hall, D. T., & Kram, K. E. (2008). Peer coaching: A relational process for accelerating career learning. *Academy of Management Learning & Education, 7*(4), 487–503.

Reicher, S., Haslam, S. A., & Hopkins, N. (2005). Social identity and the dynamics of leadership: Leaders and followers as collaborative agents in the transformation of social reality. *The Leadership Quarterly, 16,* 547–568.

Rippin, A. (2007). Stitching up the leader: Empirically based reflections on leadership and gender. *Journal of Organizational Change Management*, 20(2), 209–226.

Roberts, L. M. (2012). Reflected Best Self engagement at work: Positive identity, alignment, and the pursuit of vitality and value creation. In S. David, I. Boniwell, & A. C. Ayers (Eds.), *Handbook for happiness*. London, UK: Oxford University Press.

Roberts, L. M., Dutton, J. E., Spreitzer, G. M., Heaphy, E. D., & Quinn, R. E. (2005). Composing the Reflected Best-Self portrait: Building pathways for becoming extraordinary in work organizations. *Academy of Management Review*, 30(4), 712–736.

Taylor, S. S., & Ladkin, D. (2009). Understanding arts-based methods in managerial development. *Academy of Management, Learning & Education*, 8(1), 55–69.

Tucker, B. A., & Russell, R. F. (2004). The influence of the transformational leader. *Journal of Leadership and Organizational Studies*, 10(4), 103–111. doi:10.1177/107179190401000408

Wicks, P. G., & Rippin, A. (2010). Art as experience: An inquiry into art and leadership using dolls and doll-making. *Leadership*, 6(3), 259–278. doi:10.1177/1742715010368767

Woodward, J. B., & Funk, C. (2010). Developing the artist-leader. *Leadership*, 6(3), 295–309. doi:10.1177/1742715010368768

Wordle.net. (2011). *Home page*. http://www.wordle.net/

Chapter Seven

Leadership Embodiment and Resistance

The Complex Journey of Latin American Pentecostal Women Pastors

Nora Méndez and Fernando Mora

Many women become influential leaders in Pentecostal churches all over the world, especially in Latin America. They access pastoral positions through the most varied and unthinkable paths, which disrupt the organizational dynamic of patriarchal Pentecostal denominations, especially when they start planting and leading their own churches and ministries. In spite of their entrepreneurial drive, these women exercise their leadership with doubts and fears because they are embodying a role that traditionally has been ascribed to men. Under this tension these women have to make sense of who they are and what they represent to their followers, and in the process embody their identities as leaders.

In this chapter our purpose is to explore how leaders embody leadership identity, specifically through power struggles and resistance. More specifically, we study how Pentecostal female pastors construct their leadership identity in the context of the power struggle that exists within their male-dominated local churches and denominations. This struggle crafts their subjectivity over a long journey or pilgrimage that starts at home and continues as they go to school, work, marry, and become active participants in religious activities. To understand the embodiment of leadership for these women pastors, we examine the formation of their subjectivity as a construct of their fantasies, thoughts, intuitions, beliefs, spirituality, feelings, connections and relationships, experiences of oppression, resistance, and liberation.

Identities are created through the interactions of individuals with their social environments. In other words, identities are socially constructed and recognized through speech, actions, and performances (Gee, 2000). However, these identities depend upon language, discursive resources, and narratives, which are produced by a subjectivity that is evolving and always changing. It is through their bodies that these women connect, negotiate, and express their subjectivities—in symbolic, emotional, and physical dimensions—in a way that gives sense to their emerging leadership identities (see, for example, Ladkin & Taylor, 2010) as women pastors. Leadership is embodied through a discursive practice that springs forth from their inner self, involving caregiving, spiritual disciplines, regular preaching, and the exercise of spiritual gifts or charismas, all enmeshed with emotions and body gestures (Lawless, 1988, 2003; Méndez, 2009). For these leaders, faith becomes evident through the language of their bodies, which creates a strong connection with their followers.

Women Pastors in Latin American Pentecostal Churches

Within contemporary Christianity, Pentecostalism is by far the movement that has experienced the largest and fastest growth in the world, identified by Jenkins (2002) as "perhaps the most successful social movement of the past century" (p. 8). It might be possible to affirm with a high degree of certainty that in Latin America one of every four persons is Pentecostal (or Charismatic) in some form of its expressions or ecclesial traditions (Pew Research Center, 2006). The majority of these are women, totaling up to 70 percent in certain metropolitan areas of the continent (Machado, 2005). Pentecostalism can be characterized as urban, poor, and with a youthful and female face (Chesnut, 2003). Because the rate of growth is so fast, new expressions of leadership are continually appearing.

The key to the understanding of the development of women leadership in Pentecostal churches has to do with the evolution of the prophetic role within the communities. From the start of the movement in 1904, its incipient theological basis placed importance on gender equality in the exercise of prophetic gifts (Barfoot & Sheppard, 1980). Typically the Pentecostal woman leader emerges spontaneously from the community without major requirements other than having been "called" to serve. God-given revelations and "gifts" or talents, personal charisma, and extraordinary experiences are much more important to her leadership than academic or theological credentials. Women see this calling as powerful and overwhelming, usually describing it with the narrative structure of the biblical prophets. Edith Blumhofer (2006) has said that historically the main obstacle in the recognition of female leadership within Pentecostal denominations has been the role of pastor, not the pulpit. Stephenson (2011) framed it perhaps more clearly by saying that "women are granted access to ministering authority, but not governing authority" (p. 410). Even from the beginning of the Pentecostal movement, the leadership role and place of women within the church have been quite uncertain.

We argue that the characteristics, practices, and theology of the Pentecostal movement open new spaces of participation, provide symbolic resources, give a new language that stimulates women's participation, and therefore promote the rise of women pastors. However, all of this happens in tension with the dominant religious views that give men exclusivity in leadership. Women end up relegated to secondary positions and accepting marriage and maternity as the essential and desirable roles for them. In spite of the theological limitations placed on female members, the breakthroughs of women who are challenging tradition by embracing Pentecostal practices have been recognized and studied; for instance, experiences of conversion, transformation, healing, and deliverance that affect their families and social networks (Drogus, 1997). Also, the embodiment of women's leadership within these churches and surrounding communities by some sort of self-authorization is attributed to the anointing power of the Holy Spirit, without legitimating male intervention (Bandini, 2008; Lawless, 1988; Machado, 2005).

During a period of nearly two years (2008–2009), one of the authors held conversations with, participated in different activities with, and collected the life stories of three Pentecostal women pastors from poor parishes in the metropolitan area of Caracas, Venezuela. These women were chosen for the study because of their experience as senior leaders with ultimate responsibility for the operations and ministry of the church; they were not auxiliary ministers or pastors' wives, typical roles of women in Pentecostal denominations in Latin America (Bandini, 2008). Pastor Febe (real names have been changed, and New Testament names of female leaders were used) is a middle-aged single woman with twenty-four years of accumulated experience as a religious leader. She is the director of a network of four urban churches and several prayer and welfare ministries. Pastor Junia, the oldest of the three, is married and has several children and grandchildren; she has been a pastor for more than fifteen years and leads a nationwide movement of small churches that she founded. Pastor Priscilla is a middle-aged married woman with many years of experience in church leadership. She graduated from a local theological seminary and has been a senior pastor for more than two years.

Their stories were thoroughly documented, providing descriptions of their leadership journey by means of several sessions of semi-structured interviews, complemented with spontaneous conversations; phone calls; cell phone SMSs; and reading and analysis of written journals, and in some cases of their church brochures, books, and written materials. Also, the author participated in several of their services, activities, and ceremonies and held shorter conversations with some members of their congregations. All the material was assembled in three separate documents (approximately eighty pages each) organized by the authors such that it was possible to access the material in an easier way. The whole study encompassed four dimensions that were chosen to characterize women pastoral leadership, namely: care, leadership, preaching, and symbology. This chapter discusses one of the results obtained regarding the leadership dimension.

Resistance Leadership

One paradigm that has been used for the study of power relations in leadership has been the consideration of Michel Foucault's (1988) ideas about the interaction between *power* and *resistance*. Power is a "process" that becomes real when human beings interact, and it is continually negotiated and challenged between two parties (Williams, 2009). For Foucault, power and resistance coexist in the constitution of relations between active subjects, the one that exercises the power and the other who resists. However, this model has to be considered carefully from a feminist standpoint, because women as resisters have specific experiences of power and a less articulate process of empowerment (Deveaux, 1999). For example, in the Pentecostal church, women are usually bound by practices, disempowering conventions, and theologies that limit their interaction with those exercising power over them. For a Foucaldian analysis to be useful, on the one hand it requires the recognition of certain women's experiences or practices that counteract hegemonic power or represent a difference from traditional church structures but that may not be too evident. On the other hand, an understanding of the progressive development of their subjectivity and their identity as leaders is necessary.

According to Hollander and Einwohner (2004), four elements must be present in the study of resistance: *action* and *opposition*, *recognition*, and *intent*. They suggest that resistance requires some form of active behavior, verbal, cognitive, or physical. Actions can be expressions of contradiction, anger, rejection, subversion, opposition, disruption, and so on, that somehow challenge or oppose oppression, subordination, or hegemonic power. Recognition involves the discovery of the resistance act, which could be self-evident or visible but many times is hidden or even embedded in everyday acts. Finally, the idea of discovering the intent becomes important when considering situations in which resistance is not overt, because the motivations behind public displays or demonstrations are generally expressed by resisters. Here the subjectivity of the resister comes into play in the perception of the oppression and in the production of the resistance act.

Williams (2009) found the previous conceptualization of resistance problematic and defined three dimensions that describe tensions, such as: passive/active, micro/macro, and covert/overt. The first defines the intentions and level of agency of resisters, the second the context of resistance, and the third the characteristics of the act itself. The idea of the use of these tensions is to avoid the urge to categorize the acts of resistance and instead have a range of possibilities to be observed and identified, especially in leadership studies. This also prevents the bias in favor of public demonstrations of resistance by considering them more important, in contrast with other forms that are more private, hidden, disguised, individual, disorganized, spontaneous, or seemingly trivial, and yet which produce very important consequences and represent turning points in the formation of leadership subjectivity, identity, and embodiment.

Vinthagen and Lilja (2007) linked acts of resistance to empowerment, describing it as the process through which self-confidence, self-esteem, and identity unite to produce an action.

In leadership development, this process can be seen at work in the growth of self-confidence, dignity, and authority, allowing individuals to make decisions and act in the midst of adversity and obstacles.

In looking at leadership as an emergent and organic process, Collinson (2005) considered a set of dialectical interactions like power/resistance, consent/dissent, and men/women. This approach serves to identify emerging leadership by considering mutuality and coproduction in the relationships and practices of leaders and followers as well as the complexities and contradictions involved in these relational dynamics. Zoller and Fairhurst (2007) have expanded these concepts by including additional tensions and by better describing resistance leadership dynamics within the range of possibilities in each key dialectic tension proposed. The importance of this analytical approach is that it allows exploring more clearly the multiplicity of possibilities through which resistance leadership emerges in different contexts.

As Commisso (2006) stated, "The place in which the thought of resistance resurfaces and is reaffirmed is language" (p. 174), and this is no other than "the language of the experience of the body" (p. 174). By careful identification of resistance acts, how they evolve and how they are continuously created through the women's embodied language, one can begin to identify how resistance practices contribute to the formation of subjectivities and to the development of leadership identities. Four topics regarding the embodiment of leadership through resistance leadership processes among Pentecostal women pastors arise: (1) the progressive emergence of female pastoral leadership by initiative taking and appropriate emotional handling of situations, seen through those resistance acts through which we see changes in the discourse of the leader, especially through the use of sarcasm and irony as well as more symbolic performances; (2) the identification of the sources of legitimization of Pentecostal women pastors as leaders, which are very much rooted in such

Pentecostal practices as the continuous appeal to the power from above, the use of scriptural authorization, and the positioning of themselves in the context of an ongoing spiritual battle; (3) how women pastors exercise agency and mobilization dynamics when they engage in service and care in ways that contradict traditional ideas about pastoral leadership and the place women should occupy in religious organizations; and (4) how emergent women pastors convey their message and disrupt the organizational meanings of the Pentecostal denominations through their preaching practices.

In the next section we turn our attention to some examples of these topics to demonstrate how the embodiment of leadership takes place in the case of Pentecostal women pastors.

Resisting Pastors

The resistance examples that we were able to document show that the women pastors are crafting their subjectivity as they confront, consciously or otherwise, the asymmetric power struggles that oppress them as women. "Subjectivity emerges and is revealed as a right to difference, to variation and to metamorphosis" (Commisso, 2006, p. 174). Each new situation of oppression that they endure along their pastoral journey brings a more clear consciousness or awareness of gender oppression. This turns out to help them to build up a more unique, enduring, and empowered self. Collinson (2003) proposed that by engaging in resistance, members of organizations can construct a more positive sense of self. However, he also warns that resistance has inherent ambiguities and possible countereffects on the resister, such as disciplinary actions or isolation. We identified such contradictory aspects, their effects, and the resulting subjectivity.

All of this complex process becomes the school that shapes their emerging identities and embodiment as leaders. It is not a linear process that follows certain preconceived and predictable paths. In fact, leadership identity is forged and embodied in these leaders progressively, through the many challenges that shape their subjectivities as women trying to cope with the *symbolic insecurities* that the Pentecostal religious system offers them. Insecurity is seen as a characteristic of the organizational system, its discourse, power relations, underlying principles, and culture (Collinson, 2003). For women leaders within a Pentecostal denomination, symbolic insecurity is derived from the uncertainty and anxiety that occupying a traditional male role brings. This leadership role is complex, filled with many possibilities to make mistakes, and lived in the continuous anguish that spiritual power and authority can be lost for the most trivial and absurd reasons.

With access to the narratives of the leadership journeys of the three women pastors, we attempted to discover their resistance acts. We defined resistance as the behaviors, actions, and interactions on the part of the women pastors that challenge power relations and the norms that support and reproduce them within their organizations (Davies & Thomas, 2001). These resisters, like many others, remain within the social system that they oppose or question through their resistance acts. In spite of that, they develop a progressively critical stance through suffering, pain, and struggle, and from this subjectivity they articulate their acts of resistance. The authors, without participation of the resisting pastors, performed the identification and classification of the resistance acts. In the remainder of this section, we present some of these acts and the associated quotes taken directly from the compiled life stories of Junia, Febe, and Priscilla.

There is a form of resistance that repeats continually during the development of these women as pastors, but in particular in the life of Junia. These are expressions of resistance through humor, sarcasm, and irony when faced with underestimation, discrimination, and abuse by male leaders and by members of their congregations. In the use of humor as a form of resistance, contradiction is emphasized, existing norms and paradigms are challenged, and a message of protest is sent (Tracy, Myers, & Scott, 2006). In the following example, taken from the transcribed life story of Junia, we can see how Junia understands her subordinate position within the patriarchal culture of the Pentecostal church. When she is summoned by the senior leader to serve in a traditionally male role, she is faced with the contradiction and ambiguity of the proposition. Junia resists with irony and sarcasm, because her dedication and work are not valued in comparison with those of her male counterparts. The response provokes a demonstration of power that appeals to the traditional androcentric and hierarchical discourse of domination (in the life story accounts of Junia, Febe, and Priscilla presented in this section, translation from Spanish to English was done by the authors):

> The pastor said, "Let's send sister Junia who is available to this mission because all the brothers are busy working and they can't travel."
>
> I said: "And what do we do with my sex?"
>
> . . . He answered, "What is wrong with you, sister? May the Lord rebuke Satan!"
>
> "I say it because I am still a woman."
>
> The pastor remained in silence and finally he told me, "Well sister, you will continue being a woman and you will keep submitted, but you must go to that place."

On another occasion, Junia adds a bit of anger to her sarcasm and ironic humor when she openly resists a more deliberate opposition to her ministry. In this case she has already overcome some of her insecurities and has grown in her leadership position. She now receives invitations to preach and work with other churches that recognize her gifts and talents. However, for each invitation, the senior pastor requires a formal letter of invitation, but in some opportunities he deliberately delayed the authorization to serve in these other places. This behavior upsets Junia and adds to her response:

> The letter was in the desk drawer more than a week. The day of the crusade came and I did not have the permission to go. I said, "Pastor, why can't I go?"
>
> [He answered], "Because you are a woman."
>
> I said, "You know what? With pastors like you, it is when I desire to be a transsexual. . . . If I had the money I would pay for a surgery to become a man and have a penis" (crying during interview).

Junia has some understanding now that God has allowed her—a woman—her pastoral work and has guided her service to others. She is not rejecting her gender, but she is expressing her frustration because the church male leadership restricts women's leadership in an arbitrary way and without convincing Christian arguments, especially when there is a need to be fulfilled. Through this act of resistance, which is essentially a direct confrontation, she is trying to make the pastor think about and somehow overcome his prejudices toward women leaders.

This feeling of growing uneasiness, sometimes expressed in words, is the mixed result of the awareness, on one side, that she is experiencing misogyny and sexism, and, on the other side, the perception that God is affirming her as woman and pastor and that she is also being confirmed as a leader by the members of the church. As she begins to reflect on, meditate on, understand, pray about, and even question these encounters and difficulties, her subjectivity as a pastor is being built up and becomes the source of vitality for the formation of her identity as a leader. Resistance is not just a senseless act or a mere passing and trivial response, but the manifestation of an internal unrest, reflection, and self-talk process. In the case of these women pastors, their consciousness of gender oppression is growing, and their acts of resistance become more effective in affecting the power relationships, as their subjectivities are strengthened through their spirituality, calling, and personal convictions. Therefore, resistance goes beyond words to produce small but significant changes (Fleming & Spicer, 2003).

In some cases their acts speak louder than their words, displaying resistance in symbolic ways, especially when they appeal to their spiritual disciplines and practices like prayer, fasting, solitude, dreams, prophetic words, and even patterns of service attendance and participation. In many situations, Junia resists and waits in prayer until she receives a response and confirmation from God to take a particular course of action. Her prayer and fasting retreats are read by her followers and the other leaders as evidence that something is not going well, while at the same time they are resistance acts because from them changes and actions follow. Additionally, Junia sees these times as moments of profound reflection, of deeper consideration of her inner life, her vulnerabilities, and especially her precariousness as a woman leader facing a patriarchal mind-set. Through fasting and prayer Junia finds answers to her contradictions and strength to press on in her calling as a pastor:

> I started to fast again and I asked the Lord, "Speak to me, what should I do?" And as time was going by, the Lord said, "It is necessary to obey God before men," and I started to meditate even more. . . .

Feminine preaching introduces a new imagination and an aesthetic of the relationship with God based upon the subjectivity of women and their awareness of the fragility, vulnerability, and relational nature of human existence. According to Lawless (2003), a woman in a pulpit transmits a semiotic change because she defies the classical masculine images of priest or pastor, not only in bodily terms but also in speech, perspective, experience, and vision. This is why Sunday sermons in Pentecostal churches become resistance spaces in which women can express their voices through "personal narratives." Theological knowledge and some sort of special skills do not limit these narratives; they involve reason, emotion, sensation, imagination, values, and communal participation to tell the story of how God intervenes in human lives or in history. Smith (1989) indicated that women's histories and sagas serve to describe reality from a feminine perspective and to inform their performance of their leadership role in front of the congregation. The topics range from their own experiences of oppression, suffering, pain, and exclusion, to their personal dialogue with God, with their families, with other leaders, with members of the church, and with the community that surrounds them.

In particular in the Pentecostal worldview, the stories of the Old Testament prophets serve as powerful rhetoric resources and models for the legitimization of the woman preacher and as a source of symbolic security in the exercise of an office dominated by men (Barfoot & Sheppard, 1980). Pastor Priscilla vividly describes her calling this way: "I fell on my knees and started to cry, because certainly it was my calling to be a prophet." This prophetic calling is a way through which the woman preacher can be bold and resist with a message that brings a challenge from God, not from her, to the congregation. Women pastors affirm their power and influence, reinterpreting the symbolic order whenever necessary, because they attribute their authority as God-given. Pastor Priscilla, fiercely criticized at the beginning of her career, responds to the challenge of a male leader who corners her: "I am in charge of the church as a pastor, because God called me, God revealed this directly to me. . . . So, if that is the case, you are going to have to fight with God for my removal."

In the midst of contradictions, the women pastors find the gaps that allow them to resist through the spoken message. From the Bible they get permission to trespass, disobey, and cross certain lines. Pastor Priscilla preaches the verse in Acts 4:19—"Which is right in God's eyes, to listen to you or to God?"—to her community, located in a poor neighborhood in a large urban center. In her interpretation she essentially gives permission to women to disobey men whenever their behavior or orders go against Christ's teachings and practices regarding human dignity within social relationships.

Authenticity in the embodiment of leadership during preaching is demonstrated by two attitudes of the woman preacher: *weeping* and *confession* (Smith, 1992). On the one hand, weeping is a way of speaking from their broken and suffering bodies their truth about pain, injustice, and oppression; on the other hand, it is a way of expressing solidarity and empathy with the grieving and oppression of others, which leads to intercession, either with humans or with God, in action and prayer, for the excluded, the oppressed, the sick, and the abused. Preaching is no longer a rhetorical exercise but becomes a redemptive experience to the listeners. Confession is a moment of sincerity, of narrating the crude realities of the women pastors' own experiences in their everyday lives at church, at home, and in society where patriarchy rules. Confession by the leader breaks the silence and denial in the followers and opens doors of liberation and transformation.

Pastor Febe's initiatives and activism are based on her profound sense of social justice. Her spiritual practices are informed by some scriptures, but also by the sociopolitical context of the poverty-stricken areas where she ministers. She resists by taking numerous risks that subvert or transgress the traditional sexual role of a passive, docile, quiet, submissive, and silent woman that her religious system celebrates. When she speaks about herself, she tells the story of how she used to sell liquor and play cards in the grocery store that she owns. Proudly she speaks of a time when she defended the store and her car at gunpoint from a street gang that tried to rob her. Even before being a Christian she was a social resister involved with the surrounding community. As a believer she gives herself completely into the service of others as a strong warrior, filled with power and completely fearless:

> One night a guy was stabbed and they wanted to take him to the emergency room. The only car they found was my old station wagon that looked like a funeral car. They threw the man in and I had to gain courage and take him to the hospital. I felt death all over him and started to rebuke it in prayer. In his agony he told me, "Save me Febe, don't let me die." And I said to him, "You will not die, you will live to be a testimony." He still lives, thanks to God's mercy.

In a way, it is a position she has taken from the start in order to protect herself from a system that rejects her as a leader, to survive in the difficult role that she has taken. To compensate, she strives to be the best in whatever she does, adopting traditional leadership identities and even developing somehow a more masculine style. When describing her beginnings as a preacher in small churches and street gatherings she shares this idealized view of herself:

> I was a threat to the leadership of the church. . . . The visiting preachers and evangelists called the senior pastor telling him, "You don't even know what God has sent to your congregation, this woman is an amazing leader."

In her study of Japanese workers, Kondo (1990) rejected the idea of a coherent and always consistent resistance but prefers to describe the continually changing and ambivalent subjectivities of workers. Similarly, we can see the ambiguous nature of Pastor Febe's resistance. Pastor Febe, the so-called amazing leader and pastor who takes risks and develops initiatives for the members of her church, at the same time assumes the role of a mother who, without physical children, cares, intercedes, and mourns for her family (the church), thereby affirming, reproducing, and legitimizing traditional sexual roles. Consequently, her identity as a resistance leader is attenuated and weakened by her commitment to the patriarchal norms and values of the church she serves, and to the need to conform to a performance- and results-oriented church style with increasing toxic activism levels. This confuses and precludes her from clearly understanding what she represents as a woman leader within an androcentric, hierarchical, and sexist religious organization. This is very well exemplified in Febe's desire to train *ideal women according to God's purpose*:

> I am also leading prayer rallies called "Mothers Cry for their Children." I ask God, "Why am I leading this if I am not a mother?" And God answers because I am the one with a mother's heart. They see me praying and crying, and mothers behind me crying, and all the sisters crying behind me, and not necessarily because I have kids.

Again, we see the ambiguity. On one side is the possibility of being disqualified for not being a biological mother. On the other side is the vitality and determination that they have to overcome conflicts and struggles that they confront as leaders. For them, the image of the strong woman, able to stand the threats of men and demons, a resister of oppression that employs irony and sarcasm, bold enough to preach and mobilize her followers, can easily be reconciled with a motherly, protective, and caregiver figure (Lawless, 1988).

This view of the caring pastor adapts well to the norms of patriarchal culture, which assigns women the primary responsibility of taking care of the home, the private issues of family and of raising children. Just as a mother is mainly responsible for the physical, emotional, and moral well-being of children, the Pentecostal women pastors end up doing almost every task in the congregation, providing for the needs of the members, and sorting out a myriad of conflicts and situations in which the congregants get involved. This strengthens the essentialist argument that relegates women to the care functions of the church while men take on more public managerial and political roles. To quote one of Febe's leaders: "Men pastors prefer to be executive, show themselves off, but the ones who take the load of the church are women." No wonder Febe protests to her members about her excessive amount of work: "I am always doing something. All of you want me to do everything. . . . You have gotten used to having the pastor present in everything."

Pentecostal women pastors refer continually to God's power through the Holy Spirit as counselor, restorer, friend, and helper, and as the one who empowers them to prophesy, preach, teach, exhort, and bring correction. Through this practice, their body in terms of physical manifestations, emotions, thoughts, and affections "becomes language" (Gebara, 2003, p. 13). They make continuous references to their religious experience, such as speaking and interpreting other tongues by the power of God in their lives, something that gives them credibility in front of male leaders with more theological training but who may fall short in this area.

In a similar way, they understand and live their daily lives as if they were in a spiritual battle between good and evil, and this is how they evaluate the emergence of their leadership. Within this cosmic battle they see themselves as playing an important role for which they have been chosen by God. As mentioned earlier, they are not left by themselves but receive the legitimization from the spiritual power that they display in the midst of their congregations. This without doubt is another space of resistance where through the symbology of battle they express their power and take control of difficult situations. The tension and also the contradiction is that many of the situations, especially those that involve gender struggles, are somewhat minimized by attributing their origin to the work of Satan.

Conclusion

When we look at the leadership development of women pastors from a resistance standpoint, we go beyond the simple inquiries about their caring, preaching, or leadership skills to dig deeper into their journeys. Analysis of the resistance acts present in their life stories allows us to discover how these women leaders have been able to cope, and to respond to the open and disguised hostility embedded in the religious systems; how they have used their creativity and imagination to be accepted, loved, respected, and recognized by churches and male peers; and how much they have invested of themselves in order to be accepted and to survive in such a patriarchal and sexist environment. At the same time it makes us ask how much of the individual has been lost in the process and what wounds have been inflicted upon them.

Resistance leadership analysis gives access to a more authentic, organic, and even dramatic view of leadership development. It portrays the manner in which the identity of a leader is embodied; demonstrates how subjectivity is crafted through many struggles, without a previously established script; and shows how, from a position of precariousness and vulnerability, the individual expresses her true self even within established hegemonic religious discourses. Generally, this uncovers women's experiences and practices that counteract dominant power but that are usually overlooked or dismissed by classical leadership studies. Additionally, it provides a deeper understanding of the progressive development of leaders' subjectivity and their identity development. This chapter contributes to the understanding of women's leadership embodiment through emotional, affective, relational, and empowermental dimensions, which can develop even within oppressive structures.

References

Bandini, C. (2008). Ministério feminino na igreja do evangelho quadrangular: Autonomia além do espaço religioso. Notas de uma pesquisa. Actas do V Congresso Português de Sociologia, Lisboa, 41–46. http://www.aps.pt.

Barfoot, C., & Sheppard, G. (1980). Prophetic vs. priestly religion: The changing role of women clergy in classical Pentecostal churches. *Review of Religious Research, 22*(1), 2–17.

Blumhofer, E. (2006). Women in Pentecostalism. In R. S. Keller & R. R. Ruether (Eds.), *Encyclopedia of women and religion in North America*. Bloomington, IN: Indiana University Press.

Chesnut, R. A. (2003). *Competitive spirits: Latin America's new religious economy*. New York, NY: Oxford University Press.

Collinson, D. L. (2003). Identities and insecurities: Selves at work. *Organization, 10*(3), 527–545. doi:10.1177/13505084030103010

Collinson, D. L. (2005). Dialectics of leadership. *Human Relations, 58*(11), 1419–1442. doi:10.1177/0018726705060902

Commisso, G. (2006). Identity and subjectivity in post-Fordism: For an analysis of resistance in the contemporary workplace. *Ephemera, 6*(2), 163–192.

Davies, A., & Thomas, R. (2001, July 11–13). From passive to active subjects: Gender, restructuring and professional/managerial identities in the UK public sector. Paper presented at the Second International Conference on Critical Management Studies, Manchester, UK.

Deveaux, M. (1999). Feminism and empowerment: A critical reading of Foucault. In S. Hess-Biber, C. Gilmartin, & R. Lydenberg (Eds.), *Feminist approaches to theory and methodology: An interdisciplinary reader*. (pp. 236–258). New York, NY: Oxford University Press.

Drogus, C. A. (1997). Private power or public power: Pentecostalism, base communities and gender. In E. L. Cleary & H. W. Stewart-Gambino (Eds.), *Power, politics and Pentecostals in Latin America*. Boulder, CO: Westview.

Fleming, P., & Spicer, A. (2003). Working at a cynical distance: Implications for power, subjectivity and resistance. *Organization, 10*(1), 157–179. doi:10.1177/1350508403010001376

Foucault, M. (1988). El sujeto y el poder. *Revista Mexicana de Sociología, 50*(3), 3–20.

Gebara, I. (2003). *Antropología religiosa. Lenguaje y mitos*. Buenos Aires, Argentina: Católicas por el Derecho a Decidir (CDD).

Gee, J. P. (2000). Identity as an analytic lens for research in education. *Review of Research in Education, 25*(1), 99–125. doi:10.3102/0091732X025001099

Hollander, J., & Einwohner, R. (2004). Conceptualizing resistance. *Sociological Forum, 19*(4), 533–554. doi:10.1007/s11206-004-0694-5

Jenkins, P. (2002). *The next Christendom: The coming of global Christianity*. New York, NY: Oxford University Press.

Kondo, D. K. (1990). *Crafting selves: Power, gender, and discourses of identity in a Japanese workplace*. Chicago, IL: University of Chicago Press.

Ladkin, D., & Taylor, S. (2010). Enacting the "true self": Towards a theory of embodied authentic leadership. *The Leadership Quarterly, 21*(1), 64–74.

Lawless, E. J. (1988). *Handmaidens of the Lord: Pentecostal women preachers and traditional religion*. Philadelphia, PA: University of Pennsylvania Press.

Lawless, E. J. (2003). Transforming the master narrative: How women shift the religious subject. *Frontiers: A Journal of Women Studies, 24*(1), 61–75.

Machado, M. D. (2005). Representações de gênero nos grupos pentecostais. *Estudos Feministas, 13*, 387–396.

Méndez, N. M. (2009). *Sucesoras de Pedro: El trabajo pastoral femenino en las Iglesias evangélicas Pentecostales del área metropolitana de Caracas*. Trabajo de Grado de Maestría en Estudios de La Mujer. Caracas, Venezuela: Universidad Central de Venezuela.

Pew Research Center. (2006). *Spirit and power: A 10-country survey of Pentecostals*. Washington, DC: Author.

Smith, C. (1989). *Weaving the sermon: Preaching in a feminist perspective*. Louisville, KY: Westminster John Knox.

Smith, C. (1992). *Preaching as weeping, confessing and resistance: Radical responses to radical evil*. Louisville, KY: Westminster John Knox.

Stephenson, L. (2011). Prophesying women and ruling men: Women's religious authority in North American Pentecostalism. *Religions, 2*(3), 410–426. doi:10.3390/rel2030410

Tracy, S., Myers, K., & Scott, C. (2006). Cracking jokes and crafting selves: Sensemaking and identity management among human service workers. *Communication Monographs, 73*(3), 283–308.

Vinthagen, S., & Lilja, M. (2007, September). The state of resistance studies. Paper presented at the European Sociologist Association Conference, Glasgow, Scotland.

Williams, P. (2009). The multidimensionality of resistance in youth-subcultural studies. *Resistance Studies Magazine*. http://www.rsmag.org

Zoller, H., & Fairhurst, G. (2007). Resistance leadership: The overlooked potential in critical organization and leadership studies. *Human Relations, 60*(9), 1331–1360. doi:10.1177/0018726707082850

Chapter Eight

Michelle Obama's Embodied Authentic Leadership

Leading by Lifestyle

Elizabeth D. Wilhoit

In February 2012, Michelle Obama did twenty-five push-ups on national television with Ellen DeGeneres. In April 2012 she worked out for twenty minutes at the White House with contestants on the reality weight loss show *The Biggest Loser* (Smith, 2012). Additionally, Obama rises early to exercise (Vaccariello, 2009a), and the first family does not eat dessert on weeknights (Moskin, 2010). Obama does all these things to model a healthy lifestyle and encourage Americans to become more healthy and active. Although such performances are rarely considered in studies of leadership, they are central to Obama's rhetoric and style of leadership and are marks of authentic leadership (AL).

In general, the body has received little attention in leadership studies (Sinclair, 2005a). By studying leadership in a disembodied way, scholars suggest that leaders are somehow superhuman and insusceptible to the limitations of the body (Sinclair, 2005b). Indeed, many past studies of the body in organizations have been centered on how bodily categories like race or sex limit actors' possibilities (Ashcraft, Kuhn, & Cooren, 2009). However, rather than being a necessary constraint or an

The author thanks Robin Jensen for her comments on earlier drafts of this chapter.

inconvenience to be overcome, the body can present a resource for leaders (Ladkin, 2008, 2012; Ladkin & Taylor, 2010; Sinclair, 2005a). Specifically, in studies of AL, and its concern with congruency among a leader's actions, goals, commitments, and morals, the role of the body is important but undertheorized (Ladkin & Taylor, 2010).

To explore the role of the body in leadership, especially AL, I use a critical rhetoric approach, working from the premise that the body can persuade and communicate. Throughout this chapter, I use the term *enacted rhetoric* to describe how Obama makes arguments through her bodily activity. This concept is drawn from Campbell and Jamieson (1978), who defined enactment as "a reflexive form . . . in which the speaker incarnates the argument, *is* the proof of the truth of what is said" (p. 9). Enacted rhetoric is an embodied way to gain credibility, a performance of argument without words. Obama enacts her rhetoric by continually presenting her lived experience, including its mistakes, as a persuasive appeal.

The overall purpose of this chapter is to extend scholarship on the role of the body in AL. To do this, I examine First Lady Michelle Obama's rhetoric in conjunction with her anti–childhood obesity campaign, "Let's Move!" Specifically, I suggest that Obama is an authentic leader and that her embodied performances demonstrate her AL style. Additionally, as Obama presents an Othered body and subject position (female and black), she uses these to her advantage, suggesting that the body may actually enable women to be authentic. Through this example, I address some of the complexities of embodied leadership, particularly how to integrate personal weaknesses (Diddams & Chang, 2012) and Othered subject positions (Eagly, 2005) into AL theories. In this, I hope to extend AL scholarship by showing that the body can be an important rhetorical resource that strengthens leaders' arguments and followers' identification.

About Let's Move!

In February 2010, Obama began the Let's Move! initiative with the goal of ending childhood obesity in America within a generation ("Let's Move! accomplishments," n.d.). The program aims to bring stakeholders together to make small changes that will result in healthier children and a stronger nation ("About Let's Move!," 2011; Obama, 2009). Although the program is relatively new, it has already achieved many goals, including passage of the federal Healthy, Hunger-Free Kids Act; a partnership with Walmart to make fresh produce more affordable and increase the nutritional value of processed food; and a plan to add salad bars to the cafeterias of six thousand schools ("Let's Move! accomplishments," n.d.). Obama said that she hopes, through these and other programs, "to change the way a generation of kids thinks about food and nutrition" (Obama, 2010b).

But as Let's Move! has made steps toward changing the future for American children, Obama has found herself the target of criticism from opponents who feel that it is the role of parents, not the government, to make choices about their children's health (see, for example, Behrendt, Nelson, & Bruce, 2010). Many of these critiques accuse Obama of inauthenticity as her adversaries search for inconsistencies between the way that she lives her life and how she tells others to live theirs. This has resulted in increasing surveillance of Obama's everyday activities. In response, Obama seems to have turned this scrutiny into a persuasive boon by drawing attention to her body and performing a healthy, balanced life to lead and persuade the nation.

Authentic Leadership and Body Possibilities

Although there has been a range of approaches and exact definitions presented for the term *authentic leadership* (Cooper, Scandura, & Schriesheim, 2005), scholars generally agree on a core set of characteristics that mark AL (Gardner, Cogliser, Davis, & Dickens, 2011). In this section, I discuss these defining traits and show that they could be enhanced by considering the body's role in AL. In this I extend Ladkin and Taylor's (2010) work to provide a more comprehensive integration of AL and embodiment. As I review past work on AL, I hope to show that the body fits naturally into this theory and that including it will enhance our understanding of leadership.

First, AL begins with the issue of authenticity. As Avolio, Gardner, Walumbwa, Luthans, and May (2004) have written, "The essence of authenticity is to know, accept, and remain true to one's self" (p. 802). Authentic leaders act from core convictions rather than a desire for self-promotion (Bass & Steidlmeier, 1999). Authentic leaders lead from their strengths, values, and goals while inspiring their followers to be authentic (Gardner, Avolio, Luthans, May, & Walumbwa, 2005; Luthans & Avolio, 2003). The identity of leader becomes an important part of an authentic leader's self-concept, and leadership is more than a role that can be put on and off (Shamir & Eilam, 2005). Looking at a leader's body, then, we should see consistency and a performance that is consistent between word and deed.

Second, authentic leaders have a high level of self-awareness. Authentic leaders can critically evaluate their personality and know their strengths and weaknesses (Ilies, Morgeson, & Nahrgang, 2005). Additionally, authentic leaders self-regulate their behaviors to meet their goals and model positive behaviors (Avolio & Gardner, 2005). However, this is more than impression management; it involves leaders' actually living out and enacting their values through behaviors (Hannah, Lester, & Vogelgesang, 2005). How one chooses to "do" one's body communicates about oneself to others (Butler, 1990). It seems that an authentic leader's embodied behaviors would be consistent with what she purports her values, goals, strengths, and weaknesses to be.

Third, authentic leaders act because they are truly passion-ate and have goals derived from personal convictions and beliefs (Sheldon & Houser-Marko, 2001). This should result in a con-cordance between authentic leaders' internal beliefs and their external behavior (Shamir & Eilam, 2005). Authentic leaders behave in a "self-expressive" manner that reflects their internal motivations (May, Chan, Hodges, & Avolio, 2003; Shamir & Eilam, 2005, p. 399). Some scholars have been concerned that in seeking authenticity, leaders might feel obligated to fit a cer-tain model of leadership that would result in inauthentic behav-iors or emotional labor (Eagly, 2005; Gardner, Fischer, & Hunt, 2009). However, an authentic leader has the goal of being true to oneself, not fulfilling expectations of leadership (Gardner and others, 2011).

In terms of the body, Ladkin and Taylor (2010) have sug-gested that it is through bodily cues that authentic leaders' con-sistency between the internal and external may be most clearly judged. Although AL scholarship differs on what the specific leadership behaviors of authentic leaders are (Avolio & Gardner, 2005), it seems that the external actions of authentic leaders cannot be manifest just through words, but that the authentic leader, acting from true convictions, would present a consistent bodily performance. Authentic leaders lead by example (Avolio and others, 2004), which entails doing, an inherently embod-ied activity. However, previous AL scholarship has neglected to describe exactly how authentic leaders lead by example. How is their behavior on display to their followers? It is at this point that AL scholarship has neglected to explore the central role of the body in the performance of leadership.

Fourth, authentic leaders have distinctive relationships with their followers that are based on trust and transparency and encourage authenticity in their followers (Avolio and oth-ers, 2004; Gardner and others, 2005). Human relationships, including those between leaders and followers, so often happen in embodied contexts and perceptions (Dale & Burrell, 2007; Turner, 1996), and we understand others through our bodies (Niedenthal, Barsalou, Winkielman, Krauth-Gruber, & Ric, 2005). For a leader to truly know his or her followers, there must be a connection of the flesh or the material (Ladkin, 2012). Therefore, it may be through the body that followers understand the experience of a leader. These mechanisms of embodied knowing and understanding have been overlooked in AL scholarship, yet may be vital for understanding how followers relate to and emulate authentic leaders.

Finally, authentic leaders have a strong positive moral or ethical component (Avolio & Gardner, 2005). This means not only having a sense of right and wrong but also having and using positive character traits (May and others, 2003). Because of the authentic leader's internal convictions and positive character traits, she has increased moral agency to act altruistically or ethically even in difficult situations (Hannah and others, 2005). Human ethical behavior (which is always manifest through interactions in our material and embodied world) is an embodied, performed activity that is deeply related to our bodies (Varela, 1999). The moral core of authentic leaders cannot be viewed only as an abstract concept, but must also be seen as an embodied and active interaction with the world.

In all these characteristics of AL, the role of the body has received little attention (for exceptions see Ladkin, 2012; Ladkin and Taylor, 2010). However, it is in the body that we find meaning (Johnson, 1990) and understand others' experiences because of the universal experience of embodiment (Merleau-Ponty, 1962). Therefore, we can better understand the nature of AL by seeing how it is enacted in daily life as it is performed and lived in the body. To do this, I now move to Michelle Obama, an authentic leader who exemplifies using the body to strengthen her leadership.

Critical Rhetoric

To analyze Obama's leadership, I take a critical rhetoric approach. Critical rhetoric seeks to understand and uncover power, especially in relation to social change. As such, it is an appropriate approach for understanding how Obama's embodied subjectivity affects her leadership (McKerrow, 1989). The study of a leader's rhetoric to understand leadership practices follows a discursive leadership approach: leadership is contextually bound and socially constructed (Fairhurst, 2008, 2009; Fairhurst & Grant, 2010). Additionally, critical rhetoric emphasizes that power is not fixed or constant and one can impose power even while being the subject of power (McKerrow, 1989). Obama has power as first lady of the United States, but she is also African American and a woman, subjectivities with a long history of subordination.

Doing critical rhetoric entails analyzing multiple fragments of texts to understand an overarching rhetoric (McKerrow, 1989). Studying Obama's lived experience requires such a method, as knowledge about how she lives does not exist in a unitary form. Therefore, studying Michelle Obama's unique rhetoric must go beyond reading transcripts of her speeches. I do draw from speeches Obama has made in conjunction with Let's Move! (for transcripts, see Obama, 2010a, 2010b, 2011a, 2011b), but I also look at news stories and press releases to understand how she lives her life and "does" her leadership and persuasion. The scope of this chapter is limited to Let's Move! because it is within this context that her embodied AL is most apparent. In this, I assume the perspective of a follower to her leadership, using the information about Obama's embodied behaviors that have been mediated and are publicly available. Through studying the information that Obama divulges about her life, we can see the body possibilities of AL.

Michelle Obama's Authentic Leadership and Enacted Rhetoric

This analysis of Michelle Obama's AL and enacted rhetoric is divided into three sections. First, I describe her AL and enacted rhetoric, providing examples to illustrate this concept. Second, I demonstrate how Obama performs her weaknesses through her body, contributing to her authenticity. Third, I discuss how Obama's embodied AL challenges cultural norms about the Othered body and allows her to draw on her body as a rhetorical resource.

Obama's Authentic Leadership

One of the primary marks of Obama's AL and enacted rhetoric is modeling the behavior she would like to see in her followers (Gardner and others, 2005). The title of her campaign is *Let's* Move! rather than, for instance, *You* Move!, suggesting that Obama is also active. Rather than *telling* Americans what to do differently to end childhood obesity, she *shows* them, providing her audience with the knowledge and tools to do the same: "When I do these things, I'm thinking, 'If people see me—the First Lady—with my shoes off, running around with kids, sweating, jumping around, making a fool out of yourself, then maybe more moms and dads will say, 'I can do that, and actually that looks fun'" ("First lady making strides," 2011). Sloop (2000) has suggested that "those things that one displays externally are taken as signifiers of impulses 'in' the body (e.g., body orientations, personality traits)" (p. 133). Here, Obama's outward displays are intended to reflect her inner character and motives, suggesting, for example, that she is not a detached leader but a caring, maternal figure. This atypical performance for a first lady may also demonstrate authenticity to her followers who can see how personal these issues are to Obama.

However, it is not only in public contexts that Obama enacts her rhetoric and models behavior for her followers, but also in her daily habits. Even though the Obama family has a team of chefs at their command and a personal trainer, Obama identifies with the average American by emphasizing her choices. For example, despite having a devoted pastry chef, the Obama family does not eat dessert on weekdays; "otherwise it's not a treat; it's just something that you do" (Kohan, 2010; Moskin, 2010; Obama, 2009).

Additionally, both Barack and Michelle Obama work out for an hour most days, getting up as early as 4:30 a.m. to do so (Vaccariello, 2009b). Despite having a gym and a personal trainer, the Obamas still need to *choose* to get up early and exercise. Although these choices are probably made for their own health, they serve to model this behavior for the American people. Michelle Obama expressed this goal when she said, "If the President of the United States can sit down with his family and have dinner, hopefully more Americans will find time to do the same thing" ("The story of the White House garden," 2009). Obama has stated that telling people how to behave will not be effective: "There is no way that the First Lady can or should go into someone's house and tell them what to eat—it doesn't work. It wouldn't work in my household—in fact, I would resent it" ("First lady making strides," 2011). Instead, Obama leads by example, modeling healthy habits for the rest of America. However, as an authentic leader Obama goes beyond being a role model, and increases identification with her followers, as she lives and demonstrates the choices and struggles involved in living a healthy life.

Authenticity and Personal Weaknesses

Although AL takes the approach from positive psychology of focusing on strengths rather than weaknesses (Avolio and others,

2004; Seligman, 2002), how authentic leaders deal with weaknesses is important (Diddams & Chang, 2012; George, 2003). Authentic leaders must accept their weaknesses without defensiveness (Diddams & Chang, 2012). Additionally, if authentic leaders seem flawless, followers will not be able to identify with them (Ford & Harding, 2011). When leaders admit their weaknesses, they encourage the development of authentic followers who are more willing to be vulnerable and enter into trusting relationships (Shamir & Eilam, 2005). When authentic leaders are transparent about their weaknesses, they will not lose the consistency between their values and actions, which is central to AL (Diddams & Chang, 2012). Obama demonstrates this by being honest about her weaknesses and reframing them as aspects of humanity rather than flaws. Although this results in accusations of inconsistency from her detractors, I argue that it actually enhances her AL.

While Obama's performance of leadership is centered on modeling positive, healthy behaviors, some disagree that Michelle Obama presents good habits. In public performances of identity, society holds one accountable, as critics look for inconsistencies (Force, 2010). For example, when the Obamas' 2011 Super Bowl party menu included cheeseburgers, deep-dish pizza, beer, and ice cream, the Obamas found themselves defending the food (CNN Political Unit, 2011). The White House faced criticism from opponents who labeled the menu hypocritical for a family concerned about both their personal health and the health of all Americans. For example, the Fox News website gave its story about the menu the headline, "Michelle Obama's Shocking Anti-Obesity Super Bowl Menu" (2011).

Obama responded not by denying her weaknesses but by arguing that life is about balance, and occasional treats for special occasions (like the Super Bowl) are fine (Kohan, 2011; Sweet, 2011). Obama enacts moderation, living by the "ninety-ten rule": watch what you eat 90 percent of the time, and enjoy special foods the other 10 percent (Moore, 2011). Through this, Obama publicly acknowledges that she is not a perfect model of health and frames these indulgences not as failings to be hidden but as occasional and anticipated pleasures. It seems that this portrayal of her human side would increase identification among followers who may have trouble identifying with someone who is superhumanly perfect (Quinn, Spreitzer, & Brown, 2000).

There are more examples of this criticism (see, for example, Bershad, 2011), which draw attention to the surveillance and objectification that Obama faces. Responses like this make her aware of the attention paid to her body and reinforce the potential that her embodied AL can have when her behavior is observed. Additionally, these examples serve as an exigence for enacted rhetoric, demonstrating the need for public figures to lead by example rather than telling their constituents what to do. In both her strengths and weaknesses, Obama leads authentically with consistency among her values, goals, speech, and action while helping her followers relate to her as she performs her humanity and ordinariness in mundane activities like eating. Her embodied weaknesses, rather than hurting her rhetoric, allow her followers to relate to her even more as they relate their embodied experiences to hers (Merleau-Ponty, 1962).

The Othered Body as Rhetorical Resource

The fact that Michelle Obama's body is Othered in multiple ways cannot be ignored. The fact that one physically exists as a black woman suggests a position with different possibilities, even if race and gender are not salient (James, 1999). As an African American woman, Obama has a body that has been historically constrained. However, through her AL and enacted rhetoric, she reconstitutes her raced and gendered body as a rhetorical resource that can speak in a way that a white, male body could not. Like when using her weaknesses to her advantage,

Obama is able to use her Othered body in a transformative way. Eagly (2005) has expressed concern that female authentic leaders might need to change their leadership style so much that they would not remain authentic. Obama's example demonstrates that the body and the subjectivities that accompany it can be a rhetorical resource, not a barrier.

As Obama enacts a healthy life, she repeatedly tells the story of what brought her family to their current lifestyle, making it clear to her audience that she has not always behaved the way she does now, again increasing identification. In this version of her narrative, Obama emphasized her position as a regular mom:

> It wasn't that long ago that I was a working mom, struggling to balance meetings and deadlines with soccer and ballet. And there were some nights when everyone was tired and hungry, and we just went to the drive-thru because it was quick and cheap, or went with one of the less healthy microwave options, because it was easy. And one day, my pediatrician pulled me aside and told me, "You might want to think about doing things a little bit differently." (Obama, 2010a)

As a result, she made changes to her family's habits, and the pediatrician saw her daughters' health improve. Obama repeatedly tells this story to demonstrate that she is motivated by personal values and change that she genuinely wants to see take place—marks of AL (Avolio & Gardner, 2005; Shamir & Eilam, 2005). Her current behaviors were learned following failure to ensure her daughters were as healthy as they could be. She does not share her story out of judgment, but to show that anyone can make healthy changes to his or her life. By using this story, Obama explains her current actions and uses narrative to share her sense of self and develop her position as an authentic leader (Shaw, 2010; Sparrowe, 2005).

In this story, she also uses her gendered and raced body to increase follower identification by emphasizing her position as a mother. By speaking as a parent, she makes her arguments more personal and she appeals to the sensibilities of other parents. This frame has been emphasized in the media, and Obama has not shied away from it. Her official White House webpage begins with this description: "When people ask First Lady Michelle Obama to describe herself, she doesn't hesitate to say that first and foremost, she is Malia's and Sasha's mom" ("First Lady Michelle Obama," n.d.). This description acknowledges and emphasizes her family and traditionally gendered roles.

Additionally, Obama often draws from racial assumptions about mothering, such as the African American community's focus on parenting in which "other mothers and nonparents" have rights in raising other children (Collins, 2000, p. 182). She is not only Sasha and Malia's mother, but also the mother of all American children. In this way, her enactment of motherhood is based in both gender and race. Obama uses this role to identify with many of the women in her audience, but in varying ways. In assuming the mother persona, Obama continues her AL, not speaking as a politician but living as a caring parent.

In this, Obama bridges the public and private, an act that is also rooted in her subjectivity as a black woman. Although the first lady is a public figure, her role is often perceived as primarily private (Watson, 2000). However, within the African American community, such public/private distinctions have historically not been possible (Collins, 2000). Black women have worked in public since slavery, and gender roles in the African American community have not always been defined based on division of labor to the extent that they have been in white culture. From a black perspective, the conflation of mother and politician, private behaviors and public surveillance, is not unusual.

This is thus another way that Obama leads from her embodied black subjectivity. She is true to her body and uses it as a site for authentic relationships with followers.

In addition to her speaking as a mother and an African American, Obama's more general enacted rhetoric is predicated on her female body. Because of the surveillance and gaze that fall on the female body (Mulvey, 1975), it would not be possible for her to enact her rhetoric in the same way from a male position. The historic objectification of women's bodies has opened to include larger questions about how they obtain that body: "the topic of how beautiful women eat has become something of a chronic national obsession" (Gordinier, 2011). The fact that a research project like this is possible is thanks to media and public interest in and surveillance of Obama's body and related actions. Still, surveillance is often viewed negatively because of the self-regulation that it encourages, especially for women (Foucault, 1977).

At the heart of all these forms of action is Obama's attempt to enact normativity, leading by modeling behavior to her followers. Despite her Othered position, she seeks to be perceived as normal, less regarding her race or sex but more in relation to general embodiment. In an environment in which disordered eating is increasingly normalized, a "normal" diet or weight can be difficult to attain or even understand. Although a few critics have labeled her as fat, most agree that Obama is a healthy size, neither impossibly thin nor overweight. As one observer wrote, "Nor, with her solid 5-foot-11 frame, does Mrs. Obama, who is 45, have a typical runway model body. That makes her image even more admirable to many women, and perhaps even attainable" (Robbins, 2009). Accessibility is what Obama seeks: she has crafted her lifestyle not to show off or craft her personal identity, but to lead in a way that aligns with her embodied subjectivities. By living her arguments and performing them in her body, Obama is an authentic leader who leads from a moral center and demonstrates that her values and actions align at the most basic levels.

Although Obama's leadership and rhetoric have been successful, they do introduce some complexities. Even as she capitalizes on structures that generally oppress the Othered body, her use of personas like black mother or woman as the subject of a male gaze reifies their employment. Many scholars have criticized the patriarchal factors that construct expectations for docile female bodily performance (Bartky, 1988; Bordo, 2004; Butler, 1990; Heyes, 2006; Warin, 2011). Through practices like diet, exercise, makeup, and fashion, women's bodies are subjected to surveillance from the self and others. As women are reduced to an ongoing concern with their appearance, they sacrifice the resources they might devote to political issues (Trethewey, 1999). It is important to consider that Obama's use of these bodily tropes might be problematic, especially as followers might imitate them (Peck, Freeman, Six, & Dickinson, 2009).

Still, Obama does reappropriate these historically oppressive body positions as she demonstrates "an embodied sense of rhetoric as a performance that one does, rather than as an analytic, objectified extension of who one is" (McKerrow, 1998, p. 323). In this, she shows that rhetoric is connected to everyday life and one's "true self," which can be manifest in leadership behaviors (Ladkin & Taylor, 2010). Seen this way, speech through embodied practices is not always a site of constraint but potentially a way to enact political power.

Implications of Rhetoric, Embodiment, and Authentic Leadership

Through Obama's rhetoric, I demonstrated how she leads by example through her embodied behaviors, uses her performances of weakness as a rhetorical example, and turns her

Othered subjectivities into rhetorical resources that increase follower identification and augment her authenticity. My goal in this chapter has been to expand AL theories by showing how many characteristics of AL are in fact enacted through the body. The body, rather than being a site for leaders to accidently reveal weaknesses, can be a resource for more effective leadership.

Specifically, I have shown how the use of the body augments AL theory for non-normative subjectivities or weaknesses that have previously been problematic for AL (Diddams & Chang, 2012; Eagly, 2005; Ladkin & Taylor, 2010; Shaw, 2010). Through embodied acts like eating French fries, Obama's presentation of her weaknesses creates a site for follower identification. Rather than being a detached leader who talks without action, Obama displays her life so that her followers can sense an authentic relationship. Additionally, Obama draws on tropes of race and gender, using her embodied subjectivities as an aspect of her authentic self. Scholars had previously questioned whether weaknesses and minority leaders could be part of AL theory (Diddams & Chang, 2012; Eagly, 2005), and Obama's example seems to suggest that they can.

More generally, Obama's example shows the role that the body can play in AL. It is through the body that leaders can show that their talk and action are not distinct, but that they live their arguments, heightening authenticity. In turn, it is through this authenticity that leaders can create relationships with their followers. As humans relate to each other through common bodily experiences, leaders can use their embodied performances as a way for followers to feel connected. As Obama makes her private life public, she shows that for her, there is not a disconnect between what she says and how she lives; she is an authentic leader. Leaders who are more open will be more persuasive (Quinn and others, 2000), and audience identification also increases persuasion (Burke, 1950). Obama performs a form of AL that positions her not as a distant and aloof leader but as a normal American.

In addition to extending scholarship on AL, I have also used a critical rhetoric approach to study Obama's leadership (McKerrow, 1989). Studying rhetoric, particularly embodied arguments, provides a focus for examining a leader's behavior. By examining Obama's leadership from a rhetorical perspective, I have been able to focus on how the use of her body in argumentation indicates that she is an authentic leader. Rhetorical methods could be used in future AL studies to continue to isolate action and persuasion.

Michelle Obama, through her AL, identifies with her audience and shows that she is not asking Americans to do something that she herself is not participating in. She uses bodily performances and embodied subjectivities to demonstrate her authenticity as a leader, more effectively persuading her public. This demonstrates the importance of considering the body in AL scholarship. By living her leadership and persuasive appeals, Obama identifies with her audience on a new level. Her goals as first lady are ambitious, and she needs an unprecedented form of leadership to match as she enlists followers.

References

About Let's Move! (2011). *Let's Move!* http://www.letsmove.gov/about.php

Ashcraft, K. L., Kuhn, T. R., & Cooren, F. (2009). Constitutional amendments: "Materializing" organizational communication. *Academy of Management Annals, 3*(1), 1–64. doi:10.1080/19416520903047186

Avolio, B. J., & Gardner, W. L. (2005). Authentic leadership development: Getting to the root of positive forms of leadership. *The Leadership Quarterly, 16*(3), 315–338. doi:10.1016/j.leaqua.2005.03.001

Avolio, B. J., Gardner, W. L., Walumbwa, F. O., Luthans, F., & May, D. R. (2004). Unlocking the mask: A look at the process by which authentic leaders impact follower attitudes and behaviors. *The Leadership Quarterly, 15*, 801–823. doi:10.1016/j.leaqua.2004.09.003

Bartky, S. (1988). Foucault, femininity and the modernization of patriarchal power. In L. Quinby & I. Diamond (Eds.), *Feminism and Foucault: Paths of resistance* (pp. 61–86). Boston, MA: Northeastern University Press.

Bass, B. M., & Steidlmeier, P. (1999). Ethics, character, and authentic transformational leadership behavior. *The Leadership Quarterly, 10*(2), 181–217. doi:10.1016/S1048-9843(99)00016-8

Behrendt, T., Nelson, R., & Bruce, M. (2010, November 10). Sarah Palin cookie protest: Calls Pennsylvania a "nanny state run amok." *ABC News.* http://abcnews.go.com/US/cookie-protest-sarah-palin -calls-pennsylvania-nanny-state/story?id=12104862

Bershad, J. (2011, February 21). Rush slams Michelle Obama for eating ribs, doubts she could get in SI swimsuit issue. *Mediaite.* http://www .mediaite.com/online/limbaugh-slams-michelle-obama-for-eating -ribs-doubts-she-could-get-in-the-si-swimsuit-issue/

Bordo, S. (2004). *Unbearable weight: Feminism, Western culture, and the body.* Berkeley, CA: University of California Press.

Burke, K. (1950). *A rhetoric of motives.* New York, NY: Prentice Hall.

Butler, J. (1990). *Gender trouble: Feminism and the subversion of identity.* New York, NY: Routledge.

Campbell, K. K., & Jamieson, K. H. (Eds.). (1978). *Form and genre: Shaping rhetorical action.* Falls Church, VA: Speech Communication Association.

CNN Political Unit. (2011, February 6). White House Super Bowl menu. *CNN Politics.* http://politicalticker.blogs.cnn.com/2011/02/06/white-house -super-bowl-menu/

Collins, P. H. (2000). *Black feminist thought: Knowledge, consciousness, and the politics of empowerment* (2nd ed.). New York, NY: Routledge.

Cooper, C. D., Scandura, T. A., & Schriesheim, C. A. (2005). Looking forward but learning from our past: Potential challenges to developing authentic leadership theory and authentic leaders. *The Leadership Quarterly, 16,* 475–493. doi:10.1016/j.leaqua.2005.03.008

Dale, K., & Burrell, G. (2007). *Spaces of organization and the organization of space: Power, identity and materiality at work.* Basingstoke, UK: Palgrave Macmillan.

Diddams, M., & Chang, G. C. (2012). Only human: Exploring the nature of weakness in authentic leadership. *The Leadership Quarterly, 23*(3), 593–603. doi:10.1016/j.leaqua.2011.12.010

Eagly, A. H. (2005). Achieving relational authenticity in leadership: Does gender matter? *The Leadership Quarterly, 16*(3), 459–474. doi:10.1016 /j.leaqua.2005.03.007

Fairhurst, G. T. (2008). Discursive leadership: A communication alternative to leadership psychology. *Management Communication Quarterly, 21,* 510–521. doi:10.1177/0893318907313714

Fairhurst, G. T. (2009). Considering context in discursive leadership research. *Human Relations, 62*(11), 1607–1633. doi:10.1177/0018726709346379

Fairhurst, G. T., & Grant, D. (2010). The social construction of leadership: A sailing guide. *Management Communication Quarterly, 24*(2), 171–210. doi:10.1177/0893318909359697

First lady making strides one year into "Let's Move." (2011, February 10). *NPR.* http://www.npr.org/templates/transcript/transcript .php?storyId=133652546

"First Lady Michelle Obama." http://www.whitehouse.gov/administration /first-lady-michelle-obama

Force, W. R. (2010). The code of Harry: Performing normativity in *Dexter. Crime, Media, Culture, 6*(3), 329–345. doi:10.1177/17416590 10382333

Ford, J., & Harding, N. (2011). The impossibility of the "true self" of authentic leadership. *Leadership, 7*(4), 463–479. doi:10.1177/1742715 011416894

Foucault, M. (1977). *Discipline and punish: The birth of the prison* (A. Sheridan, Trans.). New York, NY: Vintage Books.

Gardner, W. L., Avolio, B. J., Luthans, F., May, D. R., & Walumbwa, F. (2005). "Can you see the real me?" A self-based model of authentic leader and follower development. *The Leadership Quarterly, 16*(3), 343–372. doi:10.1016/j.leaqua.2005.03.003

Gardner, W. L., Cogliser, C. C., Davis, K. M., & Dickens, M. P. (2011). Authentic leadership: A review of the literature and research agenda. *The Leadership Quarterly, 22*(6), 1120–1145. doi:10.1016 /j.leaqua.2011.09.007

Gardner, W. L., Fischer, D., & Hunt, J. G. (2009). Emotional labor and leadership: A threat to authenticity? *The Leadership Quarterly, 20*(3), 466–482. doi:10.1016/j.leaqua.2009.03.011

George, W. W. (2003). *Authentic leadership: Rediscovering the secrets to creating lasting value.* San Francisco, CA: Jossey-Bass.

Gordinier, J. (2011, February 15). For actresses, is a big appetite part of the show? *New York Times.* http://www.nytimes.com/2011/02/16 /dining/16interview.html?

Hannah, S. T., Lester, P. B., & Vogelgesang, G. (2005). Moral leadership: Explicating the moral component of authentic leadership. In W. L. Gardner, B. J. Avolio, & F. O. Walumbwa (Eds.), *Authentic leadership theory and practice: Origins, effects and development* (pp. 43–81). Oxford, UK: Elsevier.

Heyes, C. J. (2006). Foucault goes to Weight Watchers. *Hypatia, 21*(2), 126–149. doi:10.1353/hyp.2006.0009

Ilies, R., Morgeson, F. P., & Nahrgang, J. D. (2005). Authentic leadership and eudaemonic well-being: Understanding leader–follower outcomes. *The Leadership Quarterly, 16*(3), 373–394. doi:10.1016 /j.leaqua.2005.03.002

James, J. (1999). Resting in gardens, battling in deserts: Black women's activism. *Black Scholar, 29*(4), 2–7.

Johnson, M. (1990). *The body in the mind: The bodily basis of meaning, imagination, and reason.* Chicago, IL: University of Chicago Press.

Kohan, E. G. (2010, November 23). During visit to Gingerbread House Bakery, president talks dessert policy for Malia and Sasha. *Obama Foodorama.* http://obamafoodorama.blogspot.com/2010/11/president-obama -at-gingerbread-house.html

Kohan, E. G. (2011, February 9). Reporters luncheon: First lady reflects on year one of the Let's Move! campaign. *Obama Foodorama.* http:// obamafoodorama.blogspot.com/2011/02/first-lady-michelle-obama -reflects-on.html

Ladkin, D. (2008). Leading beautifully: How mastery, congruence and purpose create the aesthetic of embodied leadership practice. *The Leadership Quarterly, 19*(1), 31–41. doi:10.1016/j.leaqua.2007.12.003

Ladkin, D. (2012, January). Perception, reversibility, "flesh": Merleau-Ponty's phenomenology and leadership as embodied practice. *Integral Leadership Review.* http://integralleadershipreview.com/6280 -perception-reversibility-flesh-merleau-pontys-phenomenology-and-leadership-as-embodied-practice

Ladkin, D., & Taylor, S. S. (2010). Enacting the "true self": Towards a theory of embodied authentic leadership. *The Leadership Quarterly, 21*(1), 64–74. doi:10.1016/j.leaqua.2009.10.005

Let's Move! accomplishments. (n.d.). *Let's Move!* http://www.letsmove.gov/lets -move-accomplishments

Luthans, F., & Avolio, B. J. (2003). Authentic leadership development. In K. S. Cameron, J. E. Dutton, & R. E. Quinn (Eds.), *Positive organizational scholarship: Foundations of a new discipline* (pp. 241–261). San Francisco, CA: Berrett-Koehler.

May, D. R., Chan, A.Y.L., Hodges, T. D., & Avolio, B. J. (2003). Developing the moral component of authentic leadership. *Organizational Dynamics, 32*(3), 247–260. doi:10.1016/S0090-2616(03)00032-9

McKerrow, R. E. (1989). Critical rhetoric: Theory and praxis. *Communication Monographs, 56,* 91–111. doi:10.1080/03637758909390253

McKerrow, R. E. (1998). Corporeality and cultural rhetoric: A site for rhetoric's future. *Southern Communication Journal, 63,* 315–328. doi:10.1080/10417949809373105

Merleau-Ponty, M. (1962). *Phenomenology of perception* (K. Paul, Trans.). New York, NY: Routledge.

Michelle Obama's shocking anti-obesity Super Bowl menu. (2011, February 6). http://nation.foxnews.com/michelle-obama

/2011/02/06/michelle-obamas-shocking-anti-obesity-super-bowl
-menu#ixzz1DHcaaRxh

Moore, P. (2011). She's a mom first. *Men's Health.* http://dad.menshealth.com
/parents/shes-mom-first.php

Moskin, J. (2010, May 11). The White House pastry chef revamps sweets. *New
York Times.* http://www.nytimes.com/2010/05/12/dining/12yosses
.html?ref=dining

Mulvey, L. (1975). Visual pleasure and narrative cinema. *Screen, 16*(3), 6–18.

Niedenthal, P. M., Barsalou, L. W., Winkielman, P., Krauth-Gruber, S., & Ric,
F. (2005). Embodiment in attitudes, social perception, and emotion.
Personality and Social Psychology Review, 9(3), 184–211. doi:10.1207
/s15327957pspr0903_1

Obama, M. (2009, October 21). Remarks by the first lady at Healthy Kids
Fair. *The White House.* http://www.whitehouse.gov/the-press-office
/remarks-first-lady-healthy-kids-fair

Obama, M. (2010a, February 9). Remarks of First Lady Michelle Obama. *The
White House.* http://www.whitehouse.gov/the-press-office/remarks
-first-lady-michelle-obama

Obama, M. (2010b, March 16). Remarks by the first lady at a Grocery Man-
ufacturers Association conference. *The White House.* http://www
.whitehouse.gov/the-press-office/remarks-first-lady-a-grocery
-manufacturers-association-conference

Obama, M. (2011a, January 20). Remarks by the first lady during Let's Move!
Walmart announcement. *The White House.* http://www.whitehouse
.gov/the-press-office/2011/01/20/remarks-first-lady-during-let-s-move
-walmart-announcement

Obama, M. (2011b, February 9). Remarks of First Lady Michelle Obama Let's
Move! launch anniversary speech to parents. *The White House.* http://
www.whitehouse.gov/the-press-office/2011/02/09/remarks-first-lady-
michelle-obama-let-s-move-launch-anniversary-speech-p

Peck, E., Freeman, T., Six, P., & Dickinson, H. (2009). Performing leadership:
Towards a new research agenda in leadership studies? *Leadership, 5*(1),
25–40. doi:10.1177/1742715008098308

Quinn, R. E., Spreitzer, G. M., & Brown, M. V. (2000). Changing others
through changing ourselves: The transformation of human systems.
Journal of Management Inquiry, 9(2), 147–164. doi:10.1177
/105649260092010

Robbins, L. (2009, March 19). She's pumped. Your turn. *New York
Times.* http://www.nytimes.com/2009/03/19/fashion/19fitness
.html?ref=michelleobama

Seligman, M.E.P. (2002). *Authentic happiness: Using the new positive psychology to realize your potential for lasting fulfillment.* New York, NY: Free
Press.

Shamir, B., & Eilam, G. (2005). "What's your story?" A life-stories approach to authentic leadership development. *The Leadership Quarterly, 16,* 395–417. doi:10.1016/j.leaqua.2005.03.005

Shaw, J. (2010). Papering the cracks with discourse: The narrative identity of the authentic leader. *Leadership, 6*(1), 89–108. doi:10.1177/1742715009359237

Sheldon, K. M., & Houser-Marko, L. (2001). Self-concordance, goal attainment, and the pursuit of happiness: Can there be an upward spiral? *Journal of Personality and Social Psychology, 80,* 152–165. doi:10.1037//0022-3514.80.1.152

Sinclair, A. (2005a). Body possibilities in leadership. *Leadership, 1*(4), 387–406. doi:10.1177/1742715005057231

Sinclair, A. (2005b). Body and management pedagogy. *Gender, Work and Organization, 12*(1), 89–104. doi:10.1111/j.1468-0432.2005.00264

Sloop, J. M. (2000). "A van with a bar and a bed": Ritualized gender norms in the John/Joan case. *Text and Performance Quarterly, 20*(2), 130–149. doi:10.1080/10462930009366291

Smith, B. (2012, April 10). Week 15. *The biggest loser.* NBC.

Sparrowe, R. T. (2005). Authentic leadership and the narrative self. *The Leadership Quarterly, 16*(3), 419–439. doi:10.1016/j.leaqua.2005.03.004

The story of the White House garden. (2009, August 31). *The White House Blog.* http://www.whitehouse.gov/blog/2009/08/31/story-white-house-garden

Sweet, L. (2011, February 8). Michelle Obama defends Super Bowl menu: Healthy eating about "moderation." *Chicago Sun-Times.* http://blogs.suntimes.com/sweet/2011/02/michelle_obama_defends_super_b.html

Trethewey, A. (1999). Disciplined bodies: Women's embodied identities at work. *Organization Studies, 20*(3), 423–450. doi:10.1177/0170840699203003

Turner, B. S. (1996). *The body and society: Explorations in social theory.* London, UK: Sage.

Vaccariello, L. (2009a, November). Michelle Obama. *Prevention, 61*(11), 136–141.

Vaccariello, L. (2009b, November). Call her the first lady of fitness. *Prevention, 61*(11), 8.

Varela, F. J. (1999). *Ethical know-how: Action, wisdom, and cognition.* Palo Alto, CA: Stanford University Press.

Warin, M. (2011). Foucault's progeny: Jamie Oliver and the art of governing obesity. *Social Theory & Health, 9,* 24–40. doi:10.1057/sth.2010.2

Watson, R. P. (2000). *The presidents' wives: Reassessing the office of first lady.* Boulder, CO: Lynne Rienner.

Part Three

Leadership By and Through the Body

Antonio Marturano

Though the practice of leadership development acknowledges some aspects of the body, with programs that focus on body language or incorporate physical activities, embodiment is a neglected topic in the academic leadership development literature. According to Walsh (2012), because leadership theories are coming from what is a hyperrational, leader-centric, cognitively biased worldview, this is, perhaps, not surprising.

In Part Three, four chapters offer ideas on embodiment in leadership development ranging from body language to metaphorical notions, providing fresh, unconventional, theoretically informed additions to the discussion. All the chapters offered here focus on leadership (not just on leaders) by exploring new ways to understand leadership embodiment.

Julie Burge, Ray Batchelor, and Lionel Cox deal, in their chapter, with leadership learning by using the tango, not only metaphorically but also in a way that allows people to understand deeply the real nature of the leader–follower relationship.

The relationship between leader and follower in the dance is not one of equals in terms of precise roles, but one of near equals in responsibilities and obligations. Moreover, in such dance, the role that emotional intelligence plays in the relationship can be better explored by both players. The chapter offers five experiential themes pertinent to leadership as well as dance: trust, the symbiotic relationship, the quality of the relationship, the role of confidence, and team dynamics. Often, as the authors point out, those themes are clearly interrelated. The chapter concludes that the physicality of the tango learning approach seems to enable a more deeply textured consideration of the duality of roles in organizations and a more sophisticated comprehension of the beliefs, wants, and needs of leaders and followers pertaining to their roles and the roles of others.

Perttu Salovaara and Arja Ropo offer an analysis of the language used by leadership development (LD) program participants, focusing on their embodied experience as a legitimate form of knowledge. Using hermeneutics, Salovaara and Ropo found four new orientations for LD: from leader-centricity toward leadership; from content to process orientation; from generic input to tailor-made processes; and from an intellectual-rational approach to an embodied one. The authors conclude that a possible way that LD can develop away from a general overemphasis on leader-centricity is to pay more attention to collective, socially constructed, and shared forms of post-heroic leadership. The issue is then not one of a choice between leadership as either an individual practice or an organizational capability, but a recognition of the importance of both.

Starting from movement psychology research and phenomenology, Helle Winther presents a study based on stories coming from a teaching context and a hospital context, whose aim is to focus on the importance of the body in leadership and professional communication. According to the author, the question is whether and how it is at all relevant to focus on the concepts of embodied professional competence and embodied leadership. The author concludes that movement psychology can bring an important contribution in regard to *how* development may be fostered in the increasing complexity of professional work in modern society. Developing embodied leadership and embodied professional competence may therefore entail necessary, challenging, and perhaps enriching potentials in relation to the development of authenticity, leadership, and professional communication tools for both contemporary and future professionals.

Kathryn Goldman Schuyler presents a novel approach to leadership development through mindfulness meditation and the Feldenkrais Method, which Goldman Schuyler proposed as an underlying "organizing principle" for consulting. The approach can be described in terms of the following four principles: noticing differences, awakeness to what is happening, body movement as a source of learning, and paying attention to what draws your interest. Mindfulness and the Feldenkrais Method approach the body as a foundation for awareness and the noticing of differences, which can then be more fully appreciated. Goldman Schuyler concludes that powerful leadership requires simplicity of action and vision; authenticity; and a rich, cognitive map of life. All of these are enhanced by mindfulness, as authentic presence is hard to imagine if someone is not living in an embodied way.

Reference

Walsh, M. (2012). Leadership and the body. *Integral Leadership Review*. http:// integralleadershipreview.com/6773-leadership-and-the-body

Chapter Nine

Shall I Lead Now?

Learner Experiences of Leader–Follower Relationships Through Engagement with the Dance

Julie Burge, Ray Batchelor, and Lionel Cox

This chapter presents the account of an experimental, experiential learning strategy that analyses and evaluates the perceived political notions of leader and follower. It demonstrates the embodiment of the leader–follower relationship, as experienced through dancing the Argentinian tango and told through the dialogic reflections of participants.

The program to which this work relates is a leadership course delivered in the south of England. Learners in this group all work in the same profession, in the same organisation. Ten learners and two faculty members participated in the dance, which was led by a third faculty member, a teacher of tango.

The Learning Context

While taking an organisational, rather than individual, training focus, each leadership program is developed specifically to suit the needs of the participating professional groups—some multi-professional, some from a single profession. Core to all programs is the expressed need to develop knowledge, behaviours, and skills that support midlevel managers to enable teams through organisational and/or practice development.

Many of these organisations have a long, cultural history, where managerialist paradigms predominate. Command-and-control cultures, shown to limit the development of professional expertise to the detriment of social outcomes (Anderson & Anderson, 2010), are common and tend to require a compliant followership (Grint & Holt, 2011). While rhetoric regarding the benefits of transformational leadership knows no bounds, distributed leadership cultures are not commonplace within large and complex public sector organisations (Currie, Lockett, & Suhomlinova, 2009). In considering teams of practitioners, where each member has equal responsibility toward exercising professional autonomy, the challenge for this learning program was to confront prevailing notions of leadership in order to support higher levels of self-government, where all team members can be both leader and follower.

The popular assumption is that followers are a consequence of leaders (Shamir, 2007, as cited in Grint & Holt, 2011). Rather than argue the roles of leader and follower, types of followers, or overt team dynamics between the two functions, this learning strategy aimed to embody the symbiotic relationship between leader and follower. It was based on the belief that effective teams (where the team's mission and vision are established) share responsibilities for goal achievement, and each member can move between each role (of leader and follower). Two main assumptions were made: that the phenomenon of leader and follower is, at best, *fuzzy* and that a team member's belief, that is, their mind-set regarding their own role and the role of others, influences their relationships.

It's All About Mind-Sets and Fuzzy Sets

Standard leadership development programs tend to maintain leader preoccupations with self-development, self-improvement, and self-awareness (Jones, 2005), which perpetuates its prevailing political identity. Fuzzy set (Zadeh, 1965) leadership development requires a paradigm shift, where followers are not subordinate to the leader, or where the leader–follower relationship is dichotomous. We asserted that comprehension of this symbiosis, paradoxical to the overarching organisational culture(s), could not be achieved unless the course participants embodied the relationships through a lived experience: in this case, the dance.

Zadeh (1965) published the original paper on fuzzy logic. In contrast to the world of mechanics, he argued, humanistic systems, given their complexity, need a more "fuzzy" characterisation; he also maintained that classes of objects encountered in the real world do not have precisely defined criteria of membership. Instead, he talks of fuzzy sets, a class of objects with a continuum of grades of membership. Zadeh's basic idea was to introduce continuous grades of membership and thus destroy the limitation of crisp or binary logic, which operates with only two values: yes (1) and no (0).

A dichotomous approach to defining leading and following would be to assume exclusive identifiable properties, taxonomies, perspectives, traits, norm features, and symbols. The current intellectual and social effort to protect and typify *leader* and *not-leader* roles bears evidence to this way of thinking. Yet there is no leadership without followership, no leader without a follower; followership is integral to leadership as well as leadership to followership. What is clear is that, in the absence of any epistemological certainty, and in an effort to make the leader concept "understandable," we attempt to make it a "thing" in itself (Küpers, 2007).

Maybe there is some primal self-need for unambiguous, clearly hierarchical structures that mandate the need for a leader identity. Part of the leadership challenge of the future will involve moving away from simple interpretations of followership by evolving into more complex and sophisticated understandings, relationships, and structures. The logical synthesis of leader and follower becomes, therefore, not only an intellectual exercise but one with practical implications too.

By definition, leadership is a social activity, through which ideas, concepts, and meanings predominantly emerge from the group, rather than from individual activity. For fuzzy logic to be deemed applicable and usable in leadership environments, not only must the concept be practical and advantageous, but a network of like-minded individuals must also be created. Leadership training, education, and development may, then, require participants to modify personal, individual, or independent beliefs, traits, and behaviours, as power, authority, and influence are given and shared between leaders and followers.

Introducing the concept of fuzzy logic to participants aimed to initiate this shift in thinking about leader–follower roles, where leading becomes a reciprocal and collaborative process and exercise. As a result, followership could be seen as an influence in a leadership–followership occasion, where power, authority, and influence are measured only by degree. This does not mean that followers would be transformed into something else completely, such as equals, given that in almost all leadership–followership occasions rank or responsibility may remain.

Shall We Dance?

The use of dance as a metaphor for understanding leader and follower roles is not unique. In 2008, Ropo and Sauer, for example, compared and contrasted the waltz with raves. In the waltz, they explained, the leader is dominant; the follower has a lesser role in defining the dance. Raves, by contrast, require neither dance steps to learn nor fixed dance partners (where one leads and the other follows). Rather than compare extremes of leadership style, we wished to demonstrate the leader–follower *exchange*, such as occurs during *Queer Tango*, created from the more mainstream Argentinian tango.

As a metaphor for leadership and followership, the tango affords advantages over other couple dances, such as the waltz, in that it is improvised from moment to moment. The waltz normally involves the serial execution of a learnt sequence of steps. The tango has such sequences or "phrases" with which both dancers will be familiar, but set phrases need not be reproduced whole; they can be broken up, used in part, augmented, played with, or even ignored by either party, or by both. Conceived in this way, a waltz resembles a recital, the tango, a conversation.

The Argentinian tango embodies power relationships. The relationship between leader and follower in the dance is not one of equals in terms of precise roles, but is one of near equals in terms of responsibilities and obligations. While popular depictions of the tango might suggest a dominant man imposing over an acquiescent woman, this representation is mostly, if not wholly, erroneous, at least insofar as the social dance is concerned. At its best and most sophisticated, it does not work like this at all. Absolute beginners, taught by good tango teachers, will normally be encouraged to understand that they have different roles, and each has different sets of responsibilities and obligations. The leader needs to give shape to the dance on the dance floor, to lead his follower clearly and to take care of her; he absolutely must not push or pull her about.

In tango, the leader must make sure that the follower is not pushed into the path of others on the floor; he needs to negotiate the dance floor, which is often crowded. The follower, by comparison, has an obligation to maintain her balance and not use the leader as a prop. The more advanced leader also understands the constraints of floorcraft, safely negotiating the way around a busy and a continually changing configuration of dance floor and other dancers. The purpose for each couple is to realise the common goal of the dance in the dynamic context of a dance floor, which provides the opportunity for couple creativity.

Both parties listen very closely to the music, which is likely to vary in tempo and mood, even within a dance, and should be *interpreted*. Among beginners, this responsibility belongs almost exclusively to the leader. "Listen" in the context of follower-ship also means to physically listen to the lead, to understand and respond to the impulses given to the dance by the whole of the leader's body. As each becomes more proficient, this near-equality becomes more pronounced. Reminiscent of contingency theories of leadership, a competent leader will dance differently with each follower he dances with, responding to different quali-ties, not just of physical makeup but also to different musical sensibilities and temperaments. Moreover, this is a symmetrical development; followers become similarly alert, open, and sensi-tive to different leaders, and their lead.

How Queer Is the Tango?

Used as a metaphor for leading and following in organisa-tions (Chaleff, 2009), the Argentinian tango takes us beyond dichotomous notions of leader–follower relationships made up of impositional or even consensual roles (Fryer, 2012). Queer Tango builds on and makes this relationship more overt. Here, leader and follower interact in a consensual *exchange* (which Ropo and Sauer [2008] referred to as *aesthetic* leadership).

Shall I Lead Now?

In Queer Tango, anyone can perform either role, at any point: women lead, men follow; women dance with other women, men with other men; and women lead men. In all cases, either can swap roles, if he or she chooses. They may choose to dance one tango in one combination and then reverse it for the next, and so on. Alternatively, if they are sufficiently proficient, they may choose to swap roles in the course of a single dance, effecting a change of hold as seamlessly as possible. Either party may initiate a change: it is also possible for the lead to pass from one party to another *without changing the hold*. Only those dancing know who is leading at any one point and who is following. In 2011, a further variation on this theme emerged out of Buenos Aires, where leader and follower experiment to the point where neither is leading or following, irrespective of the hold that might conventionally indicate the role. Both dance, both interpret the music. The dance is realised by the couple simultaneously acting as one.

Leading from the follower's position is well known among more advanced women followers, when it is necessary either to instruct their leaders in the shape of a move, or to avoid a collision the leader has not spotted. It is, perhaps, in the encouraging of role change within a single dance, or the development of the "no leader/no follower" approach, that Queer Tango is different from the mainstream, leading it to be chosen as a metaphor for this learning strategy.

Participants in this particular class are all employed in an area of service that requires a multiprofessional approach to working and, once they are competent, relies on significant levels of individual professional autonomy, in a high-risk environment. In other words, all team members need to draw on professional expertise in decision making, thereby challenging the established role of leader as the decision maker and follower as a passive voice. Both leader and follower, in the normative sense, need courage to adjust role expectations (particularly within command-and-control cultures), avoiding errors in risk judgment and/or conformity with possible flawed courses of action.

It is in this expectation and exchange of roles that Queer Tango represents a more powerful analogy with professional relationships than does a more traditional form of tango. Among beginners, the leader may have more absolute power, but unless both parties fulfil the roles ascribed to them with care, sensitivity, and great attention to the other, the dance will not happen, nor be fulfilling, nor be agreeable to either party. This is a critical feature of the dance, one that attracted the teaching team with regard to its reflection of contemporary, albeit paradoxical, leadership roles within professional teams.

Embodied Learning

Learning within this course was developmental. As part of the active learning process, participants had (1) become competent in dialogic reflection and (2) explored the role of mental models in adapting attitudes, both to changing organisational and practice environments and to their mind-sets regarding the leader role. It is our belief that these features were critical to gaining insights into their experiences of the dance. Both features of the course were supported by a subsequent two-day workshop on emotional resilience, which developed participant understanding of how emotions and cognition are both integral to decision making. The development of this emotional intelligence is critical to the role, supporting practitioners to "persist in the face of frustrations, keeping distress from swamping the ability to think" (Goleman, 1998).

The construct of resilience is also generally held to include three features: (1) risk factors, (2) protective factors, and (3) the resulting outcome (Masten, 2001). The training (for our purpose) supported the thinking process that enabled participants (potentially) to consider risk to identity (I am/I want to be a leader/This is my identity); recognise protective factors in selves and others (I don't want to be/I am not a follower/This is not my identity); and reflect on action and outcome. The resilience training (we theorised) would better prepare learners to adapt traditional beliefs; help learners overcome what they may perceive as a challenge to their roles as leaders; and, in strengthening their capacity to behave in uncomfortable ways, enable a reflective exploration of the leadership–followership dynamics experienced in the dance.

The concept of followership was introduced to learners three weeks before the dance workshop; none of the participants was familiar with the term. No specific theories were introduced at this time, to avoid the development before the workshop of any a priori assumptions regarding the leader–follower relationship (though some did undertake personal study following the event). Reflections at this time demonstrated a poorly formed comprehension of followership in terms of its relationship to their own leadership role. On the day of the dance, all learners participated in a morning workshop that introduced the concept of fuzzy logic, linking it to an area of the participants' practice. This developed their comprehension regarding the significance of rigid mind-sets to leadership development in complex environments. It was only following this session that we informed learners that they would be participating in a dance workshop, that afternoon. In the workshop the central moves and techniques of the tango were introduced and practiced. Each participant took turns in leading and following in the dance, with different partners. Reflections on the experience were subsequently invited from all participants and are narrated in the following section, organised, as far as possible, by theme.

Emerging Themes

Dialogic reflections of participants demonstrated five experiential themes: trust, the symbiotic relationship, the quality of the relationship, the role of confidence, and team dynamics. Often, themes were clearly interrelated: trust and confidence, trust and its relationship to the quality of the relationship, the symbiosis of the relationship.

Trust

"After a short while I decided to shut my eyes when following, as I was overly analysing every step I took and the relationship between us. It was wonderful! All of a sudden we were moving in sync; I felt both courageous and completely trusting. It made me realise that we do look for leaders: we want to be led by someone who gives confidence; in whom we can trust. If we have that, we can feel free to take more risks; to be courageous followers. And as leaders, we can enable this feeling in our followers in an equal relationship."

"Chong and Wolf (2010) argue that . . . older staff members will take longer to accept a position as follower; they will want to test out the leader's ability, competency, and integrity prior to taking their role as follower. Further, they would need to know that the leader had genuine concern for people to gain followers' trust. I would argue that age of staff is also reliant on experience: if an older member joins, with limited knowledge, then it is my experience that they are keen to follow. They may not trust or adopt the traits of a follower immediately, but they will follow."

"I was happiest being led when the leader was clear about the task to be carried out whilst being thoughtful of my needs and the impact of her actions on me. This is an interesting concept at this time as I am just about to have a new manager and am aware I am anxious about this as well as wanting to be able to have trust in him and establish a positive working relationship."

"I was the most effective when I had faith in the leader and was able to trust in their skills."

"I see myself now as looking for a leader I can put my trust in. I think it's also important for me to be able to have an overall vision of where I am going. This was clear when I was carrying out the dance steps, but I am aware I work most effectively when

I have clarity around where my team's activities fit with the overall plan."

"The use of the dance workshop on The Queer Tango as learning opportunity in respect of leadership and followership was extremely effective for me. Following, I was the most effective when I had faith in the leader and was able to trust in their skills. I was the least effective when the leader was anxious and slightly hysterical. It was funny, but frustrating, as I wanted to get on with the dance."

"The Tango experience highlighted to me how important it is to feel safe when you are being led, and the importance of this when you are following."

"It was interesting that I closed my eyes with a person who I had not met in my life. I felt comfortable and safe, and it did not matter to me where I was. For all I knew I could have been standing in the middle of a park. We talked about this and how this relates to trust of one another and the importance of this when you are a leader. The tango experience also highlighted the difference of feeling comfortable with one person to another and what connection you may have with one person does not mean you would have this with another. This illustrates that you can be blind led by a leader, but in my opinion only if there is enough trust."

The Symbiotic Relationship

"Fuzzy logic was also present through my reflections in relation to leader/followers. The interchangeable [nature of] and inter-links between the roles make it almost impossible to separate them. It is clear that without leaders there are no followers and without followers there are no leaders. This is taken further, as without a relationship there is no platform to form followers and leaders."

"My follower was most effective when they allowed themselves to be led but had an idea of the steps. It worked best when they were confident in my knowledge and skill."

The Quality of the Relationship

"It was so much easier with a partner that was keen to take your arm and move with you around the floor, than one that was resistant. The leader–follower roles clearly got mixed up while learning the steps; at times the follower took the leading role."

"There was anxiety as to who you would dance with and whether this was someone you felt right with. The dance was reliant on the relationship between yourself and your partner. One's own achievement and satisfaction was reliant on the person one danced with. So the outcome of the dance was not just learning the steps but a complex list of necessities, relationship, trust, experiences, opinions, and so on, all impacting on the ability to dance."

The Role of Confidence

"Given different dance partners the effect of being a leader and a follow[er] was different. When I was being led by a person who was very self-conscious and anxious I found that I had to give a lot of reassurance as the follower and tried to give her positive strokes in order to keep going. This was in contrast to being led by a confident and self-assured person; here I was able to relax into the position of follower and felt confident that I was being managed well. With one of the other leaders, I had confidence in her and although she sometimes got something wrong she acknowledged this and started the steps again."

"As a leader I found that my first partner, because of her anxiety and dislike of the actual task, needed much reassurance that she was capable of performing and I tried to persuade her that she was in fact doing okay. This reminded me of times when I was instrumental in changing the way in which work was done; some of the team members found the changes difficult as they did not have the confidence in themselves. I was able to offer support, advice, and role modeling in bringing about changes in their belief system."

"I felt most challenged by the person who presented as a strong leader as I felt I had to achieve as well as her. I can perceive that this is not necessarily a negative thing as we all need to set personal developments that we can aspire to."

"I felt I was the least effective [as a leader] when I lacked in confidence and this was picked up by the follower."

"I was least effectively led when the leader showed anxiety and was unsure what steps we should take or where we were going. I do not find it helpful to be aware of my leader's concerns and anxieties. I am happiest with a leader who has a clear view of where we are going."

"My follower was most effective when they allowed themselves to be led but had an idea of the steps. It worked best when they were confident in my knowledge and skills. This led me to reflect on whether I have a need to see those I am leading as having confidence in me."

Team Dynamics

"I have learnt that I need to show 'me' to my team, by becoming *part* of the team and not *apart* from the team; there needs to be an open and honest relationship as, until this is achieved, the other elements of the leader/follower relationship remain superficial."

"The tango was done without any verbal communication. This to me was fascinating: how much of one's body language can have an influence on other people. It also highlighted to me that a leader does not always have to have their presence known."

"I recognised that many of the elements discussed in the room while dancing mirror that of my team, as some people did not enjoy the whole concept of dancing, others struggled with the steps, became frustrated with the restrictions, did their own thing and/or just got on with what they were being told. These complexities and differences are present within teams. Chong and Wolf (2010) suggest that if the two [leadership and follow-ership] are so interlinked then to be a truly effective leader one should 'be seen to embody the group identity.'"

"The activity made me aware that others don't always have the same response and I need to be aware of the fears new ideas can engender in others. Other messages I took from this activity were the importance of me trying to maintain an air of calm when lead-ing and being able to give clear messages about where I see the team going. Lastly, I need to reflect further on how impatient I can feel when people aren't able to apply themselves to a task."

"This idea is easy to relate to leading teams. Often we are taken out of our comfort zone and having to translate ideas to the team members that we are not necessarily sure of ourselves, but we need to give an air of calm."

"When leading I was aware I was somewhat anxious and look-ing for signs that the person who was the follower had some confidence in my skills and knowledge. This led me to wonder whether I look for these signs in my team members."

Discussion

If leadership is an activity, rather than a position in an organisa-tion, then the traditional roles of leader (directing a team) and team members (subordinate to the leader) have to be tested. The relationship between the two roles (if they need to be distinguished between) is fluid, and team members often have to take either role, contingent on the situation presented. This is particularly true when each practitioner within the team has a requirement and ability to exercise a high level of autonomy within his or her professional practice.

Ropo and Sauer (2008) proposed that the metaphor of dance illustrates the corporeal nature of leadership, a feature that is echoed within participant reflective themes. Chaleff (2009) used dance, the tango in particular, as a metaphor for the role of trust in the leader–follower relationship, arguing that both partners have to dance strongly in order for the dance to work well. Dancers need to be conscious of their own actions and the actions of others in terms of perceived strengths of both the leader and follower. He argued that followers and leaders can develop a closer and more equitable relationship through the courage to give and accept support, ideas, cautionary advice, and honest feedback (Chaleff, 2011). Participants have demonstrated that the tango workshop can embody Chaleff's propositions and challenge traditional, normative codes of leadership.

The workshop challenged the perceived dichotomy of leadership and followership through the application of fuzzy logic and use of the Queer Tango, where the body became the center of political inquiry. Thus, tango is not only an apt disembodied metaphor for leadership and followership (Chaleff, 2011); it also has potential as an embodied metaphor, where the metaphorical is explored physically, through doing, through the body, and through reflecting on doing.

Rather than rely on a didactic, passive pedagogy, we were able to evaluate participants' discovery of known shared leadership principles and so develop a relationship-oriented approach to leadership. In effective leadership and followership, as in dance, success in achieving objectives hinges in part on attitude. Attitude in both contexts means the mental and emotional attitude each brings to the tasks in hand. However, in tango attitude is extended to include the physical; literally the "attitude" of the body. As some learner reflections make plain, the attitude of the body of another, experienced in the dance embrace, can be revealing, in some cases more revealing than each dancer may have intended. Clearly mental, emotional, and physical attitudes are intimately interdependent.

In enabling a culture change to support higher levels of professional autonomy, learners need to be taken through a process that challenges prevailing beliefs, behaviours, and practices. The physicality of the learning approach seemed to enable a deeper textured consideration of the duality of roles in organisations and a more sophisticated comprehension of their own beliefs, wants, and needs regarding their role and the role of others.

Palus, McGuire, and Ernst (2012) argued that interdependent leadership cultures exist where authority and control are shared, where mind-sets tend toward collaboration so that new organisational structures can emerge. Participants described how they consciously adapted their own dance with each follower they danced with, responding to different qualities, needs, and emotional states. As participants were a team of team leaders, from one professional group in one organisation, we also demonstrated that a shared experience could help develop like-minded individuals. Accordingly, experiences expressed through reflection were shared and evaluated within participant learning sets.

The undisclosed approach to the event was, arguably, necessary so that participants did not presuppose ideas and be "knowing" participants of the dance. It is unclear as to whether further exploration of the topic is possible with the same group, beyond unveiling new beliefs and behaviours leaders adopt following the experience and how "courageous" they become in the future (Chaleff, 2009) in their roles of both leader and follower.

Participant reflections demonstrate that this strategy can develop learning beyond passive metaphorical perspectives of leader–follower roles; there is much that can be learnt by moving beyond the didactic, disembodied teaching of leadership by engaging learners in the dance that *is* leading and following.

References

Anderson, D., & Anderson, L. A. (2010). *How command and control as a change leadership style causes transformational change efforts to fail*. The Change Leader's Roadmap Methodology. Durango, CO: Being First.

Chaleff, I. (2009). *The courageous follower: Standing up to and for our leaders*. San Francisco, CA: Berrett-Koehler.

Chaleff, I. (2011). Courageous followers: Should we stand up to or for our leaders? *Leadership Excellence, 28*(4), 2.

Chong, E., & Wolf, H. (2010). Factors influencing followers' perception of organisational leaders. *Leadership and Organisational Development Journal, 31*(5), 402–419.

Currie, G., Lockett, A., & Suhomlinova, O. (2009). The institutionalisation of distributed leadership: A "catch-22" in English public services. *Human Relations, 62*(11), 1735–1761. doi:10.1177/0018726709346378

Fryer, M. (2012). Facilitative leadership: Drawing on Jürgen Habermas' model of ideal speech to propose a less impositional way to lead. *Organizsation, 19*(1), 25–43. doi:10.1177/1350508411401462

Goleman, D. (1998). *Working with emotional intelligence*. London, UK: Bloomsbury.

Grint, C., & Holt, C. (2011). *Followership in the NHS*. London, UK: King's Fund.

Jones, A. (2005). Ritual process, liminality and identity in leadership development programs: A cultural analysis. Paper presented at the Sixth International Conference on HRD Research Practice Across Europe, Leeds Metropolitan University, West Yorkshire, UK.

Küpers, W. (2007). Perspectives on integrating leadership and followership. *International Journal of Leadership Studies, 2*(3), 194–221.

Masten, A. S. (2001). Ordinary magic: Resilience processes in development. *American Psychologist, 56*, 227–238.

Palus, C. J., McGuire, J. B., & Ernst, C. (2012). Developing interdependent leadership. In S. Snook, N. Nohria, & R. Khurana (Eds.), *The handbook for teaching leadership: Knowing, doing, and being* (pp. 467–495). Thousand Oaks, CA: Sage.

Ropo, A., & Sauer, E. (2008). Dances of leadership: Bridging theory and practice through an aesthetic approach. *Journal of Management and Organization, 14*(5), 560–572.

Zadeh, L. A. (1965). Fuzzy sets. *Information and Control, 8*(3), 338–358.

Chapter Ten

Embodied Learning Experience in Leadership Development

Perttu Salovaara and Arja Ropo

More and more businesses are taking customer experience seriously—so seriously that they want to personalise their service instead of creating only generic offerings, the way, for instance, Facebook does it. Yet after several decades, the products and services of the leadership development (LD) industry offer generic content instead of tailor-made or individualised program content (Buckingham, 2012). Since its beginnings, leadership research has focused on individual leaders, but recently an ever-growing body of literature has claimed that there should be more attention to leadership's relational and social nature (Crevani, Lindgren, & Packendorff, 2007, 2010; Denis, Langley, & Sergi, 2012; Hosking, 2007; Ladkin, 2010; Uhl-Bien, 2006). In particular, LD is still hanging on to the image of leader-centricity, whereas leadership research is finding new avenues. Evaluations of LD tend to measure a program's impact from a neutral, objective, external perspective (Burke & Collins, 2005; Dexter & Prince, 2007). This approach misses the participants' personal narratives about relational and embodied experiences of change and development.

Anybody familiar with the reality of LD will assert that as easy as it is to proclaim *the* definitive steps to change, it is extremely difficult to fulfill the promise of these easy steps and to develop oneself. Thus, the research question we explore is, *How do leaders experience their learning path?* By *experience* we first mean embodied, sense-based perceptions of leaders as they relate to each other, issues at hand, and the learning environment. Second, sensuous experiences typically involve emotions, such as joy, anger, fear, or disappointment. We think that these emotions also describe the learning path of leaders. Third, embodied experience has been seen as a mode of lingering, staying with the perceptions and coming back to them instead of hurrying forward (Ladkin & Taylor, 2010). We think that LD needs lingering, taking time and space. Finally, people come to an LD program from various backgrounds and personal histories. Embodied experience in LD also calls for reflecting on the past (Bathurst, Jackson, & Statler, 2010). We illustrate our points by drawing from an empirical LD study that focuses on leaders who want to develop their coaching skills. It is assumed that feedback makes people more aware of their flaws, and that this heightened awareness leads them to develop themselves in practical terms (Atwater, Brett, & Waldman, 2003). But Ardichvili and Manderscheid (2008) reminded us that feedback to leaders does not automatically foster development. The present study also supports the view that self-awareness and good intentions are often just a minor part of adult learning.

We first provide a brief outline of research on leadership development. After that we discuss popular notions of learning in organisation research, such as the knowing–doing gap (Pfeffer & Sutton, 2000); turning knowledge into action (Turnbull James & Collins, 2008); the problem of translation (Barker, 1997); problems of implementation (Kornberger & Clegg, 2003); and weakness of will (Searle, 2001).

Based on the research question How do leaders experience their learning path?, our illustration of an LD program will reveal unexpected difficulties the participants encounter when trying to achieve their goals, even when these goals have been intentionally self-accepted and self-constructed. In our illustration, participants of the LD program seem to create paths for themselves that are extremely difficult to follow. These paths are at the same time personal, relational, and embodied.

Leadership Development Research: A Critical Overview

Literature on leadership theory and practice is expanding continually, and leadership is seen as a competitive advantage for a company's success. Effective leadership is hailed as one of the key characteristics of successful organisations (Day, 2001; Kellerman, 2012; McCall, 1998). LD takes various forms, ranging from formal training to action learning, mentoring, job assignments, 360-degree feedback, coaching, networking, and on-the-job experiences (Day, 2001; Murphy & Riggio, 2008; Parry & Sinha, 2005). Despite the devotion, not too many LD reviews have been published within the past ten years (Ardichvili & Manderscheid, 2008; Day, 2001, 2011; Riggio, 2008). As valid as the work of Day (2001) and Ardichvili and Manderscheid (2008) is, they did not discuss what we would call new developments in leadership theorising, such as socially constructed, shared, post-heroic, embodied, aesthetic, or plural approaches to leadership. Riggio (2008) noted that *leadership* development is in much shorter supply than *leader* development and lamented the lack of good research on LD. Day (2011) stated that developing individual leader skills does not guarantee better leadership, yet he emphasised that both are needed to enhance overall leadership effectiveness.

The way leadership is viewed has an impact on what LD focuses on. We identify two main foci in the current literature. First, the majority of LD research and programs consider leadership as an individual issue rather than a collective, shared one. Seen critically, this approach leads to the development of individuals and their competencies, and maintains the old-fashioned heroic leader concept. From an ontological point of view, leader development separates its subjects from the reality in which their roles are constructed. Second, there is an overemphasis on competency frameworks. This tendency has been increasingly criticised (Bolden & Gosling, 2006; Carroll, Levy, & Richmond, 2008; Denis and others, 2012; Probert & Turnbull James, 2011). One point of criticism is that a competency approach (qualities, traits, behaviours) to leadership assumes that there are universal leadership competencies that should be taught to leaders in LD programs. Although the importance of context has been recognised—for instance, in contingency theories (Fiedler, 1964); situational leadership (Hersey & Blanchard, 1969); relational leadership (Uhl-Bien, 2006); the aesthetic leadership approach (Hansen, Ropo, & Sauer, 2007); and a contextual theory of leadership (Osborn, Hunt, & Jauch, 2002)—with few exceptions (for example, Pinnington, 2011) most of this does not show in LD. Bolden and Gosling (2006) have summarised five commonly mentioned weaknesses of the competency approach to LD: (1) the reductionist way in which this approach fragments the management role rather than representing it as an integrated whole; (2) the universalistic/generic nature of competencies that assumes a common set of capabilities no matter what the nature of the situation, individuals, or task; (3) the focus on current and past performance rather than future requirements; (4) the way in which competencies tend to emphasise measurable behaviours and outcomes to the exclusion of more subtle qualities, interactions, and situational factors; and (5) the rather limited and mechanistic approach to education (p. 150).

In our reading of LD research of the past decade, we became increasingly concerned about a growing separation between LD and leadership research. Ideally LD practices should be informed by leadership theory, but that has not necessarily been the case recently. Olivares, Peterson, and Hess (2007) noted, "Although individual-based leader development is necessary for leadership, it is not sufficient. Leadership requires that individual development is integrated and understood in the context of others, social systems, and organizational strategies, missions, and goals" (p. 79). Probert and Turnbull James (2011) claimed LD to be in crisis "because it does not sufficiently incorporate the leadership concept that underpins leadership practice in organizations" (p. 147).

Bolden and Gosling (2006) compared the texts of LD programs and the words and themes the managers themselves used to talk about leadership development. They found out a remarkable difference between them. For example, vision and values, which are widely used by practicing managers, are absent in a third of the competency frameworks analysed; trust, ethics, inspiration, adaptability, flexibility, and resilience are absent in two-thirds; and beliefs, morals, courage, humility, emotion, reflection, and work-life balance are absent in more than 80 percent (p. 157).

Bolden and Gosling (2006) argued that "emphasis is frequently placed almost exclusively on observable characteristics and behaviours to the near exclusion of moral and emotional concerns, yet many authors argue that it is these dimensions that lie at the heart of leadership" (p. 158). Their findings support a "shift from individualistic notions of leadership to more inclusive and relational perspectives" (p. 160). Observing these LD accounts as academic leadership researchers, we restate that LD has not responded to the current state of leadership theories. In what follows we discuss the latest developments in leadership research and point out how LD differs from that. In the closing chapters we will apply recent leadership thinking and outline what these developments could mean for LD in practice.

Recent Developments in Leadership Approaches

Three key notions inform our conception of leadership. First, we draw a clear and analytical distinction between leader and leadership (for example, Crevani and others, 2010; Parry & Hansen, 2007; Salovaara, 2011). In the definition we adopt, these two are of a different nature, *leader* being a quality of an individual and *leadership* being a quality of an organisation and its culture. Leadership can therefore even be regarded as plural. Denis and others (2012) have laudably identified four different forms of plural leadership, which demonstrates that not only do plural approaches exist, but that there are enough of them to produce variations. Second, we join a growing number of leadership scholars who view leadership as a socially constructed and emerging phenomenon (Collinson, 2006; Fairhurst & Grant, 2010; Grint, 2005; Grint & Jackson, 2010; Gronn, 2002; Hosking, 2007; Meindl, 1995; Sandberg, 2001; Vine, Holmes, Marra, Pfeifer, & Jackson, 2008) and as meaning making (Smircich & Morgan, 1982). Because of the overemphasis of LD interventions on the individual, the organisational impact might remain ambiguous. Third, we consider leadership as an aesthetic and embodied phenomenon (Hansen & Bathurst, 2011; Hansen and others, 2007; Katz-Buonincontro, 2011; Koivunen & Wennes, 2011; Ladkin, 2008, 2010; Ropo, Parviainen, & Koivunen, 2002; Ropo & Sauer, 2008). In this literature, aesthetic epistemology legitimises sense-based data such as emotions, bodily sensations, intuitions, and mental representations as a basis for knowledge development (Strati, 2007), and embodiment does not refer to an individual leader's bodily dimensions.

A Need to Reinvent LD?

The principles of scientific management were laid down around a hundred years ago by time-and-motion studies. These approaches intended to solve the problems of efficiency, discipline, control, precision, and reliability of the production system. Hamel (2009) argued that these old models do not work well in today's environment where adaptability and creativity drive the business, and that the legacy of old management beliefs has a toxic effect on management innovations. Thus, Hamel urged a search for "positive deviants" that "defy the norms of conventional practice" (p. 187). With this he proclaimed the need for "reinventing management." Barker (1997) famously asked, "How can we train leaders if we do not know what leadership is?" We take these notions to imply that when the definition of what leaders and managers do is changing, LD needs to change accordingly.

We argue that one of the indicators of the changing face of LD in the future will be, in Hamel's (2009) words, to "defy norms of conventional practice" (p. 187). The trouble is that the current organisational systems maintain the status quo of managerial activities rather than change them. In terms of Burrell and Morgan's (1979) matrix of regulation versus radical change, LD (regardless of interpretative or functionalist emphasis) is based more on regulatory aspects than on radical change. When LD is underlining the regulatory activities, how could it then be elevated from the status of managerial education (teaching managers to take the managerial role and control organisational systems) to LD?

An estimated 75–80 percent of change attempts fail (Kotter, 1996; Lucey, 2008). Against that background the overtly positive LD accounts become questionable: How is it possible that other change attempts mainly fail, but LD produces only positive learning results and success stories? (For the few exceptions see Ready and Conger, 2003.) We observe that academic knowledge about change, learning, and leadership is to be found around disciplines, and that organisational change theories seldom seem to be informed about learning theories. Organisational change is often described in linear terms or in mechanical step-by-step models (Kotter, 1996; Lewin, 1976). Change requires learning, and then the "black box" (Kempster, 2009) of leadership emergence becomes ever more interesting. Learning can include negative knowledge (Parviainen & Eriksson, 2006); dropping off old things (Weick, 2007); or learning can take place without a corresponding change in the organisation.

So if change is about learning, how do the participants of a leadership training program experience their learning path? Literature mentions several obstacles during the learning path (not limited to leadership). These include a "knowing–doing gap" (Pfeffer & Sutton, 2000) difficulty; turning knowledge into action (Turnbull James & Collins, 2008); the problem of translation (Barker, 1997); the problem of implementation (Kornberger & Clegg, 2003; Kempster, 2009); and weakness of will (Searle, 2001). Pfeffer and Sutton observed that the "knowing–doing gap" develops between the knowledge of well-educated leaders and their practical actions. As Barker (1997) put it, "The problem of translation is based in the gap between the simplistic ways and steps, and the complexities of social and organizational processes" (p. 348). Barker defined the "problem of translation" roughly as a gap between an explicit generic model and its individual application at work. The same problem occurs when trying to turn strategy into practice, as described within strategy-as-practice literature (Carroll, Levy, & Richmond, 2008; Jarzabkowski, 2005; Whittington, 1996). "Thus, any plan realizes first and foremost the problems of implementation, the process of translation from the strategic vision to the concrete forms" (Kornberger & Clegg, 2003, p. 124). In this formulation the translation of a vision into form becomes pretty close to the knowing–doing gap.

A further obstacle of something *not* happening can be described by the concept of weakness of will, a concept discussed in Aristotle's *The Nicomachean Ethics* (2005). Weakness of will occurs when someone is willing and able to do X, but at the moment of acting on it does something else (Searle, 2001). A typical example is eating sweets: even if I know I should lose some weight and thus not eat sweets, I may "fall into a trap" of eating them. In the LD program we describe later in this chapter, weakness of will was a regular phenomenon. Even if participants knew what they should do, and they wanted to do it in a new way, they often fell back into old routines. This happened in practice when a participant wanted to use coaching and knew that he should use questions, but then soon fell into an answering mode once again and got trapped into promoting his own solutions instead of listening and thus motivating the other person to think independently.

In general, we observed that the leadership learning path is a bumpy road filled with potholes, and that failures and incompleteness emerged more often than success and perfection. The participants often got frustrated when failing, and for this they blamed the training, the trainers, the concept of coaching, the people in their organisation who "did not get it," and the company culture that did not support coaching; in short, anything but themselves.

THE CASE STUDY: SEBU TRAINING, "COACHING AS A LEADERSHIP COMPETENCE"

The empirical materials for the study were collected during an internal nine-month leadership development program at a company called "SEBU" (derived from the company's new strategic orientation: Service Business). The SEBU Coaching as a Leadership Competence program consists of six days of training plus two individual coaching sessions. During the training the participants create an individual business case, receive feedback, and then run five to seven coaching sessions for others. The program represents a *"both-and approach"* (Gaines, 2012) of action learning, coaching, and structured work experiences.

The idea of the program was not to create an extra curriculum for the participants as if work and learning process were separate entities, but to support the participants in tackling their important leadership issues; LD is part of the work, not an addition.

The program design was concerned with both leader development and leadership development. The aim of the program was to introduce the idea of moving from leader-centricity toward thinking about leadership as a quality of other members of an organisation too. Collectively shared leadership approaches mean that the team members can contribute to leadership and also assume leadership responsibilities (Ladkin, 2010; Pearce & Conger, 2003).

Ontology of Leadership Learning

Following the definition of leadership as a social construction, what is leadership learning about? The key question concerning the nature of LD we want to raise is, Where does the leadership content come from? LD is traditionally based on the best-practice type of model that Buckingham (2012) called "the formulaic model" (p. 88). In this particular case the participants' training content was derived from participants' real-life leadership situations. The idea is that participants do not actually join a training program but a training program joins their process. It goes without saying that people's social leadership situations are very different. The differences mean that what they will actually learn or take as their leadership learning cannot be determined in advance. In ontological terms, that which is being learned reveals itself during the process. The object of LD from this hermeneutic perspective is a process rather than predefined content.

Heidegger (1962) linked being (ontology) with time, and insisted that entering the process of learning and understanding is the most decisive aspect in defining the "being." "What is decisive is not to get out of the circle but to come into it in the right way. In the circle is hidden a positive possibility of the most primordial kind of knowing" (p. 195). Heidegger here refers to the hermeneutic circle of understanding, which equates with the discussion earlier about joining a process. Accordingly, instead of concentrating on what to get out of the LD program for individual participants (which we cannot determine anyway), we must consider how they *enter* and join the process. This is an ontological issue, because it defines that which the participant is about to study or, rather, about to enter. In this manner the ontology of LD is intimately linked with the way the participants are allowed and required to join the process through their embodiment.

We are here at the verge of how hermeneutics relates to embodiment; if leadership content is to affect understanding, it must in the first place be conceptualised as personal knowledge instead of explicit knowledge. In Gadamer's (2004) words: "It is enough to say that we understand in a *different way, if we understand at all*" (p. 296). Leadership learning in this respect requires primarily a readiness to challenge one's own prejudices, and it is only secondarily about explicit knowledge claims. Personal previous experiences function as a necessary pre-concept of what we come to understand about new leadership concepts, such as plural forms of leadership, leadership as a social construction, and aesthetic and embodied aspects of leadership.

We shall now present three examples from the materials where the hermeneutic view of LD introduces new themes to leadership discussions. The examples are: (1) participants knew the feedback, (2) the learning process starts prior to the training, and (3) LD is unique.

1. Participants Knew the Feedback

The real crux comes with an observation that the participants made about the personal feedback they received. As afraid as participants seemed to be about the feedback, afterwards all commented that there was *not too much new in the feedback; they knew most of it in advance*! A very commonsense question, then, is: Okay, if they know at a personal level what they should be doing, why haven't they done it yet? And from a pedagogic perspective one has to ask: If they have not been able to do it so far, how could they now?

Knowledge, in the participants' view, is not the problem, but to translate the knowledge into practice surely is. This means that the program ought to focus on something they already know and possess, and maybe on weakness of will. From the fundamental familiarity it follows that instead of taking a traditionally input-oriented and teacher–pupil-centered (realist) approach, the training ought to be learner driven, concentrating on personal knowledge and following a bottom-up rather than a top-down approach. Recognising one's own development as a participant means returning to the personal daily issues. The training thus starts with recalling familiar issues and being confronted with known practices instead of being confronted with new leadership formulas or externally determined best practices. In other words, the training need is about "How do we know about leadership?" rather than "What is leadership?"

2. The Learning Process Starts Prior to the Training

When we take the process view, the training does not start on the first day of the program: for the participants, the process starts *prior* to the training. In the tradition of philosophical hermeneutics we could say that "we belong to history" (Gadamer, 2004, p. 278), and thus any understanding is built upon prejudices (positively seen) (pp. 268–271). In this manner, "The interpretation doesn't start, it constitutes" (Figal, 2006, p. 74). The same applies to LD participants; a beginning is always a constitution, a unique personal achievement and a creation. Participants enter the training with the understanding and presumptions, i.e., their personal history, that they carry with them, and the training program is based on this pre-understanding. To start something is not to start from scratch, because to separate the present from the previous is, in human learning, not possible. Learning aims at a restart and preparing for a new attempt (Figal, 2009).

Nevertheless, there is a possibility not to go back to the original practice but to rely on that which they already know and have experienced, and which reveals itself during discussions (digesting) as a phenomenon. Modern organisation theorists share this hermeneutic rule that one enters a cycle of interpretation. Weick (1995), in his classic *Sensemaking in Organizations*, illustrated sense-making in a similar fashion:

> Sensemaking never starts. The reason it never starts is that pure duration never stops. People are always in the middle of things, which become things, only when those same people focus on the past from some point beyond it. . . . There is widespread recognition that people are always in the middle of things. What is less well developed are the implications of that insight for sensemaking. (p. 43)

The participants are in the middle of their local routines of practice, the nitty-gritty and unheroic battles of the workplace (Whittington, 1996). The main aim for the participants becomes making sense of their leadership challenges. Again, this observation turns the focus of training from *content* to the *processes* the participants are in.

3. LD Is Unique

Rather than generalising leadership into abstract formulas, new LD approaches should join the participants' process, and only after that should they touch base with any new revelation. In other words, LD should keep the subjective experience and the possibility to create new phenomena alive as long as possible, and only then to generalise. This co-creation by participants and the process does not categorise the content too early. As the content is derived from the participants, it has by nature connections with their life experiences and does not feel like explicit training content. However, the downside of personalised accounts of leadership is that it is difficult to provide general notions on leadership. Uniqueness calls for studying the phenomena, not creating one more general, grand leadership theory. With that aim in mind, leadership research as we know it now might, indeed, be misplaced (Alvesson & Sveningsson, 2003a, 2003b) and thus replaced by another kind of research that acknowledges the phenomenon.

Uniqueness is a term that is related to phenomena. Phenomenology, the study of what appears to us as a phenomenon, "recognizes the subjective nature of knowledge and pays close attention to lived experience as a valid source of knowing. Many of the more traditional ways of exploring leadership attempt to describe it 'from the outside' in accordance with accepted social science methods and assumptions about validity and objectivity. In contrast, phenomenology embraces the significance of meaning within human sense-making processes" (Ladkin, 2010, p. 6).

When we consider leadership as a unique, invisible, and informal phenomenon, it means that very little can be taken for granted. As a phenomenon, the perceived world appears at first unique, as never-seen-in-this-form-before, and only after that can it be categorised, defined, modeled. The central quality of the social world is its uniqueness: to be precise, there are no two similar individuals, needs, actions, or social situations. In practice, leadership always takes place in unique circumstances that never happened before or never will happen again in exactly the same manner.

Embodied Experience as an Extension of the Epistemological Stance

Burrell and Morgan argued in 1979 that most of the sociological research is based on objective epistemology, and we have already stated that mainstream LD research aligns with that definition; leadership is often treated as a known and quantifiable object. Yet the new streams in leadership research take a more extended view on the ontology and epistemology of leadership. Relational leadership approaches see that leadership is acted out together, and each member of the organisation is embedded in it and represents it. Leadership is found in practices, interactions, and relations (Crevani and others, 2010; Dachler & Hosking, 1995; Hosking, 2007; Uhl-Bien, 2006). The aesthetic leadership approach also regards (apart from rationality) senses and felt meanings as valid sources of information (Hansen and others, 2007; Ladkin, 2010; Ladkin & Taylor, 2010; Strati, 1999, 2007). In Merleau-Ponty's (1945/2012) phenomenology the body is treated and reflected upon in more tactual-kinesthetic terms. By talking about "body-subject" Merleau-Ponty referred to the subjective bodily experiences that we have. Using the example of the phantom limb, he illustrated how body and bodily sensations are not fully under our control. Merlau-Ponty illustrated the spatiality of one's own body by showing how we implicitly (kinesthetically, tactually) know about its limits and movements (pp. 79–99). He also included sexuality and bodily fluids in his discussion.

We see two reasons for the knowing–doing gap in leadership. The first is that the mainstream knowledge of leadership is in the first instance created in a rather symbiotic relationship between business and business schools. The knowledge that business schools, as attached to schools or departments of economics, produce is largely relying on realist knowledge claims. This knowledge is by definition abstract and objectified, detached from the particularities and obscurities of doing and acting. The second reason is that to overcome the gap requires taking embodied knowing seriously. As long as knowledge is constructed as a head-subject only, it remains as an abstraction. Neither learning nor leadership nor consciousness should be subsumed or reduced into events in the nervous system, since we are actually "out of our heads" as Noë (2009) put it. Learning as an embodied experience touches emotions, experiences, and prejudices, that is, the whole embodied person. To ensure its internal progress, LD knowledge in this respect could include more embodied and experiential elements. Schein (2009) described his experiences in the field as follows:

> In my career as a professor and sometimes consultant I often reflect on what is helpful and what is not, why some classes go well and others do not, why coaching and experiential learning are often more successful than formal lectures. When I am with organizational clients, why does it work better to focus on process rather than content, or how things are done rather than what is done? (p. 1)

Embodied experience presents an epistemological expansion for the functionalist approaches (Ropo & Parviainen, 2001), yet we do not consider it as a cure-all. "People don't automatically learn from experience. They can come away with nothing, the wrong lessons, or only some of what they might have learned" (McCall, 2004, p. 128). Yet, embodied learning can also be uncomfortable, Turnbull James and Ladkin (2008) remarked, as it sometimes very concretely touches identity and deeply held beliefs.

Creating a connection between bodily movement and emotions is one of the key features of outdoor exercises, in a similar way that dancing can be undertaken as a technical exercise or as performing bodily knowledge that is related to emotions (Parviainen, 2010). Embodied learning comes with the possibility to create something that one remembers and through which a new image that is more preferred than the previous one emerges. The participants know that through felt experience.

Discussion and Implications

To sum up, according to our analysis of an LD program as an embodied experience, the main empirical observations and their implications for LD are summarised in Table 10.1.

Table 10.1   Implications of Empirical Observations for LD

Empirical Observation	Interpretation of the Observation	Implications for LD
Feedback is basically familiar.	The knowing–doing gap is already there and needs attention. Instead of underlining the need for external knowledge input, more attention should be given to personal knowledge of participants.	Move from content to process orientation
Learning is a continuum of past, present, future.	There is a need to connect with the life process the participant is involved in ("learning never starts, it rather continues"). Individual circumstances are always unique.	Move from generic input to tailor-made processes
A return to personal embodied knowledge is required.	Embodied practices can be connected to daily actions, whereas purely intellectual input tends to create a knowing–doing gap. Embodiment means a return to what the participant already knows and has experienced.	Move from intellectual-rational input to embodied experience as the body of knowledge
Training efforts should be directed toward practice and action learning.	Touch the base at work and learn from the system you are part of, not just concentrating on the individual leader as the sole agent of leadership, but seeing leadership-in-practice as collective action patterns.	Move from leader-centricity toward leadership

When LD concentrates on individual leaders, it creates a somewhat artificial distance between leaders and their (work) environment and practices. Academic leadership research is theoretical, but the current approaches could provide fruitful alternatives for closing the gap.

We began by discussing the role of LD in organisations and stated that as long as it supports the current managerial thinking, LD will only maintain the status quo of an organisation. If LD should serve as a means of developing leaders and leadership, it ought not to concentrate on delivering external input but to enable the participants to connect with their daily issues and routines.

We take the view that a way in which LD can develop out of a general leader-centric and intellectual orientation is in future to pay more attention to collective, socially constructed, and shared forms of leadership (post-heroic) that are inherently also embodied through personal experiences. The focus is then not on leadership as either an individual practice or organisational capability, but rather on how both need to be taken into account as well as on the ways leaders' experiences are embodied as emotions, reflections, and history.

We introduce hermeneutics as an alternative for connecting leader and leadership development on a theoretical level. Hermeneutic epistemology enables a connection to be made with the embodied personal experience. This is an expansion of current LD theories and practices that concentrate on leadership as a rational, intellectual activity, and where emotions, if accounted for, are linked with emotional intelligence, as if rational head activity were in control of emotions too. Minds are mapped over the whole body, and LD, if it is to catch up with current leadership definitions, needs to take that human condition into account in a more holistic manner. Instead of the current societal tendency of being obsessed with the brain (Noë, 2009), should we, in times when well-being and innovation are becoming ever-growing organisational issues, pay more attention to that which carries the intellectual talking head from one meeting to another, that is, our body?

References

Alvesson, M., & Sveningsson, S. (2003a). The great disappearing act: Difficulties in doing "leadership." *The Leadership Quarterly, 14*(3), 359–381. doi:10.1016/S1048-9843(03)00031-6

Alvesson, M., & Sveningsson, S. (2003b). Managers doing leadership: The extra-ordinarization of the mundane. *Human Relations, 56*(12), 1435–1459. doi:10.1177/00187267035612001

Ardichvili, A., & Manderscheid, S. V. (2008). Emerging practices in leadership development: An introduction. *Advances in Developing Human Resources, 10*(5), 619–631. doi:10.1177/1523422308321718

Aristotle. (2005). *Aristotle: The Nicomachean Ethics* (H. Tredennick, Ed., J.A.K. Thompson, Trans.). London, UK: Penguin Books.

Atwater, L. E., Brett, J. F., & Waldman, D. (2003). Understanding the benefits and risks of multisource feedback within the leadership development process. In S. E. Murphy & R. E. Riggio (Eds.), *The future of leadership development* (pp. 89–106). Hillsdale, NJ: Lawrence Erlbaum Associates.

Barker, R. A. (1997). How can we train leaders if we do not know what leadership is? *Human Relations, 50*(4), 343–362. doi:10.1177/001872679705000402

Bathurst, R., Jackson, B., & Statler, M. (2010). Leading aesthetically in uncertain times. *Leadership, 6*(3), 311–330. doi:10.1177/1742715010368761

Bolden, R., & Gosling, J. (2006). Leadership competencies: Time to change the tune? *Leadership, 2*(2), 147–163. doi:10.1177/1742715006062932

Buckingham, M. (2012, June). Leadership development in the age of the algorithm. *Harvard Business Review*, pp. 86–94.

Burke, V., & Collins, D. (2005). Optimising the effects of leadership development programmes: A framework for analysing the learning and transfer of leadership skills. *Management Decision, 43*(7–8), 975–987.

Burrell, G., & Morgan, G. (1979). *Sociological paradigms and organizational analysis*. London, UK: Heinemann.

Carroll, B., Levy, L., & Richmond, D. (2008). Leadership as practice: Challenging the competency paradigm. *Leadership, 4*(4), 363–379. doi:10.1177/1742715008095186

Collinson, D. L. (2006). Rethinking followership: A post-structuralist analysis of follower identities. *The Leadership Quarterly, 17*, 179–189. doi:10.1016/j.leaqua.2005.12.005

Crevani, L., Lindgren, M., & Packendorff, J. (2007). Shared leadership: A postheroic perspective on leadership as a collective construction. *International Journal of Leadership Studies*, 3(1), 40–67.

Crevani, L., Lindgren, M., & Packendorff, J. (2010). Leadership, not leaders: On the study of leadership as practices and interactions. *Scandinavian Journal of Management*, 26(1), 77–86. doi:10.1016/j.scaman.2009.12.003

Dachler, H. P., & Hosking, D. M. (1995). The primacy of relations in socially constructing organizational realities. In D. M. Hosking, H. P. Dachler, & K. J. Gergen (Eds.), *Management and organisation: Relational alternatives to individualism*. Brookfield, VT: Ashgate/Avebury.

Day, D. V. (2001). Leadership development. A review in context. *The Leadership Quarterly*, 11(4), 581–613. doi:10.1016/S1048-9843(00)00061-8

Day, D. V. (2011). Leadership development. In A. Bryman, D. Collinson, K. Grint, B. Jackson, & M. Uhl-Bien (Eds.), *The SAGE handbook of leadership* (pp. 37–50). London, UK: Sage.

Denis, J-L., Langley, A., & Sergi, V. (2012). Leadership in the plural. *Academy of Management Annals*, 6(1), 211–283. doi:10.1080/19416520.2012.667612

Dexter, P., & Prince, C. (2007). Evaluating the impact of leadership development: A case study. *Journal of European Industrial Training*, 31(8), 609–625.

Fairhurst, G. T., & Grant, D. (2010). The social construction of leadership: A sailing guide. *Management Communication Quarterly*, 24(2), 171–210. doi:10.1177/0893318909359697

Fiedler, F. E. (1964). A contingency model of leadership effectiveness. In L. Berkowitz (Ed.), *Advances in experimental social psychology* (Vol. 1, pp. 149–190). New York, NY: Academic Press.

Figal, G. (2006). *Gegenständlichkeit. Das hermeneutische und die philosophie*. Tübingen, Germany: Mohr.

Figal, G. (2009). *Verstehensfragen*. Tübingen, Germany: Mohr.

Gadamer, H.-G. (2004). *Truth and method*. London, UK: Continuum.

Gaines, K. (2012). Leadership development: Let's all take a fresh look at the field. *Leadership Excellence*, 29(1), 8.

Grint, K. (2005). Problems, problems, problems: The social construction of "leadership." *Human Relations*, 58, 1467–1494. doi:10.1177/0018726705061314

Grint, K., & Jackson, B. (2010). Toward "socially constructive" social constructions of leadership. *Management Communication Quarterly*, 24(2), 348–355. doi:10.1177/0893318909359086

Gronn, P. (2002). Distributed leadership as a unit of analysis. *The Leadership Quarterly*, 13, 423–451.

Hamel, G., with Breen, B. (2009). *The future of management*. Boston, MA: Harvard Business School Press.

Hansen, H., & Bathurst, P. (2011). Aesthetics and leadership. In A. Bryman, B. Jackson, D. Collinson, K. Grint, & M. Uhl-Bien (Eds.), *The SAGE handbook of leadership* (pp. 255–266). London, UK: Sage.

Hansen, H., Ropo, A., & Sauer, E. (2007). Aesthetic leadership. *The Leadership Quarterly, 18*(6), 544–560. doi:10.1016/j.leaqua.2007.09.003

Heidegger, M. (1962). *Being and time.* Oxford, UK: Blackwell.

Hersey, P., & Blanchard, K. H. (1969). Life cycle theory of leadership. *Training and Development Journal, 23*(5), 26–34.

Hosking, D. M. (2007). Not leaders, not followers: A post-modern discourse of leadership processes. In P. Shamir, R. Pillai, M. Bligh, & M. Uhl-Bien (Eds.), *Follower-centered perspectives on leadership: A tribute to the memory of James R. Meindl.* Greenwich, CT: Information Age.

Jarzabkowski, P. (2005). *Strategy as practice: An activity-based approach.* London, UK: Sage.

Katz-Buonincontro, J. (2011). How might aesthetic knowing relate to leadership? A review of the literature. *International Journal of Education and the Arts, 12* (SI 1.3). http://www.ijea.org/v12si1/

Kellerman, B. (2012). *The end of leadership.* New York, NY: HarperCollins.

Kempster, S. (2009). *How managers have learnt to lead: Exploring the development of leadership practice.* Basingstoke, UK: Palgrave Macmillan.

Koivunen, N., & Wennes, G. (2011). Show us the sound! Aesthetic leadership of symphony orchestra conductors. *Leadership, 7*(1), 51–71. doi:10.1177/1742715010386865

Kornberger, M., & Clegg, S. (2003). The architecture of complexity. *Culture and Organization, 9*(2), 75–91. doi:10.1080/14759550302804

Kotter, J. P. (1996). *Leading change.* Boston, MA: Harvard Business School Press.

Ladkin, D. (2008). Leading beautifully: How mastery, congruence and purpose create the aesthetic of embodied leadership practice. *The Leadership Quarterly, 19*(1), 31–41. doi:10.1016/j.leaqua.2007.12.003

Ladkin, D. (2010). *Rethinking leadership. A new look at old leadership questions.* Cheltenham, UK: Edward Elgar.

Ladkin, D., & Taylor, S. S. (2010). Leadership as art: Variations on a theme. *Leadership, 6*(3), 235–241. doi:10.1177/1742715010368765

Lewin, K. (1976). Frontiers in group dynamics. In D. Cartwright (Ed.), *Field theory in social science: Selected theoretical papers by Kurt Lewin.* Chicago, IL: University of Chicago Press.

Lucey, J. L. (2008). Why is the failure rate for organisation change so high? *Management Services, 52*(4), 10–18.

McCall, M. W. (1998). *High flyers: Developing the next generation of leaders.* Boston, MA: Harvard Business School Press.

McCall, M. W. (2004). Leadership development through experience. *Academy of Management Executive, 18*(3), 127–130.

Meindl, J. R. (1995). The romance of leadership as a follower-centric theory: A social constructionist approach. *The Leadership Quarterly*, 6(3), 329–341. doi:10.1016/1048-9843(95)90012-8

Merleau-Ponty, M. (2012). *Phenomenology of perception* (D. A. Landes, Trans.). London, UK: Routledge. (Original work published 1945)

Murphy, S. E., & Riggio, R. E. (Eds.). (2008). *The future of leadership development*. Mahwah, NJ: Lawrence Erlbaum Associates.

Noë, A. (2009). *Out of our heads: Why you are not your brain, and other lessons from the biology of consciousness*. New York, NY: Hill and Wang.

Olivares, O. J., Peterson, G., & Hess, K. P. (2007). An existential-phenomenological framework for understanding leadership development experiences. *Leadership and Organization Development Journal, 28*(1), 76–91. doi:10.1108/01437730710718254

Osborn, R. N., Hunt, J. G., & Jauch, L. R. (2002). Toward a contextual theory of leadership. *The Leadership Quarterly, 13*(6), 797–837. doi:10.1016/S1048-9843(02)00154-6

Parry, K. W., & Hansen, H. (2007). The organizational story as leadership. *Leadership, 3*(3), 281–300. doi:10.1177/1742715007079309

Parry, K. W., & Sinha, P. N. (2005). Researching the trainability of transformational organizational leadership. *Human Resource Development International, 8*(2), 165–183. doi:10.1080/13678860500100186

Parviainen, J. (2010). Choreographing resistances: Spatial-kinesthetic intelligence and bodily knowledge as political tools in activist work. *Mobilities, 5*(3), 311–329.

Parviainen, J., & Eriksson, M. (2006). Negative knowledge, expertise and organizations. *International Journal of Management Concepts and Philosophy, 2*(2), 140–153.

Pearce, J. L., & Conger, J. A. (Eds.). (2003). *Shared leadership: Reframing the how and whys of leadership*. Thousand Oaks, CA: Sage Publications.

Pfeffer, J., & Sutton, R. I. (2000). *The knowing–doing gap: How smart companies turn knowledge into action*. Boston, MA: Harvard Business School Press.

Pinnington, A. H. (2011). Leadership development: Applying the same leadership theories and development practices to different contexts? *Leadership, 7*(3), 335–365.

Probert, J., & Turnbull James, K. (2011). Leadership development: Crisis, opportunities and the leadership concept. *Leadership, 7*(2), 137–150.

Ready, D. A., & Conger, J. A. (2003). Why leadership development efforts fail. *MIT Sloan Management Review, 44*(3), 83–88.

Riggio, R. E. (2008). Leadership development: The current state and future expectations. *Consulting Psychology Journal: Practice and Research, 60*(4), 383–392. doi:10.1037/1065-9293.60.4.383

Ropo, A., & Parviainen, J. (2001). Leadership and bodily knowledge in expert organizations: Epistemological rethinking. *Scandinavian Journal of Management, 17*(1), 1–18. doi:10.1016/S0956-5221(00)00030-0

Ropo, A., Parviainen, J., & Koivunen, N. (2002). Aesthetics in leadership: From absent bodies to social bodily presence. In K. W. Parry & J. R. Meindl (Eds.), *Grounding leadership theory and research: Issues, perspectives and methods: Vol. 1. Research in leadership horizons*. Greenwich, CT: Information Age.

Ropo, A., & Sauer, E. (2008). Corporeal leaders. In D. Barry & H. Hansen (Eds.), *The SAGE handbook of new approaches in management and organization* (pp. 469–478). London, UK: Sage.

Salovaara, P. (2011). *From leader-centricity toward leadership: A hermeneutic narrative approach*. Tampere, Finland: TUP.

Sandberg, J. (2001). The constructions of social constructionism. In S.E. Sjöstrand, J. Sandberg, & M. Tyrstrup (Eds.), *Invisible management: The social construction of leadership* (pp. 28–48). London, UK: Thomson Learning.

Schein, E. H. (2009). *Helping: How to offer, give and receive help*. San Francisco, CA: Berrett-Koehler.

Searle, J. R. (2001). *Rationality in action*. Cambridge, MA: MIT Press.

Smircich, L., & Morgan, G. (1982). Leadership: The management of meaning. *Journal of Applied Behavioural Studies*, *18*(3), 257–273.

Strati, A. (1999). *Organization and aesthetics*. London, UK: Sage.

Strati, A. (2007). Sensible knowledge and practice-based learning. *Management Learning*, *38*(1), 61–77. doi:10.1177/1350507607073023

Turnbull James, K., & Ladkin, D. (2008). Meeting the challenge of leading in the 21st century: Beyond the "deficit model" of leadership development. In K. Turnbull James & J. Collins (Eds.), *Leadership learning: Knowledge into action* (pp. 13–34). Basingstoke, UK: Palgrave Macmillan.

Turnbull James, K., & Collins, J. (Eds.). (2008). Introduction. *Leadership learning: Knowledge into action*. Basingstoke, UK: Palgrave Macmillan.

Uhl-Bien, M. (2006). Relational leadership theory: Exploring the social processes of leadership and organizing. *The Leadership Quarterly*, *17*(6), 654–676. doi:10.1016/j.leaqua.2006.10.007

Vine, B., Holmes, J., Marra, M., Pfeifer, D., & Jackson, B. (2008). Exploring co-leadership talk through interactional sociolinguistics. *Leadership*, *4*(3), 339–360. doi:10.1177/1742715008092389

Weick, K. E. (1995). *Sensemaking in organizations*. Thousand Oaks, CA: Sage.

Weick, K. E. (2007). Drop your tools: On reconfiguring management education. *Journal of Management Education*, *31*, 5–16. doi:10.1177/1052562906293699

Whittington, R. (1996). Strategy as practice. *Long Range Planning*, *29*(5), 731–735. doi:10.1016/0024-6301(96)00068-4

Chapter Eleven

Professionals Are Their Bodies

The Language of the Body as Sounding Board in Leadership and Professional Communication

Helle Winther

The body lives, breathes, senses, and experiences. The language of the body develops in the small child long before spoken language, and in all human relationships, bodily communication is both a personally and culturally toned mother tongue (Halprin, 2002; Winther, 2009). Thus, more focus on embodiment may be of great importance to leadership, empathy, and communication in many professional capacities. The theoretical basis flowing through this chapter comes from movement psychology research.

Movement psychology as developed by Winther (2008, 2009, 2012) has a wholeness-oriented understanding of the body that is also inspired by the work of both Rudolf Laban (1980)

This chapter is part of a larger project on the embodied professional. The project examines embodied leadership in professional communication, as well as developing and testing out educational programs and developing practical courses for embodied professional competence in teacher education, university education, health care workers' education, and postgraduate education and developmental programs for these groups. The project is a collaboration among the Research Group for Body, Learning and Identity at the University of Copenhagen, teacher education at University College Copenhagen (Blågaard), and the nursing school at the Diakonisse Foundation in Copenhagen. This chapter is written with data from the postgraduate education, developmental programs and the teacher education. Linda Hejselbak Jensen, Mathias Berg, Betina Hansen, and Tina Thilo have contributed to gathering data.

and Stéphano Sabetti (2001; Sabetti & Freligh, 2001), as well as by Merleau-Ponty (1962/2002), one of the phenomenology-oriented theoreticians who focused on the body and our perceptual openness to the world as our basic condition of existence.

Movement psychology furthermore regards the body as a multidimensional and also energetic organism, which, through sense-based communication, constantly reflects, expresses, and sometimes represses personal dynamics, feelings, vulnerabilities, and lived life (Lowen, 2006; Sabetti & Freligh, 2001; Winther, 2009, 2012). Thus, the body communicates continually, throughout life. Professionals, too, *are* their bodies. Therefore, it is also relevant to examine the relationship between personal, bodily, and professional dimensions in leadership and communication.

Sharing Stories: About the Methods

This chapter is based on bodily based qualitative research that examined individuals' experiences, feelings, and identity processes through stories from practice (Dadds, Hart, & Crotty, 2001; Jarvis, 1999; Sparkes, 2002; Winther, 2012).

The presented stories come from a teaching context and a hospital context and are written by students and professionals. The accounts build on the principle of *sharing stories* and that of elucidating what is essential in a phenomenon by "zooming in" on important situations that only a person working in the practical field can create (Dadds and others, 2001).

In addition, inspiration comes from phenomenology, which is a living philosophical practice in constant development, as well as from newer postmodern-inspired texts on scientific theory (Todres, 2007; Winther, 2008). According to Todres, phenomenological descriptions may hold both the uniquely personal and qualities that are commonly characteristic of human existence in a given field. The stories in this text are selections from a larger empirical compilation on the importance of the body for professional competence for teachers, leaders, and health care professionals in particular (Berg & Thilo, 2012; Hejselbak Jensen & Winther, 2012; Winther, 2012). They are used, as Todres (2007) pointed out, as unique examples of living practice that still may lead to broader reflections on embodied leadership and embodied professional competence.

The Connection Between the Bodily, Personal, and Professional Dimensions

The personal in the professional is an area that in recent years has been given more and more attention and relevance (Avolio & Gardner, 2005; Avolio, Walumbwa, & Weber, 2009; Ladkin & Taylor, 2010; Nielsen, Marrone, & Slay, 2010; Plauborg, Andersen, Ingerslev, & Fibæk Laursen, 2010).

In spite of the fact that increasingly more focus has been given to personal, emotional, and relational work in the professional room, the importance of embodiment for this dynamic, paradoxically enough, has been given relatively little attention, including in leadership studies (Ladkin & Taylor, 2010; Meekums, 2007). Nevertheless, the importance of the bodily is especially visible in the contexts of teaching and leadership, in which emphatic bodily communication is of importance for authority and authenticity.

The bodily is also of great importance in professions that involve confidentiality, trust building, and senses-based attention to patients or clients (Winther, 2012). Here, professionals must be extremely aware of how they move in the vulnerable inter-body space; optimally, this must be done with presence and respect. In these professions, all bodies—the professionals' included—become more visible, and the body language dynamics, which always exist, are experienced more distinctly (Andersen Kjær, 2011; Meekums, 2007; Payne, 2008; Winther,

2012). Here, the bodily communication is at once both personal and professional. It is personal because basic communication, at its deepest level, is based in the individual's body. It is professional because in various areas, depending on profession and context, there are certain unwritten rules, habits, and expectations to professional communication. It is exactly this triad—between the bodily, personal, and professional dimensions—with which this chapter is concerned. And Jacob, whom we now shall meet, encounters this triad as soon as he takes his first steps into the role of leader and teacher.

Leadership and the Magnified Body

Jacob is twenty-one years old, a student teacher. This is one of the first times he is trying to teach. Already before the session starts, he notices the first bodily signals.

> I notice the first butterflies that just begin to come. When the pupils arrive, I get nervous though, I notice it in the front of my chest, like a pressure in my chest that won't go away.

> My mouth feels incomprehensibly immovable, and it's difficult for the words to come out of my mouth.

> I stand at the blackboard and am about to instruct the pupils. It feels like forever, but doesn't last more than half a minute. After the first couple of sentences have passed my lips, it loosens up. I can notice a feeling of joy from the pupils in fact taking in what I present. The joy feels like a stream of warmth filling my body, starting from my legs and ending up in a smile at the other end.

From Jacob's story

To be able to stand in front of others. To be able to meet, lead, and get a group together. To be able to sense and read the language of the body. In many professional contexts, these qualities are of great importance and are profoundly connected to the body. For Jacob this situation is a big challenge that creates a dance between a nervous pressure on the one hand and a stream of joy on the other.

While relationships between friends, siblings, and partners are often characterised by a high degree of symmetry, most professions feature asymmetrical relationships in communication (Thornquist, 2005). Here, professionals have a great responsibility for the situation, the building of trust, and the communication process with the individuals with whom they work. That is why the student's, patient's, client's, or colleague's processes should be in the foreground. At the same time, professionals who work with others as such, taking into account their profession, position, responsibility, and authority, receive a form of *magnified* attention to their bodily and emotional communication (Andersen Kjær, 2011; Winther, 2012). That is, the bodily expression of the teacher, leader, nurse, or therapist comes through with a different strength, visibility, and importance compared to when the person sits talking to a friend in a cafe.

Therefore, professional communication finds itself, as mentioned, in a continually present triad that is at once bodily, personal, and professional (Winther, 2009). One does not exist without the others, but may display itself with varying strength. When personal communication is characterised by clarity, sensitivity, and consciousness of professional responsibility, it may be experienced as a sounding board that fosters trust in the relationship. But the personal dimension may also be so forward and even private as to cause the professional aspect to disappear. As the personality lives through its bodily existence, the body is therefore omnipresent and thus an unavoidable co-creator of trustworthy and authentic leadership (Ladkin & Taylor, 2010; Winther, 2012).

If the teacher dares to enter the classroom with his or her body and living movements, this person might radiate an involvement and presence that could have a motivating effect on the teaching situation. Here, the three dimensions will continually stimulate each other and create a clear professional communication.

However, in a challenging situation or in a period of significant existential private processes, that same teacher may become vulnerable and unclear of his or her own position and footing. This too may be noticed and expressed through the body.

This is what Thomas, an otherwise very experienced teacher, comments on in his story, written during a difficult period in his private life:

> I felt that there was something wrong with me as a person. I felt that I should try to hide the person I was, and instead let my professionalism and radiation as a teacher shine through. During that period, it was all a big act when I went into the classroom to teach. I had a profession and therefore some clear things I was going to do, and that I knew I could manage, but it was just survival. When I was teaching, I put on a mask and had to hold the pupils half a step further away, so that they weren't allowed to touch my personality. There was no surplus left for me to get involved. It was pure survival, while I waited for it all to come into balance again.

From Thomas's story

These lively stories, from both young Jacob and an experienced teacher, Thomas, testify to a need to make explicit the body's importance for leadership and professional competence. This is what the concept of *embodied professional competence* expresses.

Embodied Professional Competence

As a continuation of these stories and of this chapter's both empirical and movement psychological foundation of the body's importance in professional communication and leadership, a new concept may be developed: embodied professional competence. This concept expresses heightened focus on *the body* as a sounding board in leadership and professional communication.

Embodied professional competence may be defined as a combination of the following:

- *Self-contact*: Contact with one's own body and personal feelings; the ability to be focused and present; the ability to include one's heart and still keep a professional focus and a private boundary
- *Communication reading and contact ability*: The ability to see, listen, sense, and notice; the ability to read both verbal and bodily communication; the ability to create trustful and empathic contact with others; the ability to contain and manage conflicts
- *Leadership in groups or situations*: Professional overview, radiation, centering, and clear leadership of the group or situation; the ability to enter or hold a space with a trustworthy and bodily based authority and humility

The individual's challenges with embodied professional competence may be the starting point for years-long professional development and maturing. As a professional, one may meet many challenging interpersonal boggles along the way, though they may never develop further unless also seen as learning situations.

When *all* three levels of embodied professional competence begin to be in play all at once, *embodied leadership* may develop. This might be a long journey. The development of embodied leadership, as in Jacob's case, may start with the student's first experiences in a course of study, and be rounded off when the person ends his or her working life. The meaning of the three levels will be further illustrated.

First Level: Self-Contact Through the Body

Ladkin and Taylor (2010, p. 66) stated that in order to evolve an authentic leadership, a person's basis for awareness of self, both in a somatic and a symbolic sense, must be experienced and expressed through the body.

Embodied professional competence is thus also about training as a professional, first and foremost, in being able to be in emotional contact with one's own body as sounding board, and thus being able to sense, read, and listen to others in a clear professional communication. At this level of self-contact and self-awareness, especially, it is important to be able to be personal without becoming *private*. The asymmetrical relationship plays a decisive role here. In the practical situation itself, the professional may also be aware of self-contact. If the self-contact is syntonic, it may be experienced as a flowlike state in which contact with others feels life giving and easy. When self-contact is disturbed, it may be experienced as very energy demanding because a large part of one's professional attention, as in Thomas's case, is being used to fight with one's own personal state and mood. In such situations, muscle tensions and restraints on breathing and the expression of movement may be a universal emotional and social defence mechanism (Thornquist, 2005; Lowen, 2006). In everyday language we often say "to lose yourself." Here even familiar meetings and situations may feel heavy or insurmountable, and the professional may experience himself or herself as tense, insecure, or emotionally overwhelmed. But even in difficult situations, the body can be a teacher and show the way. Here the professional may listen to his or her own senses and direct more attention to the breath and to the feeling of coming down into the body.

As Thornquist (2005) wrote, "Movements may be spontaneous and understood as immediate expressions of feelings, and it is widely acknowledged that feelings are expressed bodily. Hardly as widespread is the opposite acknowledgment: that we regulate our emotional life through the body" (p. 132, my translation).

Thomas chose to go through a two-month course of working on his professional and personal development and self-awareness through the body. This was coupled with a larger focus on the importance of the body for leadership and teaching. He describes some of his learning themes:

> For a long time, I had defined myself based on a lot of labels that I had put on myself, because I thought that I had to be all of those things in order to be worth anything, but it occurred to me that the labels you put on your own back don't change who you are. . . . I have found some calmness. I breathe more easily and can better rest in myself. I have now some security that what I do is actually good enough. I really think that I am much more *me*. Now I define the roles, instead of before, when the roles defined me.
>
> **From Thomas's story**

Thomas's story shows how important, and also challenging, self-contact is. And how calmness, emotional balance, and—perhaps, in the most literal sense—freer breathing also may be of importance for the empathic communication in diverse professional contexts. This is what the second level of embodied professional competence is about.

Second Level: Communication Reading and Contact Ability

While in professional–personal contexts there is magnified attention to the professional's bodily communication, attention to the very smallest of the body's movements is decisive for the *encounter* itself. We can often choose for ourselves what we will say, and when we will be silent, and most often there is one person speaking at a time. However, the body—even though it carries life experiences, societal norms, and culture—is also connected to the moment (Fuchs, 2012; Merleau-Ponty, 1962/2002; Sabetti & Freligh, 2001; Winther, 2009). The body is always communicative and multi-sensing, and often the body expresses something that is not told completely in words (Andersen Kjær, 2011; Fuchs, 2012; Lowen, 2006; Winther, 2009). Finding the tone between two or more people is described in various contexts by concepts related to *harmony* (Løgstrup, 1983) and *resonance* (Sabetti & Freligh, 2001). Harmony is a metaphor and refers to the voice, to tone, and to atmosphere. The concept of harmony has been developed by Løgstrup and designates the phenomenon that the individual, in meetings with others, has an open, receptive attitude. A characteristic of harmony is that it is related to feelings, which in a movement psychological framework have a direct connection to an openness in the body's energy and vitality. When two or more individuals are in harmony together, the same phenomenon is termed resonance. When they are not in harmony, dissonance occurs (Sabetti & Freligh, 2001). Resonance and dissonance may be experienced clearly in music and in the way musical instruments sound together, but also in and between people; we speak in everyday life of "good or bad vibrations." We talk about "tuning in to" each other, and it is often possible to describe when "it" is "in sync" or not. Consciousness of what is in play in even small moments may also be strengthened by being attentive to the body's energy and movement in professional communication. These movements are both sensed and revealed by, among other things, small body language signs and sense-based movements which contain physical, emotional, and social meanings; thus, these are also openings to change (Winther, 2008). Sabetti (2001) termed these movements "micromovements."

Getting in harmony with each other and finding the point at which the contact has resonance may then demand a great deal of attention to the body's very smallest of movements and may develop the professional's sense of *emotional intelligence*, which is the ability to understand and manage moods and emotions in the self and others (Goleman, Boyatzis, & McKee, 2002). In professional contexts, it is the professional who has the most responsibility for communication being trustful and for the interpersonal *dance* being successful. This dance too may be filled with episodes of sunshine, humour, vulnerability, happiness, or crisis. And in a hospital, the scene may shift from one moment to the next. This may challenge both the professional's self-contact and his or her ability to make contact with others. A physical therapist tells about that here.

> I hear his voice before I see him standing in the doorway. The voice is gruffer than it usually is, on the verge of being agitated.
>
> It was not good news: how the X-rays turned out.
>
> He is already on the way down the corridor. His canes can almost not manage to follow him; he's walking faster than he usually does. Yells at the doctor.
>
> I walk there beside him—have a strong impulse to put one hand on his arm, as something calming, comforting. But I sense that I would then "break the wall down," and tears would trickle out. I know him well enough to know that he will not cry when anyone is looking—it's a defeat. Lack of steadfastness, of manliness.
>
> My hand therefore hangs down at my side. . . . He almost runs out of the ward—out where he can breathe and most probably cry. I leave there with the feeling of having had my fingers in a big wad of cotton that just grew, and that I couldn't gather together. It just ran out between my fingers.
>
> My own body feels the opposite of cotton, like stone—I concentrate on "getting my breath back." And getting air.
>
> **From Betina's story**

For health care professionals or therapists, it may be, as in this story, important to be able to both *sense* and *read* micromovements in order to give optimal support and care. Teachers and leaders too can train themselves to understand participants' micromovements, body positions, and small interpersonal body language movements. Are the person's eyes lively and open, or are they dull and with an unsteady gaze? Do the movements feel resonant, or is there resistance and dissonance that can be seen in tense muscles or a dejected or restless body expression? If teachers and leaders train themselves to both sense and read the body, they may gain meaningful information and insight into both individual and group processes and moods, and perhaps find optimal opportunities for actions that create resonance and empathic communication far in advance of the participants' saying anything and far in advance of any disagreements' developing into conflicts. Even as self-contact (as the first level) and communication reading and contact (as the second level) are important for developing a trustworthy professional competence, they are not sufficient for the development of leadership. As Ladkin and Taylor (2010) stated, "An individual can reveal their 'true' self and relate well to others and the particular moment, but still not be perceived as an authentic leader because they are not experienced as embodying leadership in a way perceived by the group to be 'leaderly'" (p. 71).

Therefore, the third level of embodied professional competence is important: namely, leadership.

Third Level: Leadership—Taking a Space

In both teaching and leadership, it is important to be able to be in movement (Kirkeby, 2004). Here it is about entering and filling a space or room and balancing between the personal, bodily, and professional. It is easier said than done, and both experienced and new teachers must constantly train in leadership. In connection with performance, the concept of *stage presence* is often used, and we speak of "being on." These are at their deepest level energy concepts that are about role awareness, presence, radiation, timing, feelings, and being comfortable with one's own bodily communication (Winther, 2012).

. In every professional context, there is namely an important space. The space is never empty but is charged with atmosphere, energy, meaning, possibilities, and disturbances. People also communicate bodily in space (Sabetti & Freligh, 2001). Therefore, the way we enter, create, and hold the professional space is important for credibility, authority, and creating relationships. In order to be personal, powerful, bodily and professionally present, it is important to be able to bear the magnified bodily communication, for it is through the body that authority in the room is negotiated (Thornquist, 2005).

The competence of entering a space may be strengthened by bodily consciousness of the point of balance, which in martial arts, body psychology, and movement psychology is termed the *center*: a physical, psychological, and emotional point of energy in the middle of the body, just under the navel (Lowen, 2006; Sabetti & Freligh, 2001; Winther, 2009).

When a professional has good contact with his or her own center, this person may be experienced as an individual who rests in himself or herself and has the competence, in the most literal way, to be the center of others' processes through leadership and in chaotic or conflict-filled situations as well as in harmonious ones. If contact with the center is lost, then the focus, orientation, overview, and thus control and leadership of the situation are also lost. Thus, the first step may be, again, working with the first level of embodied professional competence: one's own self-awareness, that is, the level of self-contact, perceived through the body. In this way, there is a possibility for composure and thus leadership to be reestablished.

Even though the competence of taking a space is of significant importance in various professions if the professional is to be perceived as leaderly, leadership is not only about developing a healthy *authority*. It is also about creating a space of *humility*.

Leadership and Humility: Holding a Space

In some situations, leadership as a professional is about creating and *holding* a space. This may be especially relevant in professional contexts where people are in vulnerable situations in connection with, for example, illness, crisis situations, or therapy. Also, in research on charismatic leaders, humility and the sense of "others" orientation is developing as an important theme (Nielsen, Marrone, & Slay, 2010). Here, too, it is about the professional taking the responsibility for the space and filling it with his or her bodily presence. This demands much more humility, but also an ability to be in oneself and use the body as a sounding board, so that another person may sense that there is security there and space to share what is difficult. The physical therapist tells about this here.

> I sit down beside her, and ask if there is anything I can do for her today? She shakes her head—but puts her hand out. Has no breath to say anything. I take her hand, and then we just sit there.
>
> I am touched by the intense mood, and have to blink a few times so as not to have such watery eyes. Her breathing gets quieter, she relaxes a little more, breathes also more deeply. And as if, it's enough now—she then lets go of my hand.
>
> I leave with a feeling of having done very, very little, and still made a difference.
>
> **From Betina's story**

Here, the physical therapist was successful in both keeping her self-contact and finding a contact, with presence, to the patient. She is thus in emotional, sensual, and kinesthetic contact with both her own and the patient's bodily energy and expression, at the same time as she shows leadership in the situation and helps the patient to become calm. The ability to hold a space, to sense and understand the bodies' *speaking*, and to let authority and humility walk hand in hand is also important for teachers and leaders.

An individual's unique soma and energy may be felt in all his or her actions and movements (Lowen, 2006; Sabetti & Freligh, 2001; Winther, 2012). The energy may be seen in the particular way a person walks. It may be sensed in his or her bodily *being* and noticed in his or her handshake or be heard in rolling cascades of laughter. The energy is also connected to the individual's Earth connection or grounding, and even though the movements in the physical therapist's story are very small, grounding takes place in both persons (Lowen, 2006; Winther, 2009). Grounding is understood within a philosophical, body psychological, and movement psychological framework as an energetic concept, which is about not only a physical but also a psychological, emotional, and social footing (Lowen, 2006; Sabetti & Freligh, 2001; Winther, 2009). All individuals develop throughout life a personally toned grounding that may be more or less stable (Lowen, 2006). One's personal grounding is connected to one's body structure, life experiences, personality, and culture. Some individuals radiate a deeply rooted calm and living vitality. Others experience personal frailty or an irascible temperament, and feel that they quickly lose their footing and become stressed, nervous, or overcome by their own feelings in challenging situations. A nurse, therapist, leader, or teacher has thus his or her own unique, personal grounding as the basis of his or her professional communication, at the same time as grounding is also both a situational and trainable phenomenon. In professional contexts, grounding is the ability to be present and clear and keep one's composure in what may be difficult situations, in which patients, pupils, children, clients, or colleagues are uneasy, in emotional chaos, in crisis, or stressed or unbalanced. The better the professional knows himself or herself and his or her own bodily signals in various situations, the easier it will be to keep or regain grounding. In stressful, chaotic, or very emotionally charged situations, one's grounding may disappear. Breathing may become shallow and body language uneasy, the voice may fail, and the situation may suddenly seem confusing or chaotic. If the patient, pupil, colleague, or client loses his or her grounding, it may be important that the professional can master the situation and is able to keep his or her own footing. On the deepest level, this is about being down in the body and directing more attention to the breath, to eye contact, and perhaps, as in Betina's story, to the meeting of one's hands with the patient. The professional may thus, through bodily attention in self-contact, strengthen his or her own physical and emotional grounding, and find a calm that can spread itself through the room, so that the client, pupil, colleague, or patient may have the possibility to regain his or her own grounding.

Embodied Leadership—with the Body as Sounding Board

As these stories show, embodied professional competence is not just something one "has." It is a continually moving and also very personal competence that may be developed, made conscious, and matured. It is noticeable and expressed to a large degree through the body. It may shine through the person's personality and particular knowledge of others; get shaken or lost in vulnerable or confronting situations; be found again through the body; and be coloured by golden, often unpredictable moments when a professional meeting is really successful. The individual may have both resources and challenges within all three principles, or experience that there is a lot to learn in especially one of these areas. The three levels of embodied professional competence will, as the chapter shows, always be connected and often be mutually challenging, and in the first phases of an individual's professional development it may be difficult to be aware of all three levels at once while still keeping a relevant occupational focus. Through continual and conscious training and maturing, however, the professional in leadership professions may gradually develop embodied leadership, in which the three levels continually fertilise and enrich each other. Here the body can be a continually present sounding board, so that the professional may quickly regain his or her composure when personal feelings flood the situation, or when contact or leadership is lost.

The three levels may also be used as a feedback guide for teaching, reviews of practical work, and professional supervision. However, there is no quick shortcut to mastering the language of the body and developing unique personal and professional communication and competent embodied leadership. There are no correct answers, no easy tricks or body language phrases one may put on like a new shirt. The individual must find his or her own way. But no one should travel alone. Therefore, both contemporary and future education, as well as higher-level education and research, must focus more on embodiment and leadership, as well as focus on *how* to work with this concept in practice. As the concepts of embodiment, grounding, and centering may be applied to various movement settings, the fields of movement techniques and research in embodied leadership are relatively virgin territory. Ladkin and Taylor (2010) suggested that theatre techniques may be one possible area of development. Furthermore, methods from movement, martial arts, dance, and body therapy, as Winther (2012) showed, can be building blocks in this new landscape of professional training practice.

The Importance of Embodied Leadership in Modern Society

The chapter has thus far focused on the importance of the body in leadership and professional communication. The question is,

Is it at all relevant to focus on the concepts of embodied professional competence and embodied leadership?

Another question is whether we have time and energy enough to *not* consider it. With the increase of individualism in our postmodern era, human identity is being transformed from something relatively given and unproblematic into a challenging lifelong process that demands extensive resources of the individual (Giddens, 1991). This identity process also affects the professional–personal field. Previously, a net of meaning formed a background that also contained many internalising norms and values, by which an authority could be supported, with the consequence that the person in the professional field gained some benefit from this background of meaning (Ziehe, 1989). If the authority, credibility, and trust that previously were inherent in institutions and educational systems now must be created through each individual's relational work in various professional contexts, this has consequences. It carries great responsibility, and a risk. The danger of education (at all levels) primarily focusing on its subjects and theoretical content is that educational institutions leave the responsibility for all of the communicative work to the individual. The most risky consequence might be that highly competent individuals experience that they lack communication tools for mastering chaotic situations or creating trust, authenticity, and leadership in their professional practice. The risk is that the lack of these tools, which in the deepest sense also have a bodily sounding board, creates a personal frustration resulting in these individuals, in spite of their being very competent in their fields, not managing to stay in the profession for too long a time.

Future Research: Challenges and Possibilities

Therefore, heightened attention to bodily communication from both the magnified and actual body, to resonance, micromovements, centering, and grounding, could be part of movement psychology's contribution in regard to *how* development may be fostered in the complexity of professional work in modern society.

Increased insight into the importance of developing embodied leadership and embodied professional competence may therefore entail necessary, challenging, and perhaps enriching potentials in relation to the development of authenticity, leadership, and professional communication tools for both contemporary and future professionals. However, it is a challenging task to do research on embodied leadership. It is difficult to grasp small, fleeting moments that disappear as soon as they arise. It is a challenge to document larger streams of professional embodied experience, which often live in an unspoken landscape. This chapter is only a small drop in the ocean in this field. Much more research is needed. More empirically based research in which competent leaders, nurses, teachers, and other professionals are followed through golden moments and vulnerable critical situations in their professional lives could contribute to the growing research field on embodiment and leadership. More research is needed to clearly describe *how* embodied professional competence and leadership may be gained, lost, found, and developed through the body. Research is also needed in the field of development of new practice-based educational methods that may be used in future professional training. Ideally, this should be innovative and moving research with deep relevance and close connections to professional practice. Professionals are their bodies.

References

Andersen Kjær, T. (2011). Nærvær som omsorgens fundament. In R. Birkelund (Ed.), *Ved livets afslutning* (pp. 207–221). Århus, Denmark: Århus Universitetsforlag.

Avolio, B., & Gardner, W. L. (2005). Authentic leadership development: Getting to the root of positive forms of leadership. *The Leadership Quarterly, 16*(3), 315–338. doi:10.1016/j.leaqua.2005.03.001

Avolio, J., Walumbwa, F. O., & Weber, T. J. (2009). Leadership: Current theories, research, and future directions. *Annual Review of Psychology, 60*, 421–449. doi:10.1146/annurev.psych.60.110707.163621

Berg, M., & Thilo, T. (2012). At blive kastet for de sultne løver. In H. Winther (Ed.), *Kroppens sprog i professionel praksis*. Værløse, Denmark: Billesø og Baltzer.

Dadds, M., Hart, S., & Crotty, T. (2001). *Doing practitioner research differently*. London, UK: Routledge/Falmer.

Fuchs, T. (2012). The phenomenology of body memory. In S. Koch, T. Fuchs, M. Summa, & C. Müller (Eds.), *Body memory, metaphor and movement* (Vol. 7, pp. 9–22). Amsterdam, Netherlands: John Benjamins.

Giddens, A. (1991). *Modernity and self-identity: Self and society in the late modern age*. Palo Alto, CA: Stanford University Press.

Goleman, D., Boyatzis, R., & McKee, A. (2002). *Primal leadership: Realizing the power of emotional intelligence*. Boston, MA: Harvard Business School Press.

Halprin, D. (2002). *The expressive body in life, art and therapy: Working with movement, metaphor and meaning*. London, UK: Jessica Kingsley.

Hejselbak Jensen, L., & Winther, H. (2012). Fra overlevelse til nærværende lederskab. In H. Winther (Ed.), *Kroppens sprog i professionel praksis*. Værløse, Denmark: Billesø og Baltzer.

Jarvis, P. (1999). *The practitioner-researcher: Developing theory from practice*. San Francisco, CA: Jossey-Bass.

Kirkeby, O. F. (2004). *Det nye lederskab*. Copenhagen, Denmark: Børsens.

Laban, R. (1980). *The mastery of movement*. London, UK: Macdonald & Evans.

Ladkin, D., & Taylor, S. (2010). Enacting the "true self": Towards a theory of embodied authentic leadership. *The Leadership Quarterly, 21*(1), 64–74. doi:10.1016/j.leaqua.2009.10.005

Løgstrup, K.E. (1983). *Kunst og erkendelse. Metafysik II* (1st ed.). Haslev, Denmark: Gyldendal.

Lowen, A. (2006). *The language of the body: Physical dynamics of character structure*. Alachua, FL: Bioenergetic Press.

Meekums, B. (2007). Spontaneous symbolism in clinical supervision: Moving beyond logic. *Body, Movement and Dance in Psychotherapy, 2*(2), 95–107.

Merleau-Ponty, M. (1962/2002). *Phenomenology of perception*. London, UK/ New York, NY: Routledge Classics.

Nielsen, R., Marrone, J. A., & Slay, H. S. (2010). A new look at humility: Exploring the humility concept and its role in socialized charismatic leadership. *Journal of Leadership and Organizational Studies, 17*(1), 33–43. doi:10.1177/1548051809350892

Payne, H. (2008). *Supervision in dance movement psychotherapy: A practitioner's handbook*. London, UK: Routledge.

Plauborg, H., Andersen, J. V., Ingerslev, G. H., & Fibæk Laursen, P. (2010). *Læreren som leder. Klasseledelse i folkeskole og gymnasium.* Copenhagen, Denmark: Hans Reitzels.

Sabetti, S. (2001). Life energy process (L.E.P.). In S. Sabetti & L. Freligh (Eds.), *Life energy process: Forms, dynamics, principles* (pp. 3–23). Munich, Germany: Life Energy Media.

Sabetti, S., & Freligh, L. (Eds.). (2001). *Life energy process: Forms, dynamics, principles.* Munich, Germany: Life Energy Media.

Sparkes, A. (2002). *Telling tales in sport and physical activity: A qualitative journey.* Champaign, IL: Human Kinetics.

Thornquist, E. (2005). *Klinik, kommunikation, information.* Copenhagen, Denmark: Hans Reitzels.

Todres, L. (2007). *Embodied enquiry: Phenomenological touchstones for research, psychotherapy and spirituality.* Basingstoke, UK: Palgrave Macmillan.

Winther, H. (2008). Body contact and body language: Moments of personal development and social and cultural learning processes in movement psychology and education. *Forum Qualitative Sozialforschung, 9*(2), Art. 63.

Winther, H. (2009). *Movement psychology: The language of the body and the psychology of movements based on the dance therapy form Dansergia.* PhD thesis. University of Copenhagen, Denmark.

Winther, H. (2012). Det professionspersonlige. Kroppen som klangbund i professionel kommunikation. In H. Winther (Ed.), *Kroppens sprog i professionel praksis.* Værløse, Denmark: Billesø og Baltzer.

Ziehe, T. (1989). *Ambivalenser og mangfoldighed.* Copenhagen, Denmark: Politisk Revy.

Chapter Twelve

From the Ground Up

Revisioning Sources and Methods of Leadership Development

Kathryn Goldman Schuyler

The most powerful learning comes from bodily experience.

Nonaka and Takeuchi (1995, p. 239)

Mindfulness plus my *Feldenkrais* practice with children and severely disabled people are prime sources of insight for understanding people, change, and leadership. From personal experience coaching corporate leaders, I have seen that leadership requires clarity, the capacity to learn from experience, resonance with people, persistence, and powerful action. In both organizational consulting and university teaching, I have been greatly nourished by two nontraditional sources of change. Mindfulness teaches me to listen, sense the fullness of the moment, and feel a sense of spaciousness that allows for new options. The Feldenkrais Method of Somatic Learning helps me notice how I move through life, vary how I approach tasks, and start from

---

I thank Dolores Ransom for her detailed feedback on this chapter. Her willingness to discuss the chapter on short notice, combined with her background in meditation and the Feldenkrais Method, as well as her ability to see clear lines of thought, made her comments invaluable.

where I am, assuming no fixed limits to learning. Both practices remind me to be kind and open. Both speak explicitly about the value of the *ground*, yet they refer to two different kinds of ground. In the world of somatic learning, we speak of the physical ground, and gravity is one of our main teachers. During the movement sequences, our students often lie on the ground. In Buddhism, the ground refers to the foundation of being, our *buddha nature*, an aspect of ourselves that is already perfect and always present. It is the seed within all sentient beings that connects them with one another and with life, and makes enlightenment a possibility. When people are in touch with gravity and the ground of their being, it can be seen in the way they walk and the way they look in your eyes. Leaders who are grounded and nourished by the ground in this way would bring new options to politics, corporations, and society.

I have discovered that embodied learning can be incorporated into leadership development to enable radical simplicity, authenticity, and openness to innovation. This provides a rich and solid foundation for people to use themselves in new ways as leaders and brings wisdom to their leadership, so they can move through life powerfully and compassionately, whether in a corporate or a political role.

This chapter presents the theoretical foundations of the Feldenkrais Method and Tibetan Buddhism, invites readers to pause and sense themselves, presents examples, and explores implications for leadership.

Theoretical Foundations

The Feldenkrais Method

The Feldenkrais Method involves processes analogous to those that happen naturally in healthy infants when they are learning to function in the world (Feldenkrais, 1949, 1972). They learn through movement that changes their brains, creating more interconnections (Begley, 2007; Doidge, 2007). Described by thought leaders including Karl Pribram and Margaret Mead as a genius (as quoted in Fox, 1978), physicist and engineer Moshe Feldenkrais discovered how to use touch and what he called "non-habitual" movement patterns to generate change. From his understanding of physics and the martial arts, he saw and was able to teach people how to distribute movement throughout the body so that the skeleton bears one's weight and the spine and ribs move more freely. When no part of the structure has to consistently work harder than the rest, ordinary movements take on the power and grace of a martial art. Feldenkrais (1949, 1972, 1977) combined these core insights with a profound understanding of the human nervous system and the function of the brain. Earlier than most scientists, he recognized that the physical bases of learning are interdependent with the other aspects of a person: how he or she feels, what he or she senses and notices, and what he or she wants to accomplish in life (1949, 1979, 1981). Feldenkrais (1979) included far more than the physical in his understanding of the impact of his method; in exploring the meaning of *good health*, he wrote, "A healthy person is one who can live his unavowed dreams fully" (p. 27).

The Feldenkrais Method has two aspects. Individual sessions are designed specifically for each student; the practitioner gently moves the student, while the student senses how to allow movement to become effortless. In group lessons, called "Awareness Through Movement," the practitioner guides participants through one of many hundreds of movement sequences that train the brain (and body) to move more effectively and powerfully with as little effort as possible. Both aspects of the method enhance the ability to bring awareness to actions in ways that carry over into daily life activities.

Students are encouraged to experiment and attend to the *way* that they move. Rather than focus on *what* they do or the outcome, they are asked to notice *how* they approach a given task and where they hold on and use force unnecessarily. Such holding on reduces the fluidity and power of all actions. By starting with movements that are similar to those of infants (like lifting one's head while on one's stomach or rolling over) and progressing through increasingly complex and varied movement patterns, a learning process unfolds that taps into the inherent plasticity of the brain (Reese, n.d.). Practitioners are trained by doing such movements themselves for years, in order to recognize subtle shifts in the quality of movement that are imperceptible to most people. An effective practitioner becomes an extension of the student's own proprioceptive system. We convey ease and presence nonverbally through touch and our own movements when we are in contact with the learner, thereby allowing students to experience themselves "through" us. Our contact extends the sensitivity of the student's own nervous system.

I was drawn to this method because Moshe Feldenkrais, my teacher, emphasized that it addressed the mind and the self, not just "pushing bodies around." He approached the body as a physical representation of something less tangible that we were trying to touch—perhaps the mind, perhaps the self. From Feldenkrais, I learned to experience and observe movement as a way of accessing something more. Mental and cognitive functioning, emotions, and all of the deeper structures of the self are literally "embodied" in the way we hold ourselves and move through life. The method develops the capacity to move smoothly, without hesitation, retaining the ability to reverse the action, so that a person is able to meet whatever occurs. This yields a combination of strength and fluidity that is both mental and physical.

Mindfulness and Dzogchen

Mindfulness meditation practices have existed for thousands of years and were developed to lead to freedom from absorption in everyday cares. Research on mindfulness suggests its potential importance for leaders (Baron & Cayer, 2011; Kabat-Zinn, 2005; Shapiro & Carlson, 2009; Weick & Putnam, 2006; Weick & Sutcliffe, 2006). Personal statements about their meditation practice by globally respected social scientists Peter Senge (2012) and Margaret Wheatley (2012) vividly described how they have found it important in their lives. These methods can substantially enrich leadership education to develop resonant leadership, simplicity of action and vision, authenticity, and a rich cognitive map of life (Boyatzis & McKee, 2005; Cook-Greuter, 2004; Fisher, Rooke, & Torbert, 2000; George, 2003, 2007; Goleman, Boyatzis, & McKee, 2004; Wheatley & Kellner-Rogers, 1999).

To date, most outcome research on mindfulness and meditation is based on two traditions: Theravada practices from South Asia, which are the basis of the trainings introduced in health care by Jon Kabat-Zinn (2005), and Transcendental Meditation, which was brought to the United States by Maharishi Mahesh Yogi in the 1970s. Instead, I focus here on *Dzogchen*, a form of meditation that is often called *nonmeditation*: it involves moving beyond the use of any particular methods or techniques and being fully present, without reflecting on, judging, or reacting to whatever is occurring. It is regarded by many as the highest form of meditation (The Dalai Lama, 2007; Ray, 2002; Shabkar Tsokdrug Rangdröl, 18th century/1993, 18th century/1994; Sogyal Rinpoche, 1993).

Mindfulness meditation involves being quiet and attending to any object of consciousness. People are taught to begin with mindfulness of the body, particularly of breathing, but anything can be used as a focus of concentration: sounds, physical objects, and even thoughts. The goal is to steady the mind, which has been compared by many to a wild horse that dashes about in all directions and to a lively monkey (Mingyur Rinpoche, 2007; Patrul Rinpoche, 1800s/1998). The practice of mindfulness generates steadiness and emotional resilience. It is not intended only to generate calm, but primarily to develop the capacity to be fully present and alert, simultaneously relaxed and awake. This is comparable to the Feldenkrais notion of being ready and able to move in any direction with ease, instead of pushing hard or contracting under stress.

In the Tibetan traditions, Buddhist practice incorporates study of the underlying concepts and *view* (or philosophy of life) with practice (Goldman Schuyler, 2012; Ray, 2002; Sogyal Rinpoche, 1993). What we in the West call *meditation*, the Tibetans regard as *familiarization* with the workings of one's mind (Sogyal Rinpoche, 1993). In traditional Tibetan Buddhist education, years are spent training the mind, appreciating the importance of developing an ethic of compassion toward all beings, and understanding the interdependence and impermanence of all that seems so concrete and materially real in the world. In addition, meditation practice in the Buddhist tradition rigorously trains one to be alert and at ease. Being present (Senge, Scharmer, Jaworski, & Flowers, 2004) is essential in both modes of working with people.

Making It Real: Accessing Ourselves Through Movement and Attention

Sit for a moment before questioning the notion that we can learn about leadership from infants, children, and the disabled. Sense yourself present. Notice your weight in the chair, how you feel as you breathe, what you see without trying to see anything in particular. Take a few breaths and simply be. Listen. . . . Are birds singing? Children laughing? Does the heat make a soft background hum? Are there traffic sounds or sirens? What is the farthest sound you hear? Do you sense yourself and hear and see all at the same time, or are you aware of each in sequence? How is your mind as you try this experiment? Alert? Peaceful? Restless?

Brief stories about "Jenny" and "Paul" (pseudonyms) suggest how working with children and disabled adults can be relevant to leadership development. After these vignettes, I'll describe the applications and implications of these concepts.

Jenny

Jenny is a four-year-old whose mom initially brought her for Feldenkrais lessons because Jenny was staying awake at night. After a few lessons, she began to sleep well. It seems quite likely that when she is aware and comfortable, it is easier for her to sleep at night. This little girl is vibrant, full of life, and high strung. Her body and mind are lively, leaping constantly. Adults are expected to lie quietly on the table as the practitioner touches and moves them gently, but not children.

With children, most of the time learning has to be a game. Since Jenny wanted to move all over the table, I created a game that caused her to pay attention to herself as she did what she wanted to do. In other words, I applied a basic principle: seeking what interests the student. She wanted to scramble and wiggle on her back away from me to the other end of the table. I played with her so that it became a game. Even though it wasn't originally what she wanted, she was willing to allow it to become "her game." First I let her just move around in her own way. Then I said, "Now do it very slowly" in a slow and quiet manner. She'd say "No!" and I'd say, "Oh come on. Do it slowly." So she did the same movement somewhat slowly. I said, "That's wonderful! Now do it slowly and quietly." Gradually, she became willing to do it slowly and quietly. Then I pulled her back to me, slowly and quietly. Then I'd say, "Now go fast and noisy," knowing that she liked this best. Then, "Go medium and noisy." And she'd go at a medium pace, making lots of noise. I varied the two elements: the speed and the amount of noise she made. It was not easy for her to move slowly and quietly, and she didn't want to move quickly and quietly. Gradually by playing the game, she developed the ability to modulate the speed at which she moved down the table and the way that she wiggled and whether she made noise or not.

For adults, Moshe Feldenkrais created a vast number of movement variations that support people in moving in *non-habitual* ways. They are like a musician's finger exercises for the whole self: they help people discover variations they never thought of in how to move, so as to be fluid and creative in their lives. The movements we use with adults are based on movements people do naturally in infancy. In developing lessons for children, I have to find a way to draw on the principles that I know and apply them in the moment, building on what they want to do.

Does embodied learning help one change one's relationship to how one moves through the day and how one thinks and feels? Moshe Feldenkrais said yes, definitely. Does the student need to understand how it works, cognitively, as we might teach in a graduate program? Not at all; we work with infants and children who have neither the ability to learn nor the interest in learning that way. Being able to apply principles about learning and change in the moment, as needed, rather than adhering to a preestablished sequence of steps, is a skill that is fundamental for leadership development.

Paul

Paul is a man of about thirty-five years old who has used a wheelchair his whole life, with movement and speech limitations caused by cerebral palsy. Very slim with intelligent eyes, he talks by responding to questions with movements of his eyes. He looks up to mean yes, down to mean no. The smile or laughter in his eyes is palpable. He used to be able to drive his own electronic wheelchair, but now he is limited to pressing a lever that adjusts the tilt of his chair.

I began the lesson by asking him, "How are you doing, Paul? How are your arms? Any pain?" He quickly indicated no. The last time I had given him a lesson, he had also indicated that he was not in pain. That was a major shift. These were the first times in six months that he had indicated that he had no pain in his arms or his back!

What led to a reduction in pain? I had taught him to imagine doing movements, to picture color in different parts of his body, and to have imaginary conversations between (for example) the hand that felt good and the hand that didn't feel good. The hand that feels poorly can "tell" the hand that feels well how it feels, and that hand can be compassionate to the part of one's self that doesn't feel so well. The "better" hand can "listen" to what the other hand is "saying" about what's tough in being a hand in pain, or what it understands about life from being a hand in pain.

We might imagine a conversation where one arm says, "Oh, I feel so much more ease now! This is like the way I feel when I'm in the park, and it's a sunny day, and the breeze is blowing." And the other arm might say, "You do? How amazing! I feel like a rainy day—all tight and tense." Most students can make a part of themselves that feels good feel the same way as a part that is suffering. This seems backward, since all wish to feel good and well, but it is easier to copy feeling badly than to copy feeling well. By feeling ease of movement in one place, our nervous system (with its wonderfully smart and well-wired connections) can transfer that learning to other places. It's much easier for whatever part of ourselves that is feeling well to learn, than it is for parts that are uncomfortable, tight, or tense. So instead of asking Paul in his imaginary conversation to have the arm that's feeling more pain move like the one that moves easily, I'll ask him to imagine the one that moves more easily becoming like the more limited arm. I'll also use touch to bring increased awareness to various places, combining my touch and Paul's imagination.

You can experience such learning yourself. Are you sitting turned in one direction or leaning on one arm? Is your head cocked to the right or left? Notice how you're sitting right now. Now see whether you can sit in the mirror image of yourself. Notice how your weight is as you sit, how the pressure is on your feet, whether you're leaning with your upper body. Is there a twist or a tilt through your torso? Is one ear closer to one shoulder than the other? Where are you looking? Get a sense of the whole of your body as if you were sketching it. Once you have a clear sketch, switch to a mirror image. Many readers will discover that it is not easy to notice such details, and that if they can, it is even harder to replicate them precisely in the other direction. To replicate them approximately is relatively simple, but to do so precisely is not easy. You have probably been sitting, leaning, moving, twisting, walking, and distributing your weight in the same way for years. These patterns of movement are engraved in our bones, our nervous systems, and our tissues at very deep levels, and we do not even know it.

Facilitating embodied learning in such very different students has helped me to quickly see what is needed in a difficult or unexpected moment, to significantly adapt my style of relating to people from one person to the next, and to find ways to assess whether change is taking place while it is almost imperceptible. All of these skills are relevant for leaders, since they need to adapt to change; take action very quickly or quite slowly, as appropriate; modify their actions and communications to fit the varied people in their organization; and be adept at listening deeply before taking action. For me, being able to appreciate and learn from a child like Jenny and a man like Paul develops capacities useful for interacting effectively with marketing, engineering, R&D, manufacturing, and all the diverse types of people in an organization. Applying Feldenkrais principles to leadership after experiencing them creates a new view of leadership.

Implications: How Can Recognizing *Wisdom Mind* and Seeing the Moving Body as a Source of Knowledge Enhance the Study and Practice of Leadership?

In all parts of the world today, leadership at any level of business or government is challenging. The situations to be understood and managed are extraordinarily complex, with many forces that drive leaders toward overemotionality and fear. People are cynical about their leaders; many use leadership to accumulate wealth or power. Wisdom teachings provide a countervailing force that emphasizes the interconnectedness of all life. These teachings say that all beings have the same nature as the buddhas, but that we do not recognize this and thereby drift into a sense of separation from one another and then fear. This negative spiral accelerates. We quickly move from vague feelings of distance, to fear, hostility, and anger, finally seeing others as enemies. By not recognizing our underlying goodness, we have no contact with the "ease and comfort of our beautiful, spacious, minds" (The Dalai Lama, 2007; Samantabadra, n.d.), and instead, "getting and spending, we lay waste our powers" and "give our hearts away," as Wordsworth (1806) wrote two centuries ago.

The 14th Dalai Lama as an Example

The 14th Dalai Lama can be seen as an example of the way that Tibetan wisdom traditions contribute to exceptional leadership. Although he said of himself, "I am no one special; I am just a human being," he is a rare leader who has influenced the heads of many nations (The Dalai Lama & Stril-Rever, 2010, p. 7). As described by Thupten Jinpa (2012), his twenty-five-year translator, who knows him well and who has experienced both the Tibetan and Western doctoral levels of education, the 14th Dalai Lama has demonstrated the same principles and advocated consistent policies for decades. Jinpa's analysis of the Dalai Lama as a global leader shows the importance of four main themes: (1) his embodiment of compassion, (2) his understanding of the interdependence of all things as central to both Buddhist thought and practical leadership, (3) his longtime commitment to secular ethics as being critical for the West, and (4) his humility and focus on "self-examination" by leaders—things often neglected by the powerful. The Dalai Lama's stands for interdependence, the "philosophical cornerstone of the Dalai Lama's worldview" (p. 38), compassion, peace, and an ongoing dialogue between Buddhism and advanced scientists have been sustained for more than thirty years. People experience him as embodying what he advocates: he not only speaks about the equality of all beings, but manifests a warmth and closeness to people that are present regardless of people's status (Jinpa, 2012).

Jinpa (2012) attributes the Dalai Lama's leadership style and qualities to a combination of the "Tibetan cultural upbringing" and his education. He emphasizes that Tibetan classical education includes contemplative practices that integrate philosophical perspectives and "*embody* . . . them in one's very person" (p. 43, italics added), as contrasted with Western education, which emphasizes "the rational part of the brain and acquisition of knowledge and information" (p. 44). This insight is critical for revitalizing executive development. Western education can retain its excellence in conveying cognitive knowledge and become stronger by enriching what it offers with regard to contemplation, awareness, and presence.

The Feldenkrais Method and Leadership Development

I have drawn upon the Feldenkrais Method as an underlying "organizing principle" for my consulting and have taught it as an approach to change in workshops for managers and university students. It can be described in terms of the following four principles that students have appreciated and incorporated into their lives.

1. *Notice differences.* To increase the possibility of learning, reduce effort to a minimum so there is more chance of noticing slight changes. Introduce variation, which also increases the likelihood of noticing differences. Introduce choice: Feldenkrais said often that choice means having three options; when possible, seek at least three different ways to approach a task or challenge.

2. *Be awake to what is happening.* Begin where you are, creating small steps in the direction you wish to go. Experiment. Play. Notice what effects come from different attempts.

3. *Use your body and movement as a source of learning.* Notice what moves easily. See how small, varied movements can lead to greater ease and more powerful action. Instead of trying to "hold on" to what you have learned, let it go; recreate it again and again.

4. *Pay attention to what draws your interest.* Focus on places where learning and change are possible rather than on the problem. Sometimes this will be at the core of the system, sometimes at the periphery. Instead of putting pressure on yourself and others, know that learning occurs through a series of successive approximations.

When I applied this approach to coaching a manager about her career, she was able to eliminate her back pain, become (in her experience of herself) easier to be with, and gain entirely new perspectives on herself as a worker (Goldman Schuyler, 2007). She realized that she had been forcing herself to follow others' patterns and rhythms, and that she worked much more powerfully and creatively when she got in touch with herself and worked in accord with her own natural rhythms. She enjoyed working in passionate bursts of activity. We saw that this did not fit with industrial society's norms, yet enabled her to be her most creative self.

There were clear outcomes in a course entitled "The Art of Change: Somatic Awareness and Systems Thinking" that I developed and taught in two graduate schools. I introduced Feldenkrais movement sequences as a means to assist the students in bringing change to their work lives. After they experienced a few sequences, they discussed the principles and applied them to personal change projects (Goldman Schuyler, 2003). Students found that the process of paying more attention to themselves via these intricate, structured movements produced insights about how to improve other parts of their lives. Their papers reported on changes in areas ranging from a mother's relationship with her five-year-old daughter to the way the students approached pressure and leadership at work.

I have been asked whether it was the movement, discussions, reading, or personal project planning that made the difference. I believe that it was the combination that enabled students to experience such broad impact. The movements took them out of established habits, the reading helped them think about the implications of what they were experiencing, and the personal project invited them to bring new patterns to their actions. These workshops were life changing because the students carried awareness from the workshop sessions into their lives.

Conclusion

Both Buddhist meditation and Feldenkrais offer subtle methods for being aware, but their views of the body and its importance differ, as does the way they address relating to humanity. I compare them here to sharpen our thinking about how embodiment includes a person's connection to the ground, to share my experiences with the way that apparently unrelated ways of developing awareness can be more similar than they appear, and to encourage leaders to incorporate such refined and rigorous self-training in their development.

Some forms of Buddhist meditation regard the body as a "thing" that carries us around and can be discarded; a *piece of wood* is even used at times as a metaphor. From my perspective, both Dzogchen and the Feldenkrais Method approach the body as a foundation for being aware and for noticing differences, and as something to appreciate. Both include methods for shaping one's state of mind through somatic methods, such as sensing the body in movement or the movement within stillness (for example, breathing). Both draw students' attention to the rich, interdependent nature of actions, thought, and sensing, and to the impermanence and fluidity of life. *Embodiment* is not simply material and physical in either practice: it is something that one senses in itself and draws on to access the mind. Both practices nourish a person in being fully present to the body, life, other beings, and the world. Both train a person to be simultaneously at ease and alert.

They differ most in their views of what *mind* is, which is not a simple question in either domain. Feldenkrais focused on the mind and body in action; he discouraged people from speaking abstractly about the mind, out of the context of the body. Dzogchen points to a notion of mind that extends far beyond an individual person and connects with the continuity of being. While the underlying assumptions may differ, both offer highly refined methods for functioning in the world with awareness. Despite these parallels, there is an important distinction between the ways each views the *ground*, as pointed out at the start of the chapter. Relating to the ground is core for each body of practice, but they relate to different grounds.

For Dzogchen practitioners, the *ground* is the ground of our being that is beyond the rational, analytical mind's comprehension. The ground is the fundamental *nature of mind* or *buddha nature* that is in all sentient beings and has been described as being like the sky, yet knowing and luminous. In this context, *wisdom* refers to a deep appreciation of the way that nothing is fixed or certain or permanent, which is often described by the term *emptiness* in English. A wise person moves through life with this understanding, combined with an inevitable compassion for all beings who do not yet see this and therefore suffer. The purpose of Dzogchen practice is to live with such awareness and help others to do the same (The Dalai Lama, 2007; Shabkar Tsokdrug Rangdröl, 18th century/1994; Sogyal Rinpoche, 1993; Tsoknyi Rinpoche & Swanson, 2012; Tulku Urgyen Rinpoche, 1999/2004, 2006).

The realm of the Feldenkrais Method is more concrete, although Feldenkrais himself drew his understanding not only from engineering, physics, and the martial art of judo, but also from his upbringing, which was steeped in esoteric Judaism (Kaetz, 2007). In one book, he used a Tibetan story to help people grasp what he perceived about the relationship of the mind, body, and emotions (Feldenkrais, 1972, p. 54) and at least once in a major training program for new practitioners described the work itself as "practical loving" (Amherst Professional Training program, personal communication, 1980). However, the method itself focuses on developing sensitivity to oneself as a moving, sensing material person and the capacity to vary and learn from one's actions. Students literally lie on the ground and learn to roll, almost as babies do. The actual material ground becomes one's friend. The practitioner's trained sensitivity and fluidity become a means of learning for the student, and practitioners become so attuned to others that a room full of people can roll across the floor in unison without verbal communication. With no directions, they move together, sensing when to speed up or slow down, so as not to roll into one another. When practiced with such simultaneous awareness of oneself and others, the Feldenkrais Method becomes a compassion meditation in action. The "line" between meditation and Feldenkrais disappears.

Effective leaders move quickly, incorporating vast bodies of knowledge into clear actions. Their actions need to be crisp and definitive, yet sourced by deep listening to those they lead and the broader environment. They need to act on their own, yet help others to move together as one body. As stated initially, powerful leadership requires simplicity of action and vision, authenticity, and a rich cognitive map of life. All of these are enhanced by mindfulness, and authentic presence is hard to imagine without living in an embodied way. Mindfulness enables one to be in touch with the ground of one's being, while Feldenkrais Awareness Through Movement brings the grounded playfulness of a child into the adult sensibilities of a leader. Both are powerful, rigorous methods for bringing embodiment into consciousness and action.

References

Baron, C., & Cayer, M. (2011). Fostering post-conventional consciousness in leaders: Why and how? *Journal of Management Development, 30*(4), 344–365. doi:10.1108/02621211111126828

Begley, S. (2007). *Train your mind, change your brain: How a new science reveals our extraordinary potential to transform ourselves.* New York, NY: Ballantine Books.

Boyatzis, R. E., & McKee, A. (2005). *Resonant leadership: Renewing yourself and connecting with others through mindfulness, hope, and compassion.* Boston, MA: Harvard Business School Press.

Cook-Greuter, S. (2004). Making the case for a developmental perspective. *Industrial and Commercial Training, 36*(7), 275–281.

The Dalai Lama. (2007). *Mind in comfort and ease: The vision of enlightenment in the great perfection.* Boston, MA: Wisdom Publications.

The Dalai Lama, with Stril-Rever, S. (2010). *My spiritual journey.* New York, NY: HarperCollins.

Doidge, N. (2007). *The brain that changes itself: Stories of personal triumphs from the frontiers of brain research.* New York, NY: Penguin.

Feldenkrais, M. (1949). *Body and mature behavior: A study of anxiety, sex, gravitation, and learning.* New York, NY: Harper & Row.

Feldenkrais, M. (1972). *Awareness through movement.* New York, NY: Harper & Row.

Feldenkrais, M. (1977). *Body awareness as healing therapy: The case of Nora.* Berkeley, CA: Somatic Resources.

Feldenkrais, M. (1979). On health. *Dromenon, 2*(2), 25–26.

Feldenkrais, M. (1981). *The elusive obvious.* Cupertino, CA: Meta Publications.

Fisher, D., Rooke, D., & Torbert, W. (2000). *Personal and organizational transformations through action inquiry.* Boston, MA: Edge Work Press.

Fox, C. (1978). The Feldenkrais phenomenon. *Quest.* Reproduced with permission on http://www.feldnet.com/Default.aspx?tabid=85

George, W. W. (2003). *Authentic leadership: Rediscover the secrets to creating lasting value.* San Francisco, CA: Jossey-Bass.

George, W. W. (2007). *True north: Discover your authentic leadership.* San Francisco, CA: Jossey-Bass.

Goldman Schuyler, K. (2003, Winter). Awareness through movement lessons as a catalyst for change. *Feldenkrais Journal, 15,* 39–46.

Goldman Schuyler, K. (2007). Clinical sociology, career coaching, and somatic learning. In S. Dasgupta (Ed.), *The discourse of applied sociology: Vol.2. Practising perspectives* (pp. 33–50). London, UK: Anthem Press.

Goldman Schuyler, K. (2012). *Inner peace—global impact: Tibetan Buddhism, leadership, and work.* Charlotte, NC: Information Age.

Goleman, D., Boyatzis, R., & McKee, A. (2004). *Primal leadership: Learning to lead with emotional intelligence.* Boston, MA: Harvard Business School Press.

Jinpa, T. (2012). The fundamental equality of all of us: His Holiness the 14th Dalai Lama as a global leader. In K. Goldman Schuyler (Ed.), *Inner peace—global impact: Tibetan Buddhism, leadership, and work* (pp. 37–46). Charlotte, NC: Information Age.

Kabat-Zinn, J. (2005). *Coming to our senses: Healing ourselves and the world through mindfulness.* New York, NY: Hyperion.

Kaetz, D. (2007). *Making connections: Hasidic roots and resonance in the teachings of Moshe Feldenkrais.* Victoria, BC, Canada: River Centre Publishing.

Mingyur Rinpoche, Y., with Swanson, E. (2007). *The joy of living: Unlocking the secret and science of happiness.* New York, NY: Random House.

Nonaka, I., & Takeuchi, H. (1995). *The knowledge-creating company.* New York, NY: Oxford University Press.

Patrul Rinpoche. (1998). *Words of my perfect teacher* (Padmakara Translation Group, Trans.). Boston, MA: Shambhala. (Original work published 1800s)

Ray, R. (2002). *Secret of the vajra world.* Boston, MA: Shambhala.

Reese, M. (n.d.). *Feldenkrais and dynamic systems theory: A technical discussion.* http://brightfoundation.tripod.com/id4_1_1.html

Samantabadra. (2006). The prayer of Kuntuzangpo. In E. P. Kunsang & M. N. Schmidt (Eds., Translated c. 2005 by Bakha Tulku & Steven Goodman), *Quintessential Dzogchen: Confusion dawns as wisdom* (pp. 79–84). Hong Kong, China: Rangjung Yeshe Publications.

Senge, P. (2012). "Leaders should be people who are deeply involved in their own realization of being a human being." In K. Goldman Schuyler

(Ed.), *Inner peace—global impact: Tibetan Buddhism, leadership, and work* (pp. 317–328). Charlotte, NC: Information Age.

Senge, P., Scharmer, C. O., Jaworski, J., & Flowers, B. S. (2004). *Presence: Human purpose and the field of the future.* Cambridge, MA: Society for Organizational Learning.

Shabkar Tsokdrug Rangdröl. (18th century/1993). *The flight of the garuda* (E. P. Kunsang, Trans.). Hong Kong, China: Rangjung Yeshe Publications.

Shabkar Tsokdrug Rangdröl. (18th century/1994). *The flight of the garuda* (K. Dowman, Trans.). Boston, MA: Wisdom Publications.

Shapiro, S. L., & Carlson, L. E. (2009). *The art and science of mindfulness: Integrating mindfulness into psychology and the helping professions.* Washington, DC: American Psychological Association.

Sogyal Rinpoche. (1993). *The Tibetan book of living and dying.* San Francisco, CA: HarperCollins.

Tsoknyi Rinpoche, & Swanson, E. (2012). *Open heart, open mind: Awakening the power of essence love.* New York, NY: Harmony Books.

Tulku Urgyen Rinpoche. (1999/2004). *As it is* (Vol. 1). (E. P. Kunsang, Trans.). Hong Kong, China: Rangjung Yeshe Publications.

Tulku Urgyen Rinpoche. (2006). *Quintessential Dzogchen* (M. B. Schmidt & E. P. Kunsang, Trans.). Hong Kong, China: Rangjung Yeshe Publications.

Weick, K. E., & Putnam, T. (2006). Organizing for mindfulness: Eastern wisdom and Western knowledge. *Journal of Management Inquiry, 15*(3), 275–287. doi:10.1177/1056492606291202

Weick, K. E., & Sutcliffe, K. M. (2006). Mindfulness and the quality of organizational attention. *Organization Science, 17*(4), 514–524. doi:10.1287/orsc.1060.0196

Wheatley, M. (2012). Ancient wisdom, social science, and the vastness of the human spirit. In K. Goldman Schuyler (Ed.), *Inner peace—global impact: Tibetan Buddhism, leadership, and work* (pp. 329–342). Charlotte, NC: Information Age.

Wheatley, M., & Kellner-Rogers, M. (1999). *A simpler way.* San Francisco, CA: Berrett-Koehler.

Wordsworth, W. (1806). *The world is too much with us; late and soon.* http://www.bartleby.com/145/ww317.html

Name Index

Subject Index

Page references followed by *fig* indicate an illustrated figure; followed by *t* indicate a table.